D0607576

# The Essential Book of
# Home Design
# Techniques

# The Essential Book of
# Home Design
# Techniques

Consulting Editors

NICHOLAS SPRINGMAN

JANE CHAPMAN

Step-by-step authors

JULIAN CASSELL

PETER PARHAM

ANN CLOTHIER

MARSHALL PUBLISHING • LONDON

A Marshall Edition
Conceived, edited and designed by
Marshall Editions Ltd
The Orangery
161 New Bond Street
London W1S 2UF

First published in Great Britain in 2001
by Marshall Editions Ltd

**Project Editor** Jane Chapman
**Editor** Felicity Jackson
**Design** John Round & Martin Lovelock
**Managing Editor** Antonia Cunningham
**Managing Art Editor** Philip Gilderdale
**Editorial Director** Ellen Dupont
**Art Director** Dave Goodman
**Picture Researcher** Andrea Sadler
**Production Controller** Anna Pauletti
**Editorial Coordinator** Ros Highstead

Copyright © 2001 Marshall Editions Ltd

All rights reserved. No part of this work may
be reproduced or utilized in any form or by
any means, electronic or mechanical, including
photocopying, recording or by any information
storage and retrieval system, without the prior
written permission of the publishers.

A CIP record for this book is available from
the British Library.

ISBN 1 84028 399 8

Originated in Singapore by PICA
Printed and bound in Germany by Möhndruck

**Note** Every effort has been taken to ensure that all
information in this book is correct and compatible
with normal standards generally accepted at the time
of publication. This book is not intended to replace
manufacturers' instructions in the use of their tools
or materials – always follow their safety guidelines.
The authors and publisher disclaim any liability for
loss, injury or damage incurred as a consequence,
directly or indirectly, of the use and application of
the contents of this book.

# FOREWORD

The stylish interiors seen in glossy magazines can fire us with enthusiasm to make changes to our own homes, but knowing where to start can seem a daunting prospect. Whether you are decorating one room, or need to re-plan your entire living space, this invaluable sourcebook will provide you with the ideas and practical know-how that you will need.

Divided into four interrelated chapters, the book opens by looking at the many style options available. Covering a wide range of design idioms, from the traditional to the contemporary, and featuring stunning interiors from around the world, this guide will give you a clearer picture of the look that will work best for you, your home and your lifestyle.

The next two chapters will help you to turn these ideas into reality. All the important aspects of design are covered, from using colour to planning your storage needs. Expert advice, tried-and-tested decorating solutions, photographs showing an eclectic mix of styles, and useful diagrams will help you to plan each room so that it fulfils your needs and reflects your tastes exactly. You will also learn how elements such as texture, pattern, lighting, proportion and scale can be manipulated to your advantage.

The final section focuses on the practical techniques, including painting, wallpapering, flooring, working with wood and soft furnishings. Directory spreads tell you which tools you will need, how long each project is likely to take, and the level of expertise required.

By offering a wealth of design inspiration and building up your practical knowledge, *Home Design Techniques* will guide you through the decorating maze, giving you the confidence to create a home that is a pleasure to be in.

# CONTENTS

# CHOOSING YOUR STYLE

CHOOSING YOUR STYLE is an exciting but time-consuming process. Think hard about your needs, the effect that you would like to create and, more importantly, what you would feel most comfortable with. Then think about how you can achieve these goals with fabrics, colour and furniture. Packed with inspirational photographs of interiors from around the world and featuring an eclectic mix of different design idioms, this chapter will give you a flavour of some of the many options available and invite you to think about what would most complement your lifestyle, your personality and the type of house you live in.

While some people will want to replicate a particular look down to the last detail, others might integrate just one or two elements: the cool blue walls of a Swedish interior, perhaps, or the jewel-like textiles of an Eastern-inspired room. Nor do you have to adhere slavishly to one particular style. Sometimes the traditional and the modern, the ethnic and the minimalist can be combined to great effect to create a home that is stylish and full of originality.

# TRADITIONAL STYLE

From the charming simplicity of a Shaker farmhouse to the formal gentility of a Georgian townhouse, living with traditional style allows us to connect with the past and form a link with previous generations. Vernacular building materials and paints, exposed beams and whitewashed walls, furniture with a patina of age, faded embroidered fabrics, open fires and copper pans gleaming in the kitchen – these are just some of the things that conjure up a bygone age. But adopting this style is not about indulging in sentimental nostalgia. Many decorative elements from the past – the pale, chalky colours of Scandinavian interiors or the rustic quarry tiles found in country kitchens worldwide – have a timeless beauty that makes them completely in tune with modern living.

▲ The emerald-green walls in this 18th-century dining room complement the dark oak table and carver chairs. The window, with the original lintel still in place, is left uncurtained to draw the eye to the view. At night, the candles on the table and in the hanging Venetian glass holder will be reflected in the window to provide double the light.

◄ Terracotta floor tiles, a scrubbed table and chairs, exposed beams and the knotty pine door leading to the scullery beyond create a pleasing combination of texture and colour in this farmhouse kitchen. An English Gothic wall cupboard, stripped of its old paint, houses a collection of blue-and-white Cornish ware and white French porcelain. Note the end-grain butcher's block that can be moved around.

◄ Offset by the deep-pink walls, the heavily patterned antique fabrics create a mood of warmth and intimacy in this attic bedroom. The plain headboard has been loosely covered with an embroidered quilt. An old ladder-back rocking chair takes advantage of the natural light, while leather suitcases provide useful storage and are a decorative reminder of a bygone age.

▲ An enormous fireplace provides the main focal point in this light, airy Provençal room with its pale wood, stone floor and rugs, tall windows, and traditional armoire.

## LIVING ROOMS

Whether you favour a simple rustic style or a more elegant urban look, traditional living rooms offer a wealth of inspiration. Georgian style married mellow timber flooring with shades such as pink, blue, mid-green or light terracotta on the walls. Furniture was carefully arranged around the room to give a sense of balance. Fabrics such as brocade, cotton damask or *toile de jouy* completed the look. In country-style rooms, low beams, an open fireplace, white or softly coloured walls, painted or stained floors covered with rugs or kilims, and carved or painted furniture were among some of the defining decorative features.

▲ Though symmetry appears to be important in this double reception room, the second fireplace is used to store wood, rather than having a second grate. Pale rugs accentuate the contrast between the dark wood and the light walls and chair cover. Huge dark-framed mirrors echo the wide arch between the two rooms and increase the sense of space.

◀ The beamed ceiling, large flagstones, comfortable seating and simple pieces of country furniture give this room a relaxed charm. Note the old-fashioned knife sharpener and oil lamp.

## KITCHENS

The main focal point of the traditional kitchen was the fire or stove, where water was boiled, food cooked, and plates – and hands – warmed. Copper pans and other utensils were kept close by, and herbs would be hung up to dry. A scrubbed pine table would do double duty as a working and eating surface. Many of the elements that we associate with traditional kitchens are still popular today. An old-fashioned butler's sink has an inherent charm and is deeper than many modern versions. Traditional materials such as terracotta, marble and granite are still appreciated for their aesthetic and practical qualities.

◀ In a country-style kitchen, period details such as a butler's sink with hardwood draining boards, plate rack and breadbin are left proudly on display, while modern appliances are tucked away. Note the airing rack above the Aga and the conveniently positioned pan drawers to the side.

▲ An authentic bread oven is the main focal point in this rustic Greek kitchen. Typical of Mediterranean style, the small, shuttered windows and thick, whitewashed walls and white tiles are designed to keep the room cool in summer. Unglazed terracotta pots complement the blue paintwork.

### DISPLAY

● Stand plates, dishes and decorative pottery on a mellow-coloured pine dresser.

● Old-fashioned utensils such as copper pots, pans, jelly moulds, colanders, spoons or even a set of kitchen scales make decorative additions to a traditional kitchen.

● Prettily patterned cups, jugs and mugs can be hung on cup hooks screwed into shelves.

## BATHROOMS

Many of the materials that have traditionally been associated with bathroom design, such as terracotta floor tiles or white or patterned ceramic tiles, are still popular today. In countries such as the United States and Australia, tongue-and-groove boarding is a common feature, used either from floor to ceiling or as a dado, with the upper wall either bare plaster or wallpapered.

To complete the look, an elegant roll-top enamelled bath with clawed feet has an enduring appeal that fits any setting. Other options include a boxed-in bath with wooden or hardboard panels or an antique copper or zinc tub.

◀ Occupying what was once a bedroom, the pink-and-white scheme in this pretty bathroom was inspired by the handpainted, marble-topped washstand. The original cupboards, reflected in the grand, gilded mirror, now house the hot-water cylinder and are used for storing warm towels.

◀ Taking centre stage in a country bathroom, an elegant roll-top bath has been positioned to take advantage of the view through the window. The undersides of the bath have been painted the same mallard green as the timber cladding, while the brass taps pick out the sunny yellow on the walls. The bathmat is made out of an oil-cloth, while the old wall-mounted cabinet once belonged in a church.

## BEDROOMS

A beautiful old bedstead forms the centrepiece of the traditional bedroom, with styles ranging from four posters, elegant Empire beds or American arched tester beds to simpler designs in brass or painted iron. In farmhouses in many parts of Europe, beds were commonly built into alcoves, often close to the fire and usually enclosed with a curtain.

Bedlinen could include antique lace, linen or an heirloom patchwork or appliqué quilt. Decorative headboards – either handpainted, carved or simply consisting of a piece of fabric draped over a pole – were another quintessential feature.

▲ In period homes, the size of the windows serves as an indication of the original owner's wealth and standing in the community. In this bedroom, the original ceiling has been removed to accommodate the stately proportions of a four-poster bed, which would have been built for a much larger, grander residence. The exposed beams have been painted white to increase the feeling of space.

◄ Converted from an old Quaker school, two rooms have been knocked together to create an airy bedroom. A pretty Florentine headboard and mosquito net grace the bed, while an old-fashioned teacher's desk harks back to the room's previous function.

# CONTEMPORARY STYLE

The absence of clutter and over-elaborate furnishings in favour of clean lines, simple shapes and subtle use of colour in the contemporary home points to a desire to bring calm and order into our surroundings. Space is a key element. Furniture is not massed together but given room to breathe, allowing us to appreciate the beauty of its shape and form. Materials such as wood, wicker, seagrass and unbleached linen are chosen for their aesthetic qualities and textural contrasts, while window treatments are kept deliberately low key. This simple approach does not mean that the contemporary home is devoid of decoration, however. Rugs or jazzy cushions bring colour to an otherwise monochromatic scheme, while neutral walls provide a perfect canvas for modern pictures.

▲ Gradations of blue on the walls and finishing touches combine with strong, geometric shapes to create a look that is dramatic without being overpowering. The sensuous curves of the sofa are a foil for the angular shapes of the marble fireplace and panels on the walls.

▼ A fireplace can be as important an architectural feature in modern interiors as in more traditional homes. This contemporary version makes a pleasing focal point in a neutral room. Further decorative flourishes are provided by the pale blue daybed and exotic blooms.

▶ Although there is space in abundance, the hangar-like proportions of a loft space pose their own design challenges. Here, exposed brick walls and the overhead wooden beams provide texture and warmth. The sofas, rugs and soft furnishings also suggest an easy informality.

▶ It is the contrast between hard and soft textures rather than colour that gives depth and warmth to this modestly sized, box-shaped room. The floor-to-ceiling window bathes the room in light and enhances the feeling of space and airiness. A sinuously shaped coffee table picks up the gentle curves of the sofa and terracotta pot.

▼ The impressive scale of the beech-wood dining table is entirely appropriate for the proportions of this high-ceilinged room and ensures that guests do not feel dwarfed by the space. The simple blinds are in keeping with the pared-down industrial look and filter daylight to create a flattering dappled effect.

## LIVING ROOMS

Easy on the eye and relaxing to be in, the contemporary living room is a direct reaction to the highly decorated and heavily furnished style of previous decades. Linear and curvaceous shapes combine with hard finishes, while tactile fabrics are added to soften the look and also to help absorb sound.

Floor surfaces in wood, stone or even painted concrete are appreciated for their clean lines. They also make a good canvas for an eye-catching rug with a bold geometric design. For a slightly softer floorcovering, natural fibres such as sisal, seagrass and coir have an inherent tactile quality, their mellow tones complementing neutral walls and furnishings. Wool carpet is a warm, quiet option, but choose a muted sandy or biscuit shade rather than a loud pattern.

Lighting also plays an important role in the contemporary living room, where it is used to create interesting focal points and variations of mood.

▶ Two jazzy hues have been cleverly combined to create a look that is bold and modern without being jarring. The lime green used on the curtains and walls provides a dramatic backdrop for the purple sofa and chairs. Note how the same fruity shades are picked out in the cushions, rug and ornaments.

▼ Simple block shapes and a neutral palette help to define the classical proportions of this French apartment. The tall windows have been left unadorned, save for an unobtrusive blind, allowing the view to become an extension of the room. Paintings and flowers add further visual interest.

▲ A warm, harmonious colour scheme of terracotta, beige and yellow is tempered by splashes of complementary blue in this unusually shaped room. The small square windows that have been cut into the curved wall help to make the space feel lighter and less enclosed.

## WINDOW TREATMENTS

• For an uncluttered look, choose floor-length curtains in natural materials such as unbleached calico, muslin or sackcloth.

• Hang curtains from an unobtrusive pole made from wood, wrought iron, steel or bamboo (see also p.88).

• Blinds, shades and shutters have spare, clean lines that work well in a contemporary setting. Hanging two or three separate blinds can work well at a large window and also helps you to regulate the amount of light coming into the room more easily.

# KITCHENS

Today's kitchen is no longer the exclusive domain of the cook. As the cohesive heart of the home, it is where families congregate, guests are entertained and other tasks carried out. To fulfil this multifunctional role, the modern kitchen needs to be streamlined yet still welcoming. Adaptable, hardwearing work surfaces and storage that makes use of every inch of space need to be incorporated. Good ergonomic planning is required to ensure that the main elements – cooker, sink and fridge – are safe and efficient to use. Sleek task lighting is fitted to illuminate different areas of activity. Movable furniture, such as a trolley or butcher's block, is another worthwhile addition.

Taking inspiration from the professional caterer's kitchen, hard, shiny materials often predominate, with stainless-steel units and mirror-finish appliances, glass shelving, smooth ceramic tiles, slate flooring and chrome accessories.

▲ The cool blues, greys and shiny metallics in this kitchen are warmed by the blond-wood seats and work surfaces. The island table is used for food preparation and informal meals. Pots and pans are conveniently stored in the deep drawers beneath the hob.

◄ Two smaller rooms have been knocked through to create a spacious open-plan room. The central peninsula, with cupboards that open on both sides, is convenient for laying and clearing the table and helps to mark off the kitchen from the dining area without isolating the cook. The round table is conducive to relaxed, informal entertaining and softens the angularity of the rest of the space. Neat ceiling spots ensure that light is evenly distributed.

## BEDROOMS

The modern bedroom should project an atmosphere of calm and comfort. Furniture, appreciated for its clean lines and functionality, doesn't overcrowd the space. Fabrics offer reassuring tactile qualities: choose crisp linen sheets, soft velvet cushions, tweedy blankets, faux fur throws or dreamy voile curtains. A neutral palette of white, cream, taupe or biscuit, or pastels such as lilac or soft green, are conducive to a restful, soothing environment, while strong primary colours should play only a supporting role as accents on rugs or pictures.

▲ Where in the past beds were built high in order to avoid draughts at ground level, modern beds can be nearer to the floor. In a basement bedroom of almost monastic simplicity, this simple, low bed enhances the zen-like atmosphere of the space. Splashes of black help to counterbalance the purity of the white walls and bedding.

◄ Subtle injections of colour and texture bring warmth and intimacy to this high-ceilinged room. The two bedside tables, although not a matching pair, help to create a sense of balance and symmetry, while the pictures have been deliberately arranged on the lower half of the walls to make the room feel cosier.

## BATHROOMS

Although still usually the smallest room in the house, the bathroom now has more stringent demands placed on it than ever before. The contemporary bathroom should be clean and functional, suggesting hygiene, but also warm and inviting, a place where we go to pamper ourselves and recharge our batteries. We want power showers that drench us with water, baths that are long and deep enough to spread out in, basins that are the right height, good task lighting that will illuminate the planes of our faces, and plenty of storage space for our many lotions and potions.

Today's fixtures and fittings combine sleek good looks with practical efficiency. Neat ceramic, glass or aluminium washbasins with simple mixer taps are less obtrusive than the more traditional pedestal units. Wall-mounted toilets and bidets continue the streamlined look – and also ensure easier cleaning. Chrome towel holders and accessories, mirrors and glass shelving are chosen for their light-enhancing properties. Once popular, coloured suites have been replaced by more pristine white versions. For walls, ceramic tiles complement the pared-down look.

▲ Ceramic tiles are a decorative and practical choice for a bathroom. Here a chequerboard of tiles creates a strikingly geometric look that is fresh and contemporary. The tiles on the floor are not so highly glazed as those on the walls, making them less slippery when wet. A wooden bathmat is an additional safety precaution.

◀ Geometric shapes, cool, glossy surfaces and unbroken lines predominate in this serene, pared-down bathroom where all extraneous clutter is kept out of sight. Decorative detail is provided by the sculptural washbasin and simple vase of flowers. The ceiling spotlights and mirrored wall add to the sense of glamour, which is echoed by the dramatic night-time cityscape outside.

# ETHNIC STYLE

Whether they are witnessed at first hand on travels abroad or glimpsed in books or magazines, the colours, patterns, furniture, textiles and ornaments found in other parts of the world offer a wealth of design inspiration. Ethnic style is not about re-creating a particular look, but involves interpreting and adapting elements from cultures distinct from our own that appeal to us or evoke strong memories. One or two well-chosen pieces – simple unglazed pots or a tribal stool from Africa, perhaps, or handcarved Indonesian masks – can form the starting point of an eye-catching and original scheme. Draw on a rich palette of exotic colour: from the hot salsa hues of Mexico to the spice shades, such as burnt umber, cinnamon or terracotta, widely used in North Africa.

▶ Although this bathroom is actually set in the English countryside, the arched window, painted floor tiles and wall motif all conjure up a serene Moorish style.

◀ In a restful entrance hall, the combination of cool green walls and mellow timber helps to ease the transition between the interior and the exterior. Catching the breeze, the foliage rustles and delights the ear of those passing through and provides a further link with the natural world outside.

▶ In hot climates, earthy tones are widely used on walls. Here warm terracotta plaster is inlaid with pretty majolica tiles in blue and yellow on white to create a decorative surround for a fireplace.

## DYEING METHODS

Plant and vegetable dyes have long been used on fabrics to produce interesting variations of pattern and colour.

● Tie-dyeing involves knotting or tying areas of fabric so that they resist the dye.

● Batik, originating from Indonesia, is another form of resist-dying technique, where the areas of the cloth not intended to be coloured are covered in removable wax. When the dying is finished, the resist is washed out.

● In Malaysian ikat printing, distinctive patterns are created by dying either the warp or the weft threads of a fabric before weaving.

▲ The earthy tones of the walls and floor tiles throw the brightly painted chairs into vivid relief in this Mediterranean courtyard. In cooler countries of the northern hemisphere, earthy shades such as yellow ochre, peachy pink or faded terracotta are much easier on the eye than brilliant whites, which can easily look dull and grey.

◀ A stone seat and table have been installed in a shady corner of a terrace intended for informal alfresco dining. The blue colourwashed plaster helps to enforce the feeling of cool tranquillity.

## LIVING ROOMS

Ethnic style has an inherent charm and informality that translates well to rooms meant for relaxation. Choose natural materials such as stone, terracotta or dark wood to bring warmth and layers of texture to a neutral scheme. Lay coir, sisal or seagrass matting on the floor and hang gauzy muslin, jewel-coloured sari material or cane blinds or shutters at the window. Scatter brightly coloured ikat cushions over a plain sofa or wicker chair and throw richly patterned dhurries or kilim rugs on the floor. For a touch of exotic opulence, add splashes of gold with mirrors, light fittings or bowls, or pick out details on doors, walls or furniture with gold leaf. Arrange bamboo, dried grasses or tropical palms in large, hand-thrown earthenware pots or Cretan urns. Be inspired by the colours, shape or texture of ethnic pottery – a beautiful African pot or raku vase could become a focal point that will link the rest of the scheme.

◀ Eastern and Western influences mingle in this living room, where an ottoman footstool contrasts with a more formal 18th-century French chair. The alcove shelving houses an eclectic collection of treasured souvenirs brought back from trips abroad.

▶ Wooden blinds that filter out the sun's glare and cast alluring shadows, cool whitewashed walls and a towering tropical palm all combine to give this room a distinctly colonial feel. A lovely old palanquin (an oriental litter that would originally have been carried on the shoulders of four men) has been commandeered into service as a table.

◄ Simple batik cushions inject subtle accents of colour and pattern and help to link the terracotta floor with the wooden frame of the old Javanese bed. An intricate candle holder hangs in place of a central light and a huge chimney provides a strong architectural focus for the room.

▼ Echoing the shape of an adobe hut, this corner fireplace is raised on several steps in order to throw heat out more effectively.

## BEDROOMS

Create a luxurious haven with sensual fabrics from different parts of the world. Drape soft Peruvian alpaca blankets over the bed or add a richly patterned Indian throw or an exotic Chinese silk bedspread. Re-create the calm minimalism of a Japanese bedroom with cool, white cotton bedlinen and a low-slung wooden bed, futon or even a plain mattress. A bamboo screen and a tatami mat complete the look. For a more opulent effect, hang brightly coloured fabrics over a four-poster bed. A muslin canopy or mosquito net will bring a touch of tropical glamour, while a pretty Chinese lantern makes a decorative lampshade.

▲ In hot countries, simple window treatments are more appropriate than opulent, heavily patterned fabrics, that would soon fade in the sun. Here diaphanous muslin curtains are teamed with limed floors and white bedlinen to create an atmosphere of Eastern serenity in the bedroom of a Victorian house.

◀ A huge piece of African printed fabric has been hung from a pole to make an imposing bed head. Other tribal references are seen in the rugs, pots and handcarved statues.

## BATHROOMS

The electric blues and sun-bleached whites of the Mediterranean or North Africa can bring a freshness and vitality to even the smallest, gloomiest bathroom. Be bold and use large amounts of eye-catching indigo or cerulean blue on the walls, or use them as accents on towels or a painted chair. For a cool Moroccan look, create a decorative splashback with mosaic tiles in different shades of blue, or use them in swathes on the walls and floor and around the bath. White ceramic tiles or rough plaster painted white or a soft dusky pink are further options for walls, while terracotta, stone or slate floors complete the look.

◄ The mosaic tiles used on the floor have been continued on the side of the curved bath. The same blue and white tiles have been used to frame the large wall mirror, while the more muted tone of the wall tiles ensures that the scheme doesn't become overbearing. Ethnic influences are continued with the carved wooden table, low chair and pot plant.

## FLOORS AND WALLS

● For floorcoverings, choose materials such as brick, stone, rough flagstones or old, unpolished wood, which all have charming natural irregularities. For a smoother finish, you could lay quarry tiles, ceramic or encaustic tiles, marble or terrazzo.

● Traditional water-based paints, such as distemper or limewash, can be applied to bare plaster to create a matt, textured finish. These paints allow walls to breathe and can be mixed with coloured pigments to create a rich, chalky finish that makes a good backdrop for ethnic-style furniture and soft furnishings.

◄ Stone makes an aesthetically pleasing choice of material for this charming rustic bathroom. In keeping with the room's style, the two lanterns suspended from the beamed ceiling are correctly positioned on either side of the Moorish-style mirror, to illuminate all planes of the user's face.

# COMBINING STYLES

Adhering too rigidly to one particular style of interior design can often result in a space that more closely resembles a museum or stage set than a warm, welcoming home. Finding the right balance between the old and the new, the ethnic and the minimalist can be the key to creating a look that most closely reflects your tastes and lifestyle. While an ultra-modern apartment full of heavy period furniture would undoubtedly look anachronistic, and a sleek industrial-style kitchen out of place in a low-beamed farmhouse, introducing one or two elements from a different design idiom can work extremely well. The high, white walls of a modern loft space can, for example, provide the perfect backdrop for one or two pieces of antique furniture or a collection of ethnic ornaments.

◀ An eclectic mix of period furniture, modern paintings and Oriental rugs fuses harmoniously in this traditional living room with whitewashed walls and exposed beams. High-ceilinged rooms require one or two tall pieces to give a sense of proportion, provided here by the grandfather clock, the stove flue and the long curtains that are hung well above the window.

▲ Introducing one or two well-chosen pieces can be enough to conjure up a particular style. In a sparsely decorated room, with the bed as its centrepiece, a wall-hung rug and statue help to evoke the serene atmosphere of an Eastern-inspired room.

◄ An inspired choice of modern and ethnic finishing touches helps to compensate for the lack of architectural detail in a box-shaped room in a modestly proportioned modern townhouse. The glass table does not dominate the room in the way that one in a solid material would.

▲ Timber weatherboarding is used internally rather than externally on the wall between the living room and the kitchen. Evocative of Scandinavian cladding or a North American log cabin, it gives a traditional twist to a contemporary interior. The classic colour combination of soft green and sunny yellow enhances the relaxed rustic feel of the room.

## MIX AND MATCH

Combining different styles – old and new furniture, shiny, pristine surfaces with rough, weatherbeaten materials, antique pieces with artefacts brought back from travels abroad – helps to define and personalize a room.

● In a traditional kitchen with a predominance of wood fittings, shiny, metallic surfaces such as chrome or aluminium bring textural variation and help to diffuse any heaviness. A modern sink unit complements the dark wood of an old cabinet (right).

● A neutral scheme in a contemporary living room makes a good foil for brightly coloured ethnic textiles such as ikat cushions or a kilim rug. Cover an old-fashioned sofa with suede or cotton rather than fabrics such as brocade or damask. The timeless beauty of a Lloyd Loom chair will complement even the most pared down of modern living spaces.

● For a relaxed dining room, team modern seating, such as sleek aluminium Landi chairs, with their distinctive punched holes (see p.17), with a traditional refectory table. Alternatively, simple pine chairs, perhaps in an assortment of designs or painted different colours, can make informal partners to a modern glass table. For tableware, mix fine white porcelain with country-style earthenware, cut glass with chunky tumblers.

● In the bathroom, period baths and washbasins can be revamped with the latest high-tech fittings.

◀ Carved wooden artefacts and framed ethnic prints add detail to a plain modern bedroom. The antique chest of drawers, leather chair and faux fur throw on the bed add tonal and textural variation.

▶ Although well designed and fitted with modern appliances, including a six-ring hob, finishing touches such as the old chair, wicker basket and framed prints help to give this compact kitchen a feeling of relaxed informality. The tall storage units make good use of space in a small area. Notice how the lampshades echo the shape of the cooker hood.

Rather than opt for traditional furniture and furnishings, the owners of this first-floor Victorian drawing room have chosen a cool contemporary scheme that complements the proportions and architectural features of this interior. Traditional button-backed armchairs have been covered in fresh white cotton and sit side by side with a modern sculpture, a set of Arne Jacobsen dining chairs and a strikingly geometric zigzag chair. The absence of curtains enhances the feeling of light and space.

Traditional furniture fuses with contemporary art in this spacious living room, where a stunning wall of glass bricks filters light into the hall beyond. The large pots of cacti give the space a distinctly hacienda style.

# HOME DESIGN PRINCIPLES

TRENDS IN INTERIOR DESIGN come and go at an alarming rate, and with such a vast array of colours, paint effects and soft furnishings on the market, making an informed choice can be bewildering. You might be inspired by the zingy limes featured in a magazine or the coffee-and-cream shades seen in a restaurant, but shy away from using them because you are not sure how they will look in your home. The aim of this part of the book is to bolster your decorating confidence by showing you how key elements such as light, colour, texture and pattern work and interrelate with each other, and the effect they have on the senses.

Makeovers of the same living room in four different colourways will show you how profound an impact colour – be it a bright, vibrant shade or a subtle neutral – can have. There are ideas to help you create the illusion of light and space, and tips for dealing with problem areas such as awkward corners or low ceilings. You will also see how you can introduce finishing touches to bring subtle accents of colour, texture or pattern that will lift the overall scheme and bring visual unity to the room.

# COLOUR THEORY

## COLOUR TERMINOLOGY

● **Primary colours** – Red, blue and yellow at their maximum purity are the primary colours from which all other ones are made, and are the only colours that cannot be made by mixing together other colours.

● **Secondary colours** – Two primary colours mixed together in equal quantities to make green (blue and yellow), orange (yellow and red) or violet (red and blue).

● **Tertiary colours** – An equal mix of a primary colour and its next-door secondary colour. These include flame (red orange), apricot (orange yellow), lime (yellow green), turquoise (blue green), indigo (blue violet) and magenta (red and violet).

● **Neutral colours** – Black, white, grey and brown are neutral colours that are added to other colours in order to change their tone, or can be used individually to provide a neutral foil in a colour scheme.

● **Complex colours** – The millions of other colours that are created by mixing adjacent colours together.

● **Hue** – The property of a colour that differentiates it from another colour. Crimson has a bluer hue than scarlet, for example.

● **Tone** – The tonal value measures how light or dark a colour is, which affects how reflective or luminous a hue appears.

● **Tint** – A colour that has white added to it. This lightens the colour, making it more milky or pastel.

● **Shade** – A colour that has black added to it. This darkens the colour.

● **Pure colour** – A colour that has neither white, black, nor another neutral colour added to it and displays its pure intensity.

● **Saturation** – This is a measure of the intensity of a colour in terms of how vivid or how dull it is.

Colour is the most effective and affordable way to transform a room. If you understand it, you can use it to create the effect of more or less space, as well as to create the kind of atmosphere and feeling that you are looking for. Under good light, the human eye can distinguish between 10 million different colours, all of which have a precise relationship with each other. In order to make the best choice of colours, you need to understand the relationship between them all and how they affect each other. All colour is made up from three colours, red, blue and yellow, which are called the primary colours. The tone of these colours is modified by adding black to create a darker version, called a shade, or by adding white to create a lighter version, called a tint.

## THE BASIC COLOUR WHEEL

Made up of 12 different pure colours, this wheel contains all of the primary, secondary and tertiary colours. The colours are arranged to show their interrelationship, with the three primary colours being spaced at equal distances apart around the wheel. Each of the three secondary colours is located mid-point between the two primary colours from which it is derived. Between each primary and secondary colour is a tertiary colour.

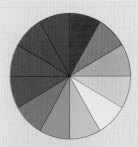
**The basic colour wheel**
This colour wheel contains a total of 12 colours. It includes all of the primary, secondary and tertiary colours.

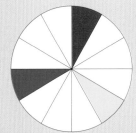
**Primary colours**
Red, blue and yellow are the only three colours that cannot be made by mixing together other colours.

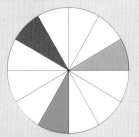
**Secondary colours**
Violet, green and orange are the three secondary colours made by evenly mixing two primary colours together.

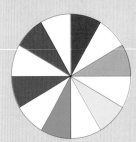
**Tertiary colours**
The six colours made from evenly mixing a primary colour with a neighbouring secondary colour.

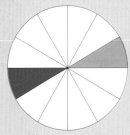
**Complementary colours**
Colours that lie directly opposite each other on the colour wheel are known as complementary colours.

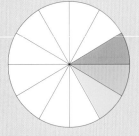
**Harmonious colours**
Colours that are adjacent on the wheel and share hues in common are known as harmonious colours.

## HUES, TONES AND SATURATION

When selecting colour, three major characteristics need to be considered. Hue defines the spectrum of colours in terms of the different proportions of base colour that are mixed together to make a colour. Tone defines a colour in terms of how light or dark it is. Saturation measures colours in terms of their intensity. Every time a colour is mixed, it loses intensity; for example, grey is produced when the three primary colours are mixed together in equal proportions. A colour sphere reveals how these three characteristics work in combination.

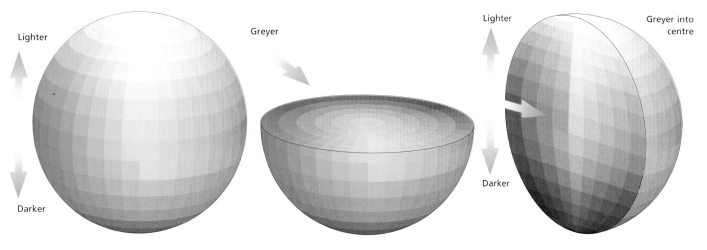

**Outer surface of colour sphere**
The outer surface shows colours arranged by hue around the circumference and their tints and shades along the meridian.

**Horizontal section through colour sphere**
This cross-section shows how the intense hues at the edge of the sphere become increasingly muted towards the centre, which is grey.

**Vertical section through colour sphere**
This cross-section shows the tints and shades of the colours as they become more muted towards the centre of the sphere.

## USING A COLOUR WHEEL

Most colour wheels contain numerous complex colours in addition to the 12 primary, secondary and tertiary colours, providing users with an extensive range of hues to choose from. The main advantage of using a colour wheel is that it shows at a glance which colours are mutually harmonious, which are complementary and whether a colour is warm or cool. The warm colours, located on the left side of the wheel, such as red and orange, all have a long wavelength, which makes them appear as if they are closer or advancing. The cool colours, located on the right of the wheel, such as blue and green, all have short wavelengths, which make them look as if they are further away or receding. This structured layout enables users to visually assess the relationship of all the hues in the wheel, and to quickly select colours with the desired characteristics for the mood and effect they want to create.

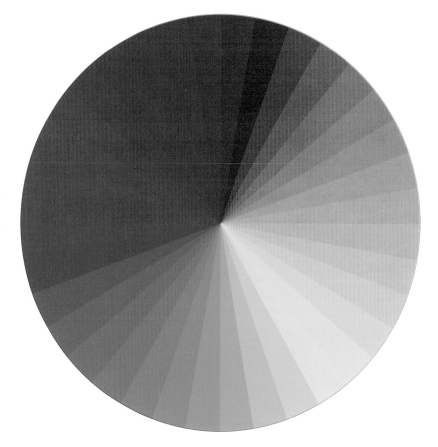

# CONTRAST AND TONALITY

## COMBINING COLOUR

Each colour has its own individual characteristics, but the impact a colour has varies depending on the other colours that surround it.

The full intensity of red is seen when set against white.

Red becomes more dramatic when seen with black.

Red and yellow are both vibrant primary colours.

The heat of red is counterbalanced by the cool of blue.

Red and green are complementary colours.

Red and maroon are harmonious colours.

Grey is neutral and does not compete with red.

Light blue is a soft colour that is dominated by red.

Both red and orange are warm, vibrant colours.

The combination of violet and red is challenging.

---

Decorating and furnishing a room in a single tint or shade of a colour is invariably a mistake because the characteristics of that colour will be overpowering. Monotony is overcome by using two or more colours to provide contrasting hues, or by employing the tints and shades of a colour to give tonal relief. Some of the different ways of using colours in combination are shown here.

## COLOUR AND PROPORTION

### TRIADIC COLOUR SCHEMES

Triadic colour schemes utilize three colours spaced at equal intervals on the colour wheel in order to create bold contrasts. As a rule, colours with a high level of contrast compete for attention if used in equal proportions, which can be unsettling. In order to achieve a more balanced effect, it is advisable to soften the colours with grey or white; allow one colour to dominate, and use smaller amounts of the other two colours to offset it.

### COMPLEMENTARY COLOUR SCHEMES

To achieve variety without producing a clash, complementary colour schemes employ two colours that are directly opposite each other on the colour wheel. Because the two colours share no base elements in common, they tend to compete for attention if they are used in equal proportions. It is therefore advisable to allow one colour to dominate, and to use the other colour to offset it. Here, indigo and green are combined in various proportions.

### HARMONIOUS COLOUR SCHEMES

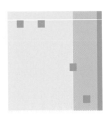

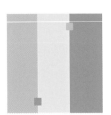

Harmonious colour schemes, also known as analogous colour schemes, use colours that lie alongside one another on the colour wheel to provide subtle variations in hue. Since the colours used have base elements in common, the level of contrast is low. As a result, harmonious colours do not compete if used in equal proportions, but if used as an accent they can get lost. Here, yellow, lime and green are combined in various proportions.

# NATURAL LIGHTING

Highly effective colour schemes can be created by using the tonal spectrum of just one colour. In these monochromatic schemes, relief is provided by the contrast of light tints, dark shades and mid tones. Tone also plays an important role in multicoloured schemes, because white or black can be used to soften the intensity of aggressive colours that normally clash in their pure form, allowing them to work well with a wide range of other hues. As a general rule, if you are using strong, contrasting colours in even quantities, then a narrow band of tones should be used. However, if the colour scheme is monochromatic, or the colours used are harmonious or neutral, then a broader range of tones should be used to provide variety.

▶ All colours have a tonal spectrum that extends between white and black. Any pure colour can be modified by adding white to create a range of tints, or by adding black to create a range of shades. As more white or black is added, the contrast between different colours diminishes.

◀ In this *en suite* bathroom and bedroom, the monochromatic colour scheme employs a range of blue tones on the walls, floor and ceiling to create a restful, coordinated effect. The consistency of colour cleverly unites the two interconnected spaces. Accents are provided by the yellow curtains around the bed, the chest of drawers and the white bathroom units.

◀ Swatches of the blue tones used in this scheme are set beside the yellow accent colour.

# CHOOSING COLOUR

## HELPFUL HINTS

● Do not put too many different colours in a room. To create interest, use tints and shades of a smaller palette of colours.

● When planning a colour scheme, it is often helpful to work out the tonal balance before selecting the hues, as the contrast of light and darkness is the main means of changing the optical appearance of a room. The best way to test the suitability of a colour is to paint a patch on a large piece of cardboard and observe it at different times of the day.

● The hue of a colour defines the atmosphere of a room. See the colour characteristics box on p.40.

● Colours with contrasting hues blend more harmoniously if the tonal value used is the same.

● Neutral and monochromatic colour schemes need tonal contrasts to provide interest.

● Use vivid colours sparingly and offset them against a large expanse of a soft colour or with a neutral shade.

● Dark floors absorb natural and artificial light and prevent it from being reflected around the room. Paler flooring helps to reflect light.

● Use colours found in nature for floors and ceilings to achieve a traditional feel. Unnatural colours can be used to give a more contemporary feel.

● Texture is an important part of your decorating scheme and should be considered in relation to colour (see pp.54–56).

When you decide to decorate a room, think in terms of the function and design of the space and the effect that you want to achieve, rather than simply picking a colour that you like. The room's size and proportions, the amount of daylight it receives and the location of prominent features will all affect your choice. Once you have established an overall plan, pick a colour that will best convey the main effect you want, whether this be to create a cool, spacious feel or a warm, intimate one. Key in all the other colours you select with this dominant colour to give the room tonal variety and balance. Before you begin, it is advisable to use a mood board to assess and refine your colour choice (see opposite page).

◄ ▼ Differences in tone are often easier to see in black-and-white photographs than they are in colour. In this kitchen, the lime green cabinets are lighter in tone than the walls, floors and work top. The contrast can clearly be seen in the black-and-white photograph, where the cabinets are seen as a light shade of grey, while the walls, floors and worktop appear as a much darker shade of grey. The chrome cooking utensils, the white lampshade and oven provide lighter-toned accents.

## USING A MOOD BOARD

The success of any decorating scheme depends not only on the blend of colours and the proportions in which they are used, but also on how well the patterns, styles and textures of items used in a room work in combination. Before decorating a room, most professional interior designers create a mood board in order to assess how well different colours, fabrics and patterns work together.

A mood board is essentially a piece of card or foam board with paint colour swatches, along with samples of carpeting, wallpaper and fabrics that will be used. These boards are easy to assemble and are the best way to avoid making the expensive mistake of buying items

that do not fit into the decorative scheme you are creating. They also give you the flexibility to experiment with your decorative scheme by adding and subtracting different elements, as well as being an effective method of establishing your own style and colour preferences.

When making a mood board, it is advisable to lay out the swatches in proportion to the amount of space they will occupy in the room. The wall covering normally occupies the largest area and should therefore take up most space on the mood board. Cushion fabrics and other elements that are to be used as accents should occupy less space on the board.

▶ The colour of the mood board should match the colour that you intend for the walls, which are the largest individual component of the room. Include a cutting of the wallpaper or paint, and number it for the key. Mark lines on the rear of any samples and trim them in line with any design. Use pinking sheers for fabrics to stop them fraying.

Where possible, try to position cuttings on the board to show where they will appear in the room. Overlap them to get an idea of how different colours, patterns and textures will work together. A swatch for a fringe for example, should be placed next to, or on top of, a curtain swatch. Do the same to see how a cushion will look with a sofa.

Taking up the largest area of the board, a swatch of wallpaper shows how a warm, neutral background colour will offset the rest of the room.

Three different shades have been chosen for the paintwork. The darkest is for the skirting board to anchor the colour scheme to the floor.

A soft tint has been chosen for the ceiling rather than a pure white so that there is less of a jarring contrast with the colour of the walls.

A faded-red paisley fabric with splashes of complementary green has been chosen for the curtains and one or two of the cushions to inject accents of colour into the scheme. The natural fabric used for the blind provides a change of texture and colour.

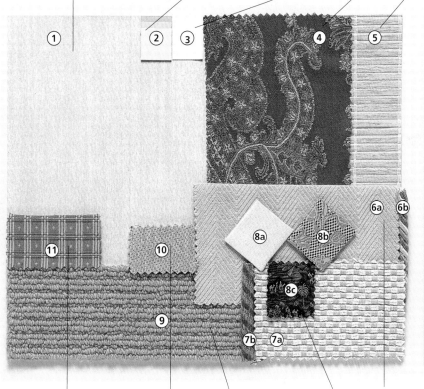

**KEY**
1  Wallpaper
2  Woodwork paint
3  Ceiling paint
4  Curtain and cushion fabric
5  Roller blind
6a  Sofa fabric
6b  Sofa piping
7a  Armchair fabric
7b  Armchair piping
8a  Cushions – sofa and armchairs
8b  Cushions – sofa and armchairs
8c  Cushions – sofa and armchairs
9  Carpet
10  Desk-chair fabric
11  Dining-chair fabric

A bright textured check fabric, rather than a neutral, is a practical choice for the dining chairs, the strong colours complementing their wood frame.

A chenille fabric has been selected for the desk chair, echoing the colour of the sofa and armchairs.

A corded carpet in a warm, neutral shade helps to anchor the scheme and creates another layer of texture.

A textured weave in a herringbone design is used for the sofa and sets off the scatter cushions. The piping chosen for the fabric picks out the tones of the fabric used on the dining chairs and curtains.

All rooms need a splash of black, here provided by the patterned cushion fabric.

# COLOUR EFFECTS

## COLOUR CHARACTERISTICS

● **Red** – Red is the warmest colour there is and in its pure form is often associated with danger and excitement. Pink and the other lighter tints of red are less aggressive. Darker shades, such as burgundy, are rich and sumptuous.

● **Blue** – Fully saturated blue is the coldest colour and has the opposite impact to red, producing a sense of calm. Tints of blue have a fresh, clean feel, while its darker shades are dignified and dependable.

● **Yellow** – At its maximum intensity, yellow is a striking and joyful colour. Light tints of yellow are luminous and refreshing, while its shades are more earthy and restrained.

● **Violet** – A combination of blue and red, violet is a challenging colour. Violet's darker tones, such as purple, have long been associated with royalty, while its tints have a nostalgic quality.

● **Orange** – A vibrant combination of red and yellow, orange is a warm, friendly colour that in its pure form is used as the international safety colour. Orange's darker tones have a warm, earthy quality, while its tints are cheerful and relaxing.

● **Green** – A soothing combination of blue and yellow, green has strong associations with nature. Its dark tones have a restrained, traditional quality, while its tints tend to be more lively and playful.

● **Grey** – An uncompetitive, neutral colour, grey can be used to calm down colour schemes employing bright, contrasting hues.

Colour not only changes the mood of a room, it can also change its optical appearance. Warm colours such as red, which have a long wavelength, or dark colours, which reflect only a small proportion of light, appear to advance and make a room seem smaller. Conversely, cool colours such as blue, which have a short wavelength, or light colours, which reflect a high proportion of light, appear to recede and make a room seem larger. Colours of contrasting hues or different tones can be used in combination to alter the optical proportions of a room. Lighting also has a major impact on the appearance of a room. Bright sunny rooms look larger than dim rooms receiving no direct sunlight.

## THE EFFECT OF LIGHT

Daylight is made up of a spectrum of hues – red, orange, yellow, green, blue, indigo and violet – and its cast (colour) changes through the course of the day. Daylight has a warm glow in the early morning, is neutral at noon when the sun is at its brightest, and becomes more blue as daylight fades. Artificial lighting also has different casts: incandescent light is yellow, fluorescent light is blue and halogen light is a bright white.

◄ The type and intensity of light alters the look of paint and fabric colours. In a room that receives direct sunlight at noon, the colours in the room retain their original hue, and subtle gradation of colours can be seen. Further interest is provided by the pattern of shadow and light that is produced.

◄ In a room lit by incandescent light, a distinctive yellow cast is produced. This has the effect of warming neutral and pale colours, making a room look more intimate. Fluorescent and halogen light work best with strong colours. They can have a draining effect on neutral or muted colours.

## OPTICAL TRICKS USING TONE

The most dramatic transformations to the optical appearance of a room are achieved by changing the tonal balance. All pale colours, including warm ones, make a room look bigger. Conversely, all dark colours, including cool ones, make a room look smaller. Below, a room is decorated using a light and a dark colour in different proportions to show some of the ways that tone can be used to alter our perception of space.

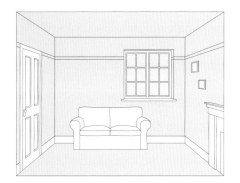

Using the same tone of colour throughout a room preserves the proportions of that room. If a light colour is used, the room will look bigger than if a dark colour is used.

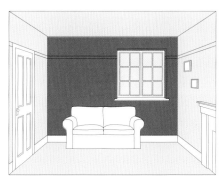

Painting one of the walls a dark colour makes that wall appear to advance. This effect can be used on end walls to optically shorten long, thin rooms or corridors.

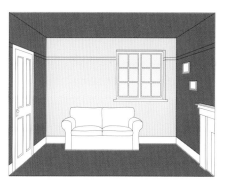

Painting one wall in a lighter colour than the other surfaces will make that wall appear to recede. This effect can be used to prevent square rooms from looking too box-like.

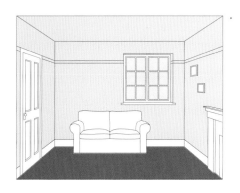

Dark colours makes a floor look smaller, while light colours make it look larger. A small room with dark floors can look cramped even if the walls are painted in a light colour.

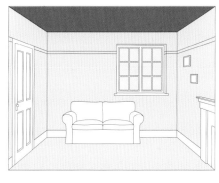

To make a ceiling appear lower, paint it in a darker colour than the walls. This effect is useful in rooms where the ceiling appears too high for the dimensions of the room.

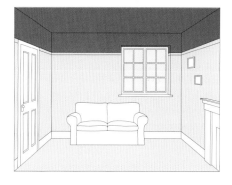

To optically reduce the height of a room still further, take the dark colour down to the picture rail. Using a light colour below the picture rail makes the room seem broader.

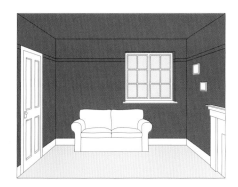

In a room where the walls and ceiling have been painted a dark colour, a light floor colour can be used to prevent the room from looking too cramped and oppressive.

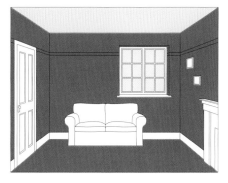

To make a room appear taller, the ceiling should be painted in a lighter colour than the walls. Using dark colours on the walls draws them closer together.

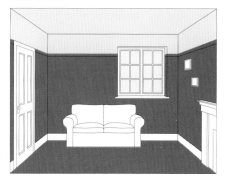

The heightening effect of using a light colour on the ceiling is diminished if that colour is taken down to the picture rail. This lowers the line of sight to the height of the picture rail.

# USING STRONG COLOURS

Once you've learned enough about colour to conquer your fear of it, you'll be eager to make full use of this potent resource in all its diverse hues and intensities. Deep, rich or vivid shades are not always an obvious choice, but they can make a powerful impression when they're used over large areas. Because they dominate their space totally, they have the potential to transform a dingy, awkward or featureless room into an irresistibly inviting one. Strong colours absorb more light than pale tints and can make a room look darker and smaller than it would with a more conventional treatment. Remember, though, that many stunning design schemes focus on cosiness, intimacy and drama rather than on size and brightness.

◀ In this living area, glowing tones of warm orange establish a strong design personality while creating an atmosphere that is not only warm but supremely relaxing. Note the choice of soft coral on architectural details such as the architrave and skirting – a bold change from the standard white or cream, and a choice that reinforces the room's exotic look.

## USING THE PALETTE

Intense colour is more suitable for some schemes than others. If you long to fill your home with radiant hues, explore sympathetic sources such as: tropical, Asian, Oriental, Moorish, Mexican or any look that has its origins in a warm, sunny climate and features colours such as bright pink, deep blue, crocus yellow, palm-leaf green or hot salsa shades. Re-create Provençal interiors using earthy reds and browns, yellows typical of sunflowers, greens found in the trees, vines and hills and blue to reflect the intense shades of the sky. Or consider bright retro looks based on the trends of the 1960s and 1970s. Be inspired by the fabrics, furniture, ceramics and art that were in fashion at the time.

◀ The rich shades of terracotta and forest green that dominate this striking scheme work well together. This is partly because their base hues, red and green, lie opposite one another on the colour wheel, and partly because they've been chosen to create an effective balance in terms of depth and intensity. As a result, neither of them overwhelms the other or the rest of the furnishings. Wisely, neutral floorcoverings and simple shapes allow the colour scheme to take centre stage.

◀ Enjoy all your meals in a carefree holiday mood for the cost of a few pots of sky-blue paint and simple curtains in sunny seaside stripes.

▶ For maximum drama, set off intricately carved furniture painted snowy white against the velvety darkness of navy walls and ceiling. Scatter cushions with a lime-green theme provide an additional layer of colour.

# USING PASTEL COLOURS

Gentle, relaxing and easy on the eye, pastel hues are one of the most popular of all colour palettes for the home. In design terms, one of their most useful qualities is that, as long as they are all equally pale, they always look good together. For this reason, never rely on commercial labelling when you are choosing your furnishings ("pastel rose" could mean anything from off-white with a slight blush to candy pink). Instead, use your own eye to assemble a collection of chalky hues that mix effortlessly in every combination and are ideal for setting off natural materials such as wicker, stone, and light or medium-toned wood; heavy dark timber, on the other hand, is likely to overpower delicate pastels.

◀ Large expanses of soft powder blue are guaranteed to look cool, fresh and light. In this large family bathroom, the scheme has been kept simple and traditional, with classic white fittings, towels and architectural detailing. The mellow tones of the natural wood floor add a touch of warmth to the blue-and-white scheme.

## USING THE PALETTE

☐ If you favour the tranquil prettiness of pastels, look to the following sources for inspiration: country-cottage schemes in which faded tints look

☐ wonderful on everything from colour-washed walls and hand-painted furniture to homespun, vegetable-dyed textiles and pretty florals; period-inspired schemes based on late 18th-to-early 19th-

☐ century styles such as Rococo, which suits feminine shades such as pink, soft blue and cream; modern styles that feature hues such as soft pistachio, eau de nil, lilac and pale lemon. Pastels look

☐ particularly refreshing when teamed with white. Use white in a two-colour scheme or use more pastel shades for greater variation. Keep the tonal values the same for the best look.

◀ Pastels are infinitely versatile: the appealing powder-blue shade that transforms this room creates a look that is fresh and energizing. Any hint of coldness is dispelled by the cosy woollen carpet and upholstery, and subtle accents in pale lemon and mauve.

◀ Without dominating the space, a band of soft yellow between the counter and ceiling helps to soften the hard edges of a modern kitchen.

▶ Use pastels to anchor monochrome schemes that feature several different tones of the same hue. The blue used on the walls of this country bedroom falls midway between the palest and darkest shades on display.

# USING NEUTRAL COLOURS

Neutral colours, often resorted to as a safe, lacklustre option in place of anything more adventurous, can be distinctly dingy and uninspiring. However, embraced with enthusiasm and skill, they can also represent the ultimate in cool, natural design sophistication.

To make neutral hues work, you must choose them as carefully as any other colours. An undisciplined mix of greenish taupe, yellowy cream and pinky beige, for example, will not blend magically just because all three are vaguely "neutral" in classification. To ensure success, stick to one basic version of each neutral colour you use (brown with a yellow rather than a red or blue cast, for example), and vary the tone, patterns and texture on each surface.

◄ Pale neutrals work well with generous proportions and graphic shapes to create an undemanding contemporary look. Here, a subtle scheme focuses attention on the outsized furnishings and fireplace and their richly textured surfaces. The jumbo scatter cushion helps to reinforce the room's chunky look and provides maximum comfort.

## USING THE PALETTE

Neutral shades feature widely in many contemporary styles such as: international modernism, the classical architectural look that features white walls, natural textures and materials, and shiny surfaces including chrome and glass; eco-chic, with its hand-woven textiles, hand-thrown pots, waxed timber and natural stone, all set off against walls brushed with distemper; and minimalism, a stark, uncompromising style from which all extraneous detail, ornament and colour have been eliminated. The neutral palette creates a calming atmosphere, across a variety of styles depending on the colour contrasts used. For the sharpest contrast of all, use black to create a harder, smarter, urban-chic style.

◄ Carefully chosen for their warmth, the scrumptious coffee, cream and chocolate tones that dominate here ensure an atmosphere that runs no risk of being sludgy or dull. The medium tone on the fireplace wall has a particularly appealing tendency to take on subtly different casts with the changing light. The earthy tones of the decorative scheme are enhanced by the natural wood floor.

◄ Many people find the purity and calm of a white bedroom perfectly conducive to rest and relaxation. However, introducing accents of colour, provided here by a jazzy throw, will ensure that the look does not become too cold and clinical.

► The stark contrast of dark-oak beams against dazzling white plaster highlights the soaring pitch of this dramatic loft space.

# COMBINING COLOURS

One of the least intimidating ways to approach colour combining is to think in terms of types or moods of colour before you consider precise hues. Colours can be grouped in many different ways: those that are found together in nature, for example, have a natural affinity with one another, as do colour families created by chemical dyes. Very pale tints mix effortlessly, as do very deep ones like wine, navy and bottle green. Once you've settled on a general type of colour, it's easier to focus on individual choices. Make full use sample pots, swatches and cards to help you see how colours work together. Some consumer paint ranges provide cross-referenced swatches or lists of recommended colour coordinations.

◀ Striking blocks of typically Art Deco colour (warm and slightly muted peach and lilac) define this strongly 1930s-inspired loft with its graphic, grid-like windows, sleek leather seating and low, clean-lined storage unit.

## USING THE PALETTE

If you don't know where to start when it comes to mixing colour, try to identify a general colour family that you particularly like. Think about: bright, citrus shades of orange, lime and lemon; autumn shades of gold, russet and brown; ice-cream tints such as rose, eau de nil, banana and aqua; earthy ochre, terracotta, chestnut and copper; intense jewel shades such as ruby, topaz, sapphire and amethyst. For a sleek, contemporary look, introduce accents of strong colours, such as bright turquoise, fuchsia pink or the primaries, into a black-and-white scheme. For a softer look, incorporate more mellow shades, such as pretty pinks and golds, into a neutral scheme based around cream and coffee shades.

◄ Vivid tropical hues can be cleverly combined to create a cool, exotic scheme. Here, intense azure blue, palm-leaf green and lavender are punctuated with warm accents of crocus yellow and crimson to produce a look that is stimulating but not jarring. Neutral tints on the ceiling and floor provide the necessary contrast and balance.

◄ In this open, airy space, fondant-hued walls define different activity areas. Contemporary art and sleek modern furniture, however, ensure that the overall effect is not sugary.

▶ An old-fashioned garden provided the inspiration for this delightful scheme. Dominant colours are rose pink, crocus yellow and wisteria blue, with blocks of appropriately leafy green for accent.

# WORKING WITH PATTERN

Like colours, the patterns you choose for a room can alter your visual perception of it, change its mood significantly, and help to create a wide range of design periods and styles. Fresh checks suggest a country theme, for example, while rich paisley swirls embody the Victorian era. When working with different patterns, the trick is to find a harmonious middle ground between the sterile and dated look of obsessively coordinated fabrics and wallpapers, and the aesthetic mayhem that results when ill-matched patterns cover too many surfaces. If you're lacking in experience, remember that starting with plain walls and floors will allow you to experiment with pattern elsewhere, and reduce the risk of expensive design disasters. Keep in mind too that most rooms contain large areas of informal pattern that are easy to overlook when you're putting a scheme together: a wall of shelves packed with books or collectables, for instance, or a wooden floor made up of intricate parquet tiles.

▲ Simple black-and-white motifs help to create a 1950s look in this contemporary Swedish living room. Note how skilfully the scale of each pattern has been linked to its use: small doodle-like shapes for the throw-cushion covers, and big bold circles woven into the striking sunshine-yellow rug.

▶ Stripes in soft shades of grey-blue adorn almost every surface in this inviting bedroom including the walls, the windows, the high-hinged screen and the narrow rug beside the bed. The painted floorboards subtly reinforce the stripy theme while providing a welcome expanse of solid colour.

## WALLS

Use pattern to change the apparent proportions of a room or to disguise any awkward architectural features. It's a design truism that vertical stripes make a room look taller, but keep in mind, too, that horizontal lines can make it appear wider. Stripes, of course, don't have to be in the form of wallpaper. In fact, if your walls or ceiling are not perfectly straight, the unforgiving geometry of printed stripes will make this more obvious. For a more flexible alternative, or to create a less formal look, employ painted lines or even tongue-and-groove cladding (fixed vertically or horizontally) to achieve a similar effect. To camouflage sloping ceilings or projecting corners, use one pattern with a small design throughout the room.

◄ In this Moorish-inspired bathroom, ceramic wall tiles in harmonious tones of blue create a subtle underwater effect. Tiles offer numerous options for creating pattern, from the simplicity of plain white clay with a grouting of similar tone to the complex designs produced by large arrays of hand-decorated squares.

▶ The unique and stylish detailing on these plain pale walls has been achieved with only a few sample paint pots and a steady hand. The vertical lines were drawn using a plumb line, then painted over. The rectangles were outlined in pencil, marked off with masking tape, then filled in.

## FLOORS

In most homes, floorcoverings use up a higher proportion of the decorating budget than any other element. It is also true that patterned floors present more design problems than plain ones, so if your confidence is faltering, stick with the simpler option. If you opt for pattern, do so only as a positive choice, not as a misguided attempt to disguise dirt: any design that is complex and colourful enough to do this is unlikely to flatter your room, and small, regular motifs make stains more, not less, obvious. There are two ways to use pattern on the floor:

● As an all-over design

● In the form of a bespoke surface that defines the room using central panels, borders or corner motifs.

▲ The richly coloured stone tiles that cover the floor (and the walls) of this bathroom provide subtle visual interest and focus attention on the intricate mosaic insets.

◄ An Op-art variation on chequerboard tiles, this practical vinyl floor sets the scene perfectly in a retro kitchen. The bold design of the flooring is offset by the plain colours and clean lines of the furnishings.

## Combining pattern

The skilful mixing of patterns that are all different, yet complement each other and their setting perfectly, is one of the hallmarks of a really stylish room. Developing a sure and instinctive eye for pattern takes time, but you can't go far wrong if you begin by limiting your choices to patterns that feature the same types of colour. For example, spring rose, leafy green, daffodil yellow and cornflower blue are all clear, fresh tints, while russet, bark, flame and ginger are all autumnal shades. Vivid pink, orange and yellow are all bright, funky hues, while fawn, lavender, grey and silvery green are subdued shades.

It is also important that the patterns you combine have broadly similar personalities. For instance, homely ticking stripes have nothing in common with stylized period ones and should not be mixed. However, patterns do not necessarily have to have similar motifs. Straightforward checks and stripes, for instance, work well together with similar patterns or with simple country florals. Varying the scale slightly between patterns displayed together will add interest to the mix, but don't go too far: tiny delicate shapes beside huge bold ones are much more likely to look disastrous than decorative.

◀ Strict adherence to ice-cream tints and straight-edge shapes gives this pattern-filled room a mellow, harmonious feel. A geometric theme is established with the customized paint treatment on the walls, which is then carried through in the designs of the framed prints, the cubical storage unit and the rug.

▲ At first glance, the only large area of pattern in this lofty bathroom seems to be provided by a Roman blind. In fact, the kaleidoscope of light and shadow made by the glow of a pierced pendant lamp falling upon trailing ivy, sinuous shelf brackets, and decorative glass bottles also creates intricate patterns.

## WINNING COMBINATIONS

Although they weren't selected from coordinated ranges, the patterns in each of the groups below work well together because they share colour families (although not precise hues) as well as general characteristics. The stripes, for example, with their muted, broken colours, have closer links with a formal drawing room than a circus tent or a seaside hut.

Sophisticated stripes

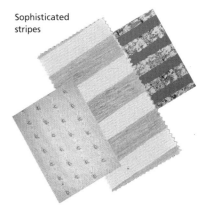

▲ The textiles that dress this high brass bed are linked by their rich, warm colouring and stylized floral motifs. Behind the bedhead, a silky Persian rug acts as an opulent wall hanging, while oriental cushions supplement the traditional pillows.

◄ In this fairytale child's bedroom, a vibrant furnishing fabric dominates the scheme. Adding interest are the tiny yellow checks on the bedlinen and curtain borders, and the pattern on the walls. Dotted among these are painted flowerpots copied from the fabric.

Country flowers

Cheerful checks

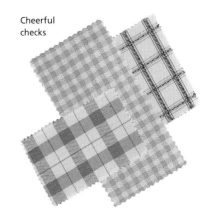

# USING TEXTURE

Introducing one or two tactile elements allows you to experience the space through touch as well as sight. Materials such as stone, brick, plaster, sisal or unbleached linen all have pleasing natural irregularities that create a reassuring three-dimensional effect. A mellow wooden floor will bring colour and warmth to a room decorated in a neutral palette, while accents such as smooth velvet cushions, a luxurious chenille throw, a knotty rug, a terracotta pot or a piece of gnarled driftwood will add further textural interest.

## FABRICS

From shiny silk, satin or taffeta to coarser materials such as hessian, felt or tweed, fabrics offer a wealth of textural interest. Think about the other furnishings and furniture in your room when choosing new fabrics. In the same way that certain colours work well together, so do different textures. Silk, for example, works very well with rough materials as well as smooth, shiny materials such as dark wood or chrome.

▲ Always consider where different textures are placed in relation to each other. In this bedroom, the bed's wooden frame and headboard help to offset the opulent texture of the bedspread, cushions and curtains.

▲ Our response to texture is not always as immediate as it is to such things as colour or pattern, but our senses do instinctively register how the surfaces of different materials look and feel, whether they are warm or cold, rough or smooth, fine or coarse. In this neutral scheme, the chair cover, curtains and tablecloth are counterbalanced by the pottery, pebbles and wooden picture frames to create interesting layers of different textures.

▶ Textural variation is particularly important in rooms where there is little background colour. In this white bedroom, subtle contrasts of texture are provided by the floaty muslin at the window and the crisp white bedlinen. Further injections of texture are provided by the low wicker table and vase of dried grasses.

## WALL COVERINGS

Your walls are an intrinsic part of your interior decoration. Use them as a neutral background for effects of colour and texture that you have created in the rest of your room, or make them a central, textural feature, either by putting up wall hangings, cladding or panelling, or by using textured wallpapers or paints. You can also add interest to your walls, particularly in older properties, by dividing them with features such as a dado rail.

▼ In a cavernous loft space carved out of a converted warehouse, the exposed brick walls bring a warmth and textural interest that wouldn't be possible if they were smoothly plastered. The rough texture of the walls contrasts with the smoother surface of the mezzanine area.

◄ Wood has an inherent tactile quality that invites you to reach out and touch it. In this dining room, the cheerful yellow on the walls helps to pick out the different grains of the wood flooring and pine furniture.

## FLOORING

Floors provide a large surface area on which to experiment with different materials such as wood, slate, stone or vinyl. However, practicality as well as style should govern your choice. Think about how much wear and tear the room will get and whether you will be happy with certain textures. Ceramic tiles, for instance, are a hardwearing choice in a bathroom, but if you hate having cold feet you may prefer a warmer, softer option.

▼ Suggesting Scandinavian country style, whitewashed floorboards make an informal, low-maintenance floorcovering that sits comfortably in either a traditional or a contemporary scheme. Placing a rug over a hard floor not only provides welcome warmth and comfort underfoot, but also creates another layer of texture.

▼ In a sparsely furnished living room, an expanse of hard-wearing textured carpet becomes a feature in its own right. The fireplace and pots provide additional textural dimensions.

## TEXTURAL CONTRAST

Hard or soft, rough or smooth, shiny or matt, variations of texture can have a profound impact on the overall look and feel of a room, especially in neutral schemes where there is little colour or pattern, or where decorative elements are kept to a minimum. Natural materials such as unpolished wood, wicker, seagrass, terracotta or cork tiles, or wool have warm, comforting properties and can help to inject some colour. Hard, shiny surfaces – glass, marble, ceramics and stainless steel – help to reflect the light and make rooms appear brighter and cooler.

## TEXTURED WALLS

Walls provide an ideal canvas on which to experiment with variations of texture, from rough plaster to smooth, silky emulsion. The new generation of textured paints offers subtle metallic, chalky and sandy finishes that enhance the walls and reflect the natural light. These tactile paints can be used on whole walls to create solid blocks of texture or combined with flat paints to bring interesting contrasts.

▲ A variety of tactile elements including leather, marble, wood, stone, cotton and wool have been cleverly combined in a living room that is coolly understated yet welcoming.

▶ A patchwork of jewel-like velvet squares on the wall, cushions and bedspread brings a touch of opulence to a bedroom.

◀ In a rustic bedroom, an antique bedspread and wall-hung rug complement the muted tones of the wood, earthenware and wicker.

▲ The mellow tones of a terracotta pot teamed with a collection of tribal masks are all that is needed to bring textural interest to a neutral scheme.

▶ Chosen for their light-reflecting properties, the chrome fittings, glass basin, vitrified ceramic tiles and mirror have transformed a small, awkward space with no natural light into a bright, stylish bathroom. The matt texture of the wood floor makes an interesting contrast to the shiny surfaces.

## SOFT FURNISHINGS

● Shiny fabrics such as silk, taffeta and moiré reflect the light and can be used for cushions, throws and curtains.

● For a tactile, natural floorcovering, consider coarse textures such as jute, sisal, coir, seagrass or rush matting; carpets that have similar textural qualities include cord and some of the more rugged wool weaves. For a smoother finish there is linoleum, rubber or vinyl.

● Rugs, throws, kilims, dhurries and rag rugs can all be used to introduce small touches of texture into a room.

● Patterned fabrics include tartan plaid, brocade, damask, chintz, embroidered tapestry, crewelwork, bouclé and toile.

# PROPORTION

When most of us are faced with designing a room or buying an item of furniture, we think first of the style, colour and size of any potential purchase. But even when a chair or a cabinet meets your requirements in all these areas, it will still look out of place if its proportions don't work with the other objects around it and the room itself.

When it comes to home design, proportion is just as much a matter of common sense as strict rules (see box opposite), and many architectural styles dictate, to some degree, their own requirements. Victorian reception rooms, for example, tend to have higher ceilings than those in newly built houses and can therefore take large, imposing items of furniture that would look wrong in a smaller, modern bungalow.

◄ The owners of this lofty Victorian drawing room have ignored the kind of high, formal furniture intended for it in favour of an exotic, laid back Eastern style. The theme is established with low daybeds that accentuate the room's vertical proportions and free the walls for prints and pictures that would otherwise look too large. The warm colour scheme reinforces the ethnic look and helps to create a cosier, more relaxed atmosphere than would have been the case with shades such as white or pale blue.

◄ A large, modern bed is in scale with the proportions of a tall, contemporary interior. Introducing items of different heights, such as the pairs of lights, helps to make the room feel less imposing.

▲ Large seating units can often work well in a small space. Here, a large daybed occupies an entire wall of a box-shaped room. The child's armchair and stool play further visual tricks with the proportions of the space.

▼ To accommodate a large-scale, ornate bed, this modestly sized bedroom has been given a simple, strong colour treatment on the walls, while the rest of the floor area remains clear.

## HINTS AND TIPS

● Never furnish a large or high room with lots of small, spindly pieces of furniture; they will always look out of place.

● King-size storage items (cabinets, shelf units, wardrobes etc.) can look fabulous filling a whole wall; if they're not valuable antiques, consider giving them the same paint treatment to achieve an almost built-in look.

● Low furniture can make rooms look higher, so if you find your ceiling oppressive, choose your seating and storage accordingly.

● To expand a small, low room visually, hang curtains from floor to ceiling and from wall to wall instead of stopping them at the window frame.

● High-ceilinged rooms should be balanced with one or two tall items of furniture.

# LIGHTING

No matter how much time and money you spend on decorating your home, if the lighting doesn't come up to scratch, then a room will never really look or feel right. Making sure that you have enough of the right kind of illumination should be one of your main priorities when you are planning the room. Begin by looking at the space from different angles and at different times of day. Even a room that gets plenty of sunlight will need some back-up on very dull days. Think about what the room will be used for and at what time of day or night and whether there are any decorative features or pieces of furniture that you would like to highlight. Consider, too, how light will affect the room's proportions and the perception of space. A tall, high-ceilinged room will feel cosier and less imposing if the source of light is directed downwards, whereas in a low-ceilinged space the light should point upwards. Placing candles in front of mirrors also helps to create a feeling of spaciousness.

▲ Simple night lights make an unusual and decorative floor-level lighting display. Note how the ceramic pots and pieces of volcanic lava help to reflect the light.

▶ Intense sunlight needs to be controlled. Here, floor-length semi-opaque curtains help to filter out the sun's rays without throwing the living room into darkness. Venetian blinds, available in a range of finishes, would also work in this modern setting, allowing the level of light to be adjusted as necessary and creating an attractive dappled effect. Note the two stylish freestanding uplighters that bathe the ceiling in light at night. Overhead, a skylight lets in more light.

## HINTS AND TIPS

● Dimmer switches allow you to control the intensity of light. Suitable for table and floor lamps and ceiling and wall lights, they are rated so that you can dim more than one light at a time.

● Install extra sockets if necessary.

● Always shade a light source to avoid glare and hard-edged shadows. Desk and table lamps should be positioned so that the bulb is not visible to the user.

● Try to plan so that each light, or group of lights, can be operated separately. Wall switches should be by the room's entrance.

▲ Natural light can become an important decorative feature in its own right. In a high-ceilinged loft space, sunlight flooding through the windows creates an alluring display of silhouettes on the large expanse of white wall.

▶ In a modern bathroom with no natural light, ceiling-recessed spotlights provide the right amount of task lighting without making the room feel cold and clinical. Glass, metallic and ceramic surfaces help to reflect the light. Bathroom lights should be enclosed if they are likely to get wet and should always be operated by a pull cord; if needed, a dimmer switch should be wired outside the room.

## NATURAL LIGHT

The intensity of daylight, and its partner, shadow, changes at different times of the day and with the seasons. The play of light affects the mood and colour of a room and should always be taken into account when planning a scheme. If possible, choose a room's function according to the quality of sunlight it gets and at what time of the day. In rooms with no natural light, such as a bathroom, you may consider having a skylight or window fitted. Choose materials that have light-reflecting properties, such as clear glass or perspex shelving, mirrors, chrome and pale wood. Use an oil-based paint and choose a finish that catches the light. This will help to create a more open feeling to the room.

▲ A large arched window ensures that this top-floor room in Brussels is not thrown into gloom during the day. The light, airy effect is reinforced by the paintwork, wood floor and large, arched mirror. Outside shutters allow the window to be left free of curtains. Artificial light is provided by the Art Deco lamps.

◄ A predominantly white scheme looks fresh and energizing in a spacious attic that is bathed in natural light for most of the day. In a room that gets little sun or loses the best light after early morning, a warmer tone such as dusky pink or pale yellow might be a more appropriate choice.

## ARTIFICIAL LIGHT

A single bulb suspended from the ceiling is seldom adequate, nor is it the most flattering option for the room or its occupants. Ideally, you should incorporate a combination of the three main types of lighting. Ambient light, in the form of pendants or up- or downlighters, throws light over a large area and provides the main background illumination in a room. Task lighting includes desk lamps or halogen spots to concentrate illumination on to a specific activity, such as cooking; the best task lighting is adjustable, allowing you to direct the illumination to where it is needed. Accent lighting picks out interesting features, such as a painting, and is provided by spots, strips or picture lights.

◀ Skilfully arranged downlighters bring pattern and tonal variation to a spare, minimalist hallway. Concealed lighting throws the stairs into relief. For safety, always light the top and bottom steps of a staircase.

▲ In an old-fashioned hallway, the red shade on a traditional table lamp casts a mellow glow that complements the staircase and beams, and a wall-mounted lamp highlights a display of plates.

### LIGHT BULBS

● Tungsten bulbs have a soft, slightly yellow cast, which illuminates colours well.

● Fluorescent bulbs have a long life and emit little heat, but their cool blue light can be rather unflattering and hard on the eyes.

● Halogen bulbs are much smaller than the alternatives. They produce a strong, clear light, without either a warm or cool cast.

# FURNITURE

Whether it is antique or stylishly modern, a family heirloom or a junk-shop find, a piece of furniture should appeal to the senses, inviting us to look at it and use it. Think about the furniture you have – or intend to acquire – when you are planning a room's layout, and consider how its shape, style, or historical or cultural references can be woven into the decorative scheme. A beautiful Art Deco dressing table could be the starting point for a period bedroom or a set of 1950s chairs the inspiration behind a retro-style kitchen. Think, too, about the size of your furniture in relation to the proportions of your room. The size of a chair or sofa may make all the difference. And remember, moving furniture is the cheapest, and often the best, way to breathe fresh life into a room.

▲ Choose furniture that reflects the room's function. A large three-seater sofa massed with plump cushions and teamed with occasional tables helps to inspire a feeling of comfort and relaxation.

◄ The sofa, chairs and ottoman have been upholstered in restful, neutral fabrics to harmonize with the rest of the living room.

▶ Arranging tables and chairs in groups in different parts of the room, rather than clustered together in the centre, can help to make a large, high-ceilinged room feel cosier and less imposing. These elegant Gustavian-style dining chairs have been pushed back, helping to make a feature of the tall window.

▶ Antique furniture can have an inherent charm that endures, where contemporary pieces can easily look dated. Here a four-poster draped in pretty toile fabric brings elegant 18th-century style to a bedroom.

## HINTS AND TIPS

● Moving furniture around from time to time can help to breathe new life into a scheme. You could bring seasonal changes to a living room, for example, by arranging the chairs around the fire in winter and then turning them to face the windows in summer.

● Buy the best quality bed that you can and ideally one that is at least 15 cm (6 in) longer than the tallest person sleeping in it. The mattress should offer good support and be covered in a natural fabric. Always lie on the bed to test it out before you buy.

● Make sure that a dining table is big enough – or can be extended – to seat the right number of people.

● When you go to buy a new piece of furniture, always have a copy of the room's measurements and a tape measure with you. Check that bulky items will fit through doors and, if necessary, up any stairs.

● There should be sufficient clearance between individual pieces of furniture so that people can move easily around and through a room.

# FINISHING TOUCHES

It is often the small touches that can bring life, warmth and unity to a room, so always think about how you can incorporate treasured possessions and appealing details when planning a scheme. An heirloom quilt, a favourite vase or one or two well-chosen cushions might, for example, help to create a visual link with the walls, furniture and soft furnishings. Observe the colours of a painting and think about how they can be repeated elsewhere – as accents on cushions or rugs, perhaps, or in larger amounts on walls or floors. You may want to pick out a particular shade with flowers or fruit. Interesting architectural features, such as an intricately tiled fireplace or ornate cornicing, can also provide a wealth of inspiration for a decorative scheme.

▲ In a bedroom with a distinctly oriental flavour, an amber-coloured glass vase picks out the mellow tones of the wooden headboard and curved bedside table with its integral reading lamp.

▼ Flowers, chosen to match the stunning shade of purple on the couch, and carefully arranged paintings help to reinforce the strong interplay of colour and symmetry in this living room. Note how the shape of the glass vases helps to define the sculptural form of the couch.

▶ In a calm, minimalist interior, a simple arrangement of twigs is not crowded out by other pieces but given plenty of space to breathe. The colours and textures are echoed in the wooden floor and table and the wicker chairs.

▶ The small, gilt-framed bird painting in the top left-hand corner was the inspiration for this scheme. The electric blue has been alluded to on the elegant Regency-style sofa, picked out with gold cushions. The colours are also picked out around the window and on the scatter cushions on the floor.

▲ The hand-painted base of a wood-topped kitchen table presented a decorative starting point for the rest of the scheme. Teamed with the whites and watery eau-de-nil shades used elsewhere, the repeated fish motif and casual arrangement of shells and pebbles help to conjure up a nautical theme. Hanging the two large pictures one on top of each other, as shown here, ensures that they become focal points, rather than being dwarfed by the proportions of the high-ceilinged room. Notice how a simple bowl of oranges adds a welcome splash of vibrant colour to the scheme.

# HINTS AND TIPS

Faced with an awkward design problem, many of us are tempted either to ignore it altogether or to splash out on a programme of redecoration that may not be necessary. In many cases, a new surface, a change of use, or simply a fresh way of looking at the situation is enough to transform a boring, awkward or wasted corner into a stylish and practical feature.

## TINY TILES

One of the most ancient forms of decoration, mosaic tiles can add colour, pattern and texture to walls, floors, furniture or work surfaces. Most complex mosaic designs are sold on a backing of paper or net so they are easy to install, but the tiles are also sold loose so you can build up your own patterns and choose your own colours to create a variety of pictorial motifs or abstract designs.

Over large areas, mosaics can be quite expensive, but they are much more affordable for floors or walls in small spaces like bathrooms, or as a way of giving a personal finish to a humdrum architectural feature or item of furniture, such as a table (see pp.162–163). If you like working with mosaics, create unusual pattern-on-pattern effects using fragments of broken china (odd or chipped plates are ideal) instead of standard tiles. (Note that this treatment is unsuitable for floors or work surfaces.)

▲ If you have an unattractive view, hang translucent blinds or curtains to preserve modesty and admit light, then add interest with an inventive trim. Here, red gerberas adorn the middle of three panels in pale muslin and provide an unusual touch.

◄ Blend a traditional fireplace into a modern scheme by painting it to match the walls (paint inside only if the flue is blocked off). Use bright, coloured mosaics to decorate the surround.

▼ An exquisite mosaic floor with classical scroll border makes this tiny bathroom look larger than it is. The all-over colour treatment also enhances this effect.

## UNDER THE STAIRS

Whether your main stairs rise from an entrance hall or a ground-floor room, the area underneath them can be difficult to utilize to its full advantage. Restricted in height and cut off from natural light, the space under the stairs tends to get boxed in to form a cave-like cupboard, or is treated as a semi-permanent dumping ground for bulky possessions in need of a home.

To maximize the potential of this awkward triangle, either draw up a room plan specially designed to accommodate its limitations (by locating a seating, dining or working area here, for example), or invest in a purpose-made storage system that allows you to see – and to reach – all the contents easily, instead of having to explore shadowy nooks and crannies to find what you want. At its most basic, such a system could involve a simple row of hooks for coats and jackets or a row of hooks fixed at increasing distances from the floor to follow the line of the staircase, and a few stylish bags suspended from them to hold unlovely necessities. For items that are too heavy or bulky to hang, add a roomy wooden, metal or wicker chest. A built-in cupboard featuring different-sized shelves could be used for storing items such as shoes.

▲ As part of an open-plan reception area, the under-stairs corner is an ideal place for a small dining table; this round one with its neat central pedestal makes it easy for diners to slip in and out of the inside chair. Overhead, a narrow beam downlighter relieves the gloom and casts a flattering glow on the setting and the food.

▶ Custom-built, and fixed on an ingenious track system, these stepped, timber-framed shelving units store a wide range of household items from shoes to bedlinen. Note the unobtrusive finger holes that take the place of conventional handles.

### STORAGE SOLUTIONS

If your rooms are overrun with clutter, investigate the storage potential of wasted spaces.

● Fix a shelf at picture-rail height across a small room or along a corridor to store items such as out-of-season clothing, family archives and old correspondence. Hide untidy collections inside stylish boxes, baskets and files.

● In a tiny bathroom install a high shelf across one wall for spare toiletries, towels and medicines; tuck a compact stool under the basin to afford easy access.

● If you need a new bed, buy one with drawers built into the base, or a hinged mattress with a roomy compartment underneath.

● Insert freestanding internal shelves into your kitchen cupboards so that you can use the wasted space above a single layer of tins, jars or glasses.

## STOLEN SPACES

When it's not possible to create the storage provision you need from completely dead space, you should consider carving it out of an existing room. If you're clever, you'll hardly notice the loss of space, and the extra storage capacity you gain may just swallow up all your excess possessions.

A dramatic example of this tactic would be a purpose-designed storage system (shelves, hanging rails, hooks, racks, baskets – whatever fills your needs) fitted wall-to-wall and floor-to-ceiling across a room. Concealed behind large doors (folding or sliding) or inexpensive curtains or blinds (made from calico, sheeting or ticking, for example), a capacious unit like this can be designed to complement any decorating style and will encourage even the most inveterate hoarder to live in a cool, clutter-free environment.

On a smaller scale, consider framing a doorway with a deep shelf unit that can hold anything from china and foodstuffs in the kitchen to toys and games in a child's bedroom or a small library of books in the living room.

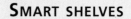

◀ This elegant shelving arch, with its architrave border, deep skirting board and witty mock keystone over the door), merges seamlessly into the room's traditional structure.

▲ One wall of this kitchen has been turned into much-needed storage, its sleek sliding doors giving easy, compact access. Internal lighting reveals the entire contents at a glance.

## SMART SHELVES

No matter how much you spend on furnishings, flimsy shelving sagging under the weight of its contents will spoil the appearance of any room.

● Make sure all your shelves (particularly those intended for books) have plenty of support in the form of strong brackets, timber battens or concealed rods fixed into the plaster. For more advice on fitting different kinds of shelving, see pp.166–175.

● Use chunky timber or man-made board (reclaimed railway sleepers, for example, make sensational shelves), or add a decorative strip along the front of each shelf to add visual weight and a quality finish (see library unit, left).

## CAMOUFLAGE TRICKS

One of the most useful decorating skills is the ability to disguise or hide inelegant – yet indispensable – features with ingenuity and flair. Whether you use folding screens, trompe-l'oeil brushwork, fabric panels, specially designed curtains and blinds, judiciously positioned furniture or custom-made carpentry, these will help you to make the most of the space and resources you have to work with. On a warning note, make sure any concealment involving services like plumbing and electricity allows quick access in an emergency.

▶ While open-plan living allows you to take advantage of light and space, it does limit your ability to hide any mess. In this fresh, citrus-bright studio, a permanent semi-circular screen made from plywood and MDF retains the sense of space while separating the main activity areas; on the kitchen side, a deep work surface allows you to leave dirty plates and saucepans out of sight of dinner party guests.

◀ Unless you can afford sleek, sculptural radiators, or you're lucky enough to have chunky, old-fashioned ones, radiators and storage heaters are charmless parts of your decor. Here, one of the offending objects is neatly boxed in with MDF, its warmth escaping through a row of curvy cut-outs.

▲ Fitted cupboards are one of the best storage solutions available, but in a tiny bedroom they can appear to be overwhelming. To render it almost invisible, this cupboard has been concealed behind a flush door papered to match the walls, fitted with a neat, unobtrusive handle and close-hung with floral prints.

# DESIGN
# IN
# PRACTICE

HAVING THOUGHT THROUGH how you would like your interior to look, and armed with ideas about how you can use elements such as texture and colour, you can now set about the exciting task of transforming your home. Whether you are planning a complete overhaul or would simply like to make one or two decorative improvements, this chapter will show you how it can be done, room by room. Inspirational photographs, before-and-after shots and practical floor plans show you what can be achieved, often for a limited outlay of time, effort and money. Helpful information boxes will guide you through tried-and-tested design solutions and steer you through some of the common pitfalls. There is advice on everything from safety and ergonomic planning to choosing the right flooring, furniture, and wallcovering. You will also see how improving the lighting and storage stystems in rooms such as the kitchen or bathroom, making some provision for a utility area and ensuring that your home office is as comfortable as possible will add immeasurably to your quality of life.

# CREATING YOUR ROOM PLAN

## HINTS AND TIPS

• Plan for clear traffic paths between the door and all the main activity areas.

• Allow plenty of clearance for each item of furniture to be used comfortably. Chest of drawers and cabinets, for example, require enough space in front of them so their drawers and doors can be opened easily.

• Note the distance between the window sill and the floor, so you know what will fit underneath.

• The alcoves on either side of a fireplace are not necessarily the same size; always measure each of them individually.

• Position large items, such as a bed or couch, first—there is likely to be a limited number of places where they can fit comfortably.

• Make sure that multifunctional items, such as a sofa bed or folding table, have sufficient clearance.

• Before you decide on a place for the television, be sure that the screen is free of glare.

• Locate electrical goods or telecommunications equipment as near as possible to their relevant outlets to avoid trailing wires.

• Always have a copy of any measurements at hand when you are buying a piece of furniture or such items as curtains—also bring a tape measure with you.

• Take careful measurements of interior and exterior doorways to make sure that bulky items such as a bed, couch, or armoire will be able to fit through.

Before you settle on a final arrangement for any of your rooms, you will probably resort to a certain amount of trial-and-error furniture moving. To keep this to a minimum, however, and to avoid any costly mistakes when it comes to buying new items, take the time to make an accurate room plan on which you can try out all the possibilities and eliminate those that are completely unworkable.

To do this, draw a scale plan of each room on a large sheet of graph paper, marking on it not only all the relevant measurements, including such objects as built-in furniture, but also the position of items such as radiators, fireplaces, power and telecommunications outlets, plumbing facilities where relevant, and the clearance needed for any doors or windows that open into the room.

## PLACING THE FURNITURE

Once you have created a basic floor plan, you can then decide where pieces of furniture—either built-in or freestanding—are to go. Take measurements of existing pieces, as well as any items you intend to buy, and, on another sheet of graph paper, using the same scale, draw and cut out templates that can be positioned onto your floor plan.

◀ For general purposes, a simple floor plan will do. If precise information about recesses and projections is required (for built-in cabinets, perhaps), a system of diagonal measurements can be used.

▲ Sketch a wall plan (an elevation) indicating permanent features and noting all relevant measurements such as the height and width of a door and the height of a radiator.

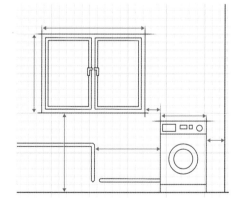

▲ With complex elements, such as water, waste, and domestic appliances, it's vital to record the exact position of existing plumbing and features such as windows.

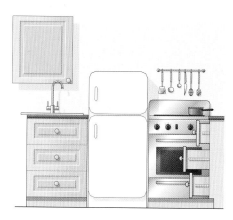

◀ Poor planning can have dire consequences. In this ill-considered kitchen, heat from the oven puts strain on the refrigerator and wastes energy. Open drawers hinder access to the oven door, and cooking utensils are kept in a dangerous position above the burners.

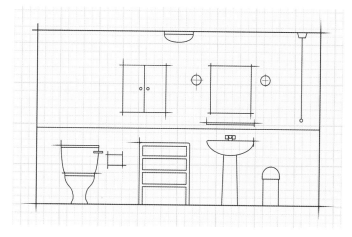

▲ For a hardworking space, such as a bathroom, an accurate elevation diagram will help you to position items attached to the walls, such as a cabinet or towel rack, logically in relation to fixed elements such as the toilet and sink (see p.101).

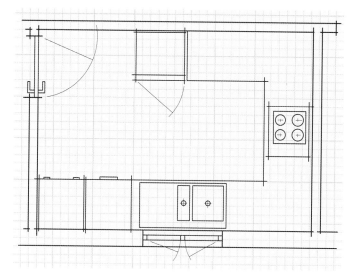

▲ A floor plan should record the position of all major furnishings and appliances. In this aerial view, the ergonomically sound kitchen has been designed around a classic work triangle (13 ft 3 in/4 m maximum) formed by the refrigerator, the stove, and the sink. Door and window swings are indicated (see p.77).

## SPACE PLANNING

▲ Clever planning allows you to make full use of the space you have. Relieve pressure on a family bathroom by turning the area under the stairs into an extra bathroom. A toilet fits neatly into the angle made by the stairs, while a miniature sink is less bulky than a standard model.

▲ Hanging the door to open outward leaves enough space inside the room for a neat storage area beside the sink. To reduce the clearance necessary, a folding door has been attached instead of a solid one; translucent glass panels allow privacy but also admit some light.

# PLANNING YOUR KITCHEN

## KITCHEN CHECKLIST

......................................................

● How large is your kitchen? Is it a living and entertaining space as well as somewhere to cook? How much time do you spend there?

● How many people use the kitchen? Will more than one person be preparing/cooking, serving or clearing up at one time?

● Are you a family? Will there be children running in and out? Even if your kitchen is small, do you need space for a baby's high chair?

● Could bulky items such as a washing machine or a freezer be housed elsewhere?

● Is a dishwasher a priority? Do you have space to stack and unstack without being cramped?

● Is the current lighting system sufficient? Do you have enough task lighting and in the right places?

● Do you want to look out of the window when preparing food or when you are at the sink?

● Do you want a single or double sink? Have you got enough space on each side to stack and drain your crockery?

● Do you need to reposition the plumbing and electrical points or put more in?

● How much storage do you need? Are there any wasted spaces that could be better used? Would drawers be easier to access?

● Do you entertain a lot? Are you happy for your guests to be in the kitchen while you are preparing a meal?

The kitchen is perhaps the most important room in a house, and regardless of whether you have a tiny galley kitchen or a spacious kitchen/dining room, making sure that the layout is well organized will add to your enjoyment of your home. Firstly you must consider how you live and what sort of kitchen you want. Look at the available space and decide what furniture, storage and equipment you will require. You may need to make adjustments to the plumbing, lighting or ventilation, or install additional power points. Careful planning will ensure that your kitchen functions efficiently and is a safe, comfortable and enjoyable place to be in.

**CASE STUDY: SMALL OPEN-PLAN KITCHEN**
Tucked into the corner of a combined living and dining area, this compact kitchen makes very good use of space and has been cleverly designed to blend with the rest of the room. The island unit has storage on both sides and can be used for preparing and serving meals. The unit also helps to screen off the main cooking area without isolating the cook. Introducing a different floor surface also serves to divide off the room's different functions. There is a good combination of open and closed storage, including drawers, cupboards and shelves. The wall cabinets have been custom-built to fit the available space and feature shelves of different heights. The kitchen also has plenty of easily accessible power points. Note how the fridge, sink and cooker are all in easy reach of each other.

## KITCHEN ORGANIZATION

There are two important principles that you should follow when planning the layout of your kitchen. One is the "work triangle" (4 m [13ft 4 in] maximum), which emphasises the need for an easy, unobstructed path between the three main activity areas: sink, cooker and fridge. The second is best understood by the motto "store, prepare, cook, wash, serve, door", which explains the linear working practice of preparing and serving a meal. Plan your storage, work surfaces and appliances according to where you use them in this sequence. There are many space-saving solutions, such as corner sinks, that will help you make the most of a small space.

◄▼ The original units in this galley kitchen have been given an instant face lift with a coat of paint and new handles. The glass shelving, splashback and counter top all make the kitchen feel lighter and less enclosed. Replacing one of the wall cupboards with open storage for pans and other utensils has also helped to open up the space.

## KITCHEN PLAN

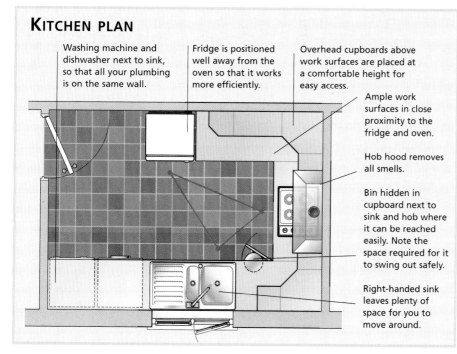

Washing machine and dishwasher next to sink, so that all your plumbing is on the same wall.

Fridge is positioned well away from the oven so that it works more efficiently.

Overhead cupboards above work surfaces are placed at a comfortable height for easy access.

Ample work surfaces in close proximity to the fridge and oven.

Hob hood removes all smells.

Bin hidden in cupboard next to sink and hob where it can be reached easily. Note the space required for it to swing out safely.

Right-handed sink leaves plenty of space for you to move around.

## KITCHEN PLANS

When you are planning the layout of your kitchen, look carefully at the space and think about the process of what you do and where and when you do it, and try to place everything in a logical position so that you never have to go far for anything.

Place your cupboards at a comfortable reaching height for you and other adults.

**Narrow galley**
A narrow galley only allows for units and electrics to be placed along one wall. Use the "store, prepare, cook, wash, serve, door" rule.

**Wide galley**
A small narrow kitchen may still allow you to have units along two sides, in which case, follow the "work triangle" rule.

**L-shaped**
The "work triangle" works well. This design can be used in a kitchen/dining room, with one arm of the "L" separating the two areas.

**Horseshoe**
This allows for the best use of the "working triangle", in which the cook literally has to move only the same distance from hob, sink and fridge.

**Island unit**
Islands suit big kitchens where they can literally be the centre of activity. They can also be used for storage and dining.

# KITCHEN STYLE

## WORK SURFACES

Choose a surface that suits your needs in terms of durability and the level of maintenance required.

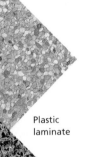

Plastic laminate

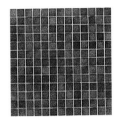

Small mosaic tiles

Granite

Patterned splashback tile

Synthetic stone

Octagonal tile

Marble

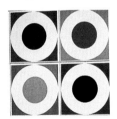

Splashback tiles

Wood

Decorative tiles

Once you have worked out what you need in your kitchen and how major units and items should be positioned, you can consider the style and precise details. The planning work that you have already done should have helped you to visualize your new kitchen and may suggest a style to you. For example, if you have a small kitchen you might choose light colours, which give a greater impression of space, or a streamlined, modern style that makes a virtue of a small space, with lots of high-tech space-saving devices. Always remember to think about who will be using the kitchen – even when you are thinking about the look. The ergonomics of your work space is of vital importance, so think about the height of the work surfaces, the sink, the oven, storage units and dishwasher.

▲ This spacious kitchen and eating area has been designed to recall the decor of a 1950s American diner, an effect achieved by the central "bar" area with integral sink, the gingham-covered stools, the hanging lamp, the woodwork and the kitsch accessories. The other island unit features ample space for food preparation on top and drawers for storage underneath.

▶ This basement open-plan kitchen-dining room receives very little natural light. To combat this, a bright, uncluttered modern scheme has been used, to reflect the light as much as possible. The touches of cool blue create interest and help to make the space look a bit bigger. Spotlights in the ceiling give overhead lighting.

◀ A stylish, modern kitchen-dining room enhances the space available by using bright, white walls that reflect the light, with touches of blue for the kitchen units to create a feeling of freshness. Natural wood, glass-fronted cupboards, modern steel chairs and an industrial-style oven keep the effect light and bright.

▲ This country-style kitchen achieves a charming, old-fashioned effect. The warm green and yellow decor, the checked gingham curtains and storage covers, the butler's sink, wooden draining board and work surfaces and the blue-and-white stove all conjure up an atmosphere of cosy informality.

## STORAGE

Having enough easily accessible storage space is one of the main ingredients of a smooth-running kitchen. The most flexible storage systems usually feature a combination of built-in and freestanding furniture, as well as a mixture of open and closed storage. Movable furniture, such as a butcher's block on castors, is another useful option. Think about the things you will need to store and how often you will use them. As well as food and cooking utensils, you may have to find a home for appliances such as food processors, cleaning equipment and oversized items such as an ironing board.

If you are not planning to overhaul your kitchen storage, but would like a new look, you can achieve a great deal simply by preparing and painting or spraying the old doors and fitting new handles. You can also update old units with new doors – useful if you decide that you want to hide away items such as the dishwasher or washing machine.

◀ Plenty of open storage is a boon to the busy cook, who can see and access ingredients and utensils in an instant. This stylish island unit features work surfaces on top and plenty of storage, so that pans and other kitchen implements can be kept conveniently close to the integral hob.

▲ A slimline, floor-to-ceiling slide-out cupboard makes good use of the available space and provides ample storage for kitchen paraphernalia, which can be tucked away out of sight when not in use. The shelves at the top of the unit are useful for storing items that are not needed on a daily basis.

## STORAGE SOLUTIONS

● Look for cupboards that incorporate pull-out trays, bins or drawers; some feature revolving carousel fittings that utilize corner space. Louvred doors allow air to circulate and are a good choice for cupboards where food is stored.

● Make sure that you incorporate plenty of cupboards and shelves of different heights so that you can accommodate items of varying sizes.

● Narrow open shelves for single-line storage make good use of any dead wall space.

● An old-fashioned plate rack mounted over the sink is a simple and time-saving storage option.

● Look for an island unit that features plenty of storage space and will double up as a table.

● A wall-mounted step-ladder for pots and pans makes good use of empty wall space.

● Hang utensils, pans and other frequently used items from butcher's hooks attached to a simple stainless steel or wooden pole.

▲ As an alternative to cupboards, which can be difficult to access, a set of wide drawers fitted with special dividers makes finding things easy. Drawers should be located close to the sink or dishwasher so that clean crockery can easily be returned to its place. Deeper drawers are useful for storing bulkier items such as pans, large dishes or electrical appliances.

◄ A combination of different storage requirements are catered for in this large family kitchen. The handsome old pine dresser and high open shelving running the length of one wall allow decorative pieces to be left on display, while other items are swallowed up by closed, fitted storage units.

## WALLS AND FLOORS

Choosing the right floor- and wall coverings can make a dramatic difference to the overall look and feel of a kitchen. Materials should, however, be selected for their practical, as well as aesthetic qualities. Surfaces should be easy to clean, durable, and resistant to water, steam and grease. For flooring, the climate and the people in the house will also help to influence your choice. Surfaces such as slate, stone, terrazzo or quarry tiles are hard-wearing, but they can

be cold to walk on if there is no underfloor heating. If you have children, you may want to opt for a softer material, such as linoleum or cushioned sheet vinyl. Polished wood is a good-looking, long-lasting choice, but floors that are not sealed properly will be damaged if spillages seep through.

For walls, choose washable paint and paper. Other options include cork, ceramic tiles, wood and vinyl, which will help to insulate against heat loss.

◄ The pretty lavender used on the walls offsets the harder, shiny surfaces of the floor, countertop and utensils. With their light-reflective properties, materials such as glass, zinc and chrome are a good choice for a room that gets little or no natural light.

▲ If you have already chosen your furniture and fixtures, use them as a starting point for your decorative scheme. Here, deep blue was used on the walls to counterbalance the striking yellow of the retro-style units. A pale floorcovering helps throw the table and chairs into dramatic relief.

▼ Neutral walls and wood flooring have been chosen for a well-organized, open-plan space designed along the lines of a professional caterer's kitchen. Although the room gets plenty of natural light, the wall lights provide artificial backup.

▼▼ Choosing two different types of flooring helps to define the two areas of activity in this kitchen-dining room. The tall, backless dresser, used for storage and serving food, also helps to screen the kitchen without closing it off entirely.

## HINTS AND TIPS

● Ventilation can be a problem in kitchens. Even if you have a big window, you will probably need a fan and a hood, which are very effective in containing and minimizing cooking smells.

● Use a fungicidal adhesive to prevent mould from forming on wallpaper.

● Conventional radiators can take up a lot of valuable space, so think about installing a system of floor, wall or ceiling heaters.

# DINING ROOMS

## TABLEWARE

Choose crockery, glassware and cutlery that are appropriate for the occasion. Team these with a tablecloth, placemats and napkins in a complementary colour.

Blue-handled
stainless-steel
cutlery

Traditional
silver plate
cutlery

Beige-handled
stainless-steel
cutlery

Ornate crystal
wine glass

Turkish
tea-glass

Two-tone
wine glass

Plain dinner service with decorative edging

Floral-patterned dinner service

When planning a dining area, think about the room and how you want to use it. Is it to be a place for regular family meals or reserved for more formal occasions? Is there scope for extending the dining table to accommodate more guests? Will you be eating there during the day or mostly after dark? You will also need to make sure that there is safe and easy access to the kitchen.

Whether you have the luxury of a separate, self-contained dining room or have to commandeer a corner of the living room, the surroundings should be relaxed and welcoming. A sturdy table and some comfortable chairs are essential, and there should be enough light without it being too harsh and glaring; a table lamp or candles will help to create a congenial atmosphere at night.

▲ Wood is a practical and aesthetically pleasing choice for a dining room. Here, a simple table, unupholstered chairs and a bare wood floor suggest an informal approach. The artefacts on display provide diners with plenty of scope for conversation.

▶ A modern version of the traditional sideboard and a freestanding unit keep crockery, cutlery and table linen organized and close to hand. A traditional dresser, armoire or simple chest of drawers would serve the same function.

◀ For comfort and easy access, this dining table is set in the centre of the room, just close enough to the fire on cold days and with the window to the side so that diners are not sitting facing or with their backs to the light.

▲ The furniture, soft furnishings and finishing touches in this wood-panelled dining room all create a mood of cosy informality.

## HINTS AND TIPS

● For maximum comfort, choose chairs with gently sloping, rather than upright, backs.

● If space is tight, choose a drop-leaf table that can be extended when you have extra guests. A pair of trestle legs and a piece of hardboard can make a useful extension. Consider coffee tables that rise to form full-height tables. Invest in a few folding chairs that can be stowed away.

● For an informal approach, group odd chairs of a similar style or shape. You can re-vamp junk-shop finds with a coat of paint or impose unity by recovering the drop-in seats (see pp.238–239). Simple slip covers in the fabric of your choice will transform a set of dining chairs (see pp.240–241).

● Place candles in front of an uncurtained window or a mirror to create a dramatic effect and double the light.

● Be aware that warm-coloured light from candles adversely affects cool colour schemes in rooms used for evening dining.

# PLANNING YOUR LIVING ROOM

## LIVING ROOM CHECKLIST

● How large is your room? How many people do you expect to be in it at any one time?

● What kind of living room would you like? Do you want to have a comfortable family/TV room? A calm, meditative retreat at the end of the day? A more formal room with which you want to impress people?

● How much direct natural light does the room get, and when? What sort of artificial light will you be using?

● Do you like to have books or objects on display? If you prefer to hide them, think about having shelved cupboards with doors that blend with your walls.

● Are you fed up with your furniture? Do you have enough of it? Or too little? Can you buy new items or upholster or alter what you already have?

● What style of architecture is your home? If features have been taken out, would you like to put them back in? Does anything need to be removed? Do the proportions need altering structurally or decoratively?

● How does the style of your home relate to what you envisage? For example, if you want flamboyant 17th-century Rococo, you might think twice if your home is modern with small, low rooms.

● What styles do you admire in other people's homes or in which magazines? Analyse the look – it may not cost you a fortune to come up with something similar.

Your living room is one of the most important areas of the house. It's primarily a place to relax – whether with friends and family or on your own – so the comfort factor is all-important. Before you embark on major purchases or decorating schemes, think about the atmosphere that you would like to create, the elements that you want to include – such as books, storage or ornaments – and who is going to be using the room. Take your time over making decisions, since errors can be costly and time-consuming. Always test colours on your walls and live with them for a while; if you are buying rugs or new carpet, take swatches away with you and see how they "grow" on you. Make sure that you measure up properly for furniture and consider its size in relation to the rest of the room.

**CASE STUDY: HOW TO COPE WITH SPACE**

Large, tall rooms can be just as difficult to plan as more confined spaces: you don't want to feel lost or overwhelmed. The owners of this lofty, gable-ceilinged living room have maintained its natural feeling of airiness and spaciousness while at the same time creating a sense of intimacy. The fireplace provides a focal point. Bookshelves fill the space on each side to a height level with the top of the window; this means that the eye stops before it follows the diagonals of the roof upwards. The effect is enhanced by hanging a large, bold poster (on the right) at the same level. The chimneybreast and shelving, which is broken up into small compartments, extends into the room, reducing its apparent length.

## MAKING YOUR SPACE WORK FOR YOU

Moving house is often the catalyst for a major overhaul. Think about what you like and dislike about the structure and decor. You might want to build around an existing feature, or might need to rip something out before you can start to decorate. Analyse the elements carefully, and be patient. You may decide to build up the look of your living room over a period of time, buying furniture as and when you can afford it; even so, to avoid mistakes you'll need to have an idea of what you want at the start. Think about the room's layout: what is the focal point? What do you like to look at when you are sitting down? How about the view from the window: do you want to gaze at it or away from it? Decorate with these points in mind.

◄ This living room is part of an open-plan space; the ottoman in the foreground creates a "wall" on one side. The main focal points are the fireplace and the tall windows; the lack of curtains ensures that the beautiful view cannot be ignored.

▲ Although this Mediterranean-style living room is used as a thoroughfare , it has been made into a cosy, intimate space  by focusing on the fireplace. The mantelpiece area is filled with plenty of visual interest.

▼ The large, square-shaped canvases on the walls of this tall, cool room prevent it from becoming overwhelming, despite its size. The comfortable and informal furniture helps to create an atmosphere that is modern and relaxed.

## FLOORING

The treatment that you give your living room floor is just as important as what you do with your walls. In terms of colour, see the floor as a fifth wall: a dark floor will make a small room seem smaller. Many designers stick to colours that are found in nature, beneath your feet. So browns, greens, greys, shades of gold, copper, ochre are all a good choice, while bright reds and yellows might be considered jarring. What kind of flooring do you already have? Can you strip and varnish or paint your existing floorboards? If you live in an apartment, you may find that bare boards are unsuitable because noise will travel to the apartment below unless you have good sound-proofing. Laminated floors, consisting of thin strips of wood glued to backing board, might be the answer, but consult your lease to make sure it is permitted. Think about your floor in relation to the furniture. And consider the texture – in terms of the look, the feel on your feet and how much wear and tear you expect it to get.

# LIVING ROOM STYLE

## CURTAIN POLES

Available in a selection of materials and diameters, and in styles ranging from antique to modern, curtain poles make an attractive alternative to tracking.

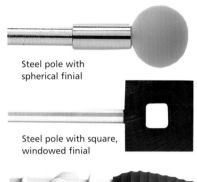

Steel pole with spherical finial

Steel pole with square, windowed finial

Wooden pole with pine-cone finial

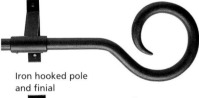

Steel pole with moulded, plaster-effect finial

Iron hooked pole and finial

Iron pole with medieval finial

Stainless-steel pole with shepherd-crook finial

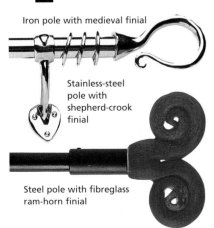

Steel pole with fibreglass ram-horn finial

With thought and careful planning, your living room can be whatever style you want it to be – regardless of size. To create the look you want, however, you need to consider the room as a whole. Think about unifying factors such as colour, soft furnishings, and the general shape and style of your furniture. And be brutal: too much furniture, or too many decorative pieces, can ruin the look, so put away anything that detracts from the desired effect. You may even want to build cupboards to hide away the TV or hi-fi when not in use. Don't forget to consider the lighting: natural light, or lack of it, will affect the way in which you design your space.

▶ A combination of traditional, contemporary and ethnic elements creates an attractive, semi-formal room. The neutral colour scheme acts as a unifying factor and allows the objects and furnishings to make an impact.

▼ The design of this cheerful living room is simple yet effective. The pale decor reflects the natural light, while the various checked patterns create a strong but not overpowering effect.

## WALLS AND WINDOWS

The way you treat your walls and windows will depend on both your own taste and the architectural space. The style of your curtains should be in keeping with the proportions of your room: heavy velvets and damasks, for example, look better in larger, more opulent surroundings. Don't forget to think about what the curtains will look like when they are both open and shut. Team your curtains with your wall colour and consider the fabric in both natural and artificial light. If privacy is not a consideration, you could think about leaving your windows bare.

Walls can make or break a room, so they need to be thought about with care. When choosing a paint colour, consider the room's proportions, how much light it receives, at what time of day you generally use the room, what colours you respond to, and how your walls might complement your furniture. Wallpaper is also an option, but be careful about choosing busy patterns. You also need to consider what you might be putting on the walls, such as pictures and shelving. Fabric, stone cladding and industrial materials all help to create a different look.

▲ Large amounts of light stream into this large, double-aspect modern interior. The tall windows and doors have been left free of detailing and curtaining so as not to detract from their geometric simplicity. Natural woods and simple contemporary furniture create a refreshing ambience.

▶ Floor-to-ceiling window shutters enhance the angular, modern look of this living room. Panels on each side of the fireplace project from what would have been recesses; this unusual feature adds interest and is in keeping with the hard, clean lines of the interior.

### CURTAIN HINTS

● Your window treatment can help alter the proportions of the room. Using a longer track can make a window look wider.

● Pelmets should be well above eye level and the tracks placed so that the fabric does not hang over the glass at the top.

● With tab-topped curtains, you can create a vibrant effect by hanging two pairs together, using muslin or sari fabric in contrasting colours. Use a "white-out" blind to block out the light.

## SHELVING AND STORAGE

The clutter of daily life is what gives a room its sense of life and prevents it from being a sterile, unlived-in space. Disorganized clutter, however, detracts from the style of a room and needs to be streamlined and contained. When it comes to storage solutions, the possibilities are almost endless. Your things can be hidden away in window seats or box-type coffee tables, or behind doors and panelling. Or you can make your storage requirements into a stylish feature – whether it be transparent open cubes that stack together, shelving made from interesting materials such as glass or reclaimed floorboards, or more traditional items of furniture such as chests of drawers, tallboys and linen presses. If you like a unified look, consider having storage built in to fit your space exactly – this is especially useful for recesses and other awkward corners. Keep an eye on the detailing, too – a modest piece of furniture can be transformed by replacing the handles with more expensive, stylish alternatives. And do not forget the little things, such as CD racks, that can introduce a stylish note into your living room at relatively little expense.

▲ This modern, built-in, boxed storage fills an awkward space under a sloping roof. Because it has been designed on two "stepped" levels, it does not make the room feel smaller, which a long built-in cupboard would have done. The useful wicker baskets are an attractive feature that could be put anywhere.

◄ Storage is always a challenge in studio flats such as this one. Here, the cupboard behind the sofa acts as a "wall" between the living room and the kitchen area – an effect underlined by hanging pictures along the back of it. The pale colours and glass-fronted storage unit help to maximize the overall sense of light and space.

▼ Custom-built furniture can be designed to suit your exact storage requirements. This stylish unit features a good combination of open and closed storage as well as surfaces for display.

▶ Shelves behind wooden panelling provide display space in this country-house drawing room. The doors can be open or closed – a look that can translate equally well to modern interiors.

## CHOOSING STORAGE

You need to think both creatively and practically when choosing storage for your living room.

● Consider your lifestyle: will you dust and look after items on open shelving? Modern storage systems, such as sleek glass shelving, need to be kept clean and well-organized for a streamlined effect.

● Think about colour and materials. Be daring and treat the back walls, or interior, of a storage area in a more dynamic way than the rest of the room.

● Decide how often you use your things and what can be stored. Box storage is most useful for items that you do not use regularly.

# PLANNING YOUR BEDROOM

## BEDROOM CHECKLIST

• Do you spend much time in your bedroom during the day? Do you need to use part of the room as a home office?

• Are there any things, such as noise, that irritate you about the room? Would it be possible to relocate to another part of the house?

• How many people will occupy the room?

• Would you like to install an *en-suite* bathroom or shower?

• Will you need to replace the bed, now or in the near future?

• At what time of the day does the room get the best light?

• Which colours would you feel happiest being surrounded by first thing in the morning and last thing at night?

• Do you like to wake up in the dark or in a room filled with direct or diffused light? This will affect the type of window covering that you choose.

• Do you like to be surrounded by possessions or do you prefer a pared-down, uncluttered look?

• How much storage space do you need? Do you prefer built-in or freestanding furniture? Can any items, such as out-of-season clothes or footwear, be kept in another room?

• Do you like to read in bed? Do you need a bedside table and a light that can be turned off when you are in bed?

The way your bedroom looks and feels can have a profound effect on the quality of your life. A bedroom is the most personal place in the house, it is where you go to relax and escape the pressures of the world and this should be reflected in how the room is arranged and decorated, and in the choice of furniture and soft furnishings. Choose lighting that will create the right ambient mood at night and organize a storage system that will help to make your daily routine run more smoothly. Small rooms in particular require careful planning; with too much furniture they can easily begin to look overcrowded and chaotic, so assess exactly what you will need. If a bedroom is to do double duty as a work space, you might want to screen off the two areas of activity.

**CASE STUDY: THE BLUE BEDROOM**

Tucked away from the home's main areas of activity, an attic room can make an ideal location for a peaceful bedroom. Here, a dormer window was added to help open up the space and allow sun to stream in during the day, while the bold blue on the walls helps to create a cosy, intimate night-time atmosphere. Painting the whole room in the same colour like this helps to mask the room's awkward proportions. A useful cupboard has been built into the wall, freeing up valuable floor space, while the light furniture, soft furnishings and flooring ensure that the room doesn't feel claustrophobic. The wall-mounted adjustable lights provide plenty of back-up illumination at night.

▲ Simple fitted shelves and a desk have transformed an alcove into a quiet correspondence corner. The daybed has been specially built to fit the length of the far wall. The soft furnishings and painted furniture suggest Swedish country style.

## CHILDREN'S ROOMS

● Always put safety first when planning a young child's room. Furniture should conform to national safety standards. A nursery needs to be situated close to the parents' room. Never position a bed or chair under a window and do not put shelves directly above a bed. Windows should be fitted with safety catches and sockets with safety covers.

● Providing enough accessible storage is essential. Look for modular units that can expand or be adapted as the child grows. Low-level storage options such as trunks, blanket boxes or freestanding bookshelves help to keep things within a child's reach and should make tidying up easier. Crates, boxes and pull-out drawers make useful under-bed storage for toys and out-of-season clothes.

● Consider a bed that combines storage and a play/work area.

● For walls, choose washable wallpapers and paints. Avoid heavily patterned papers that a child will quickly tire of or outgrow.

● Have fun with colour and pattern. Customize furniture, walls or even floors (above) with paint.

● Where there are two older children sharing, a screen such as a low bookcase will help to divide the room into separate areas.

● A teenager's bedroom will need plenty of sockets and a flexible lighting system, including a good task light for study.

## THE COMFORT ZONE

Sometimes a few simple changes can be all it takes to transform a dull, lifeless bedroom into a warm, inviting space that is full of personality. The bedroom on the right had plenty of potential, but the original decorative scheme made the room look rather cold and gloomy. A light-enhancing white was chosen for the walls and ceiling, which has helped to camouflage the room's awkward angles. Swapping the curtains for a blind has also helped to make the room feel lighter and airier. Replacing the carpet with a wood floor has given the room a stylish, contemporary edge.

▲ ▶ With a new headboard and bedlinen, the bed is now the main focus of attention. The utilitarian clothes rail has been banished in favour of a full-length mirror, transforming what was a dingy corner. Moving the blanket box away from the centre of the room has also helped to enhance the overall feeling of spaciousness.

# BEDROOM STYLE

## BEDSIDE LIGHTING

Shaded lamps help to set an ambient night-time atmosphere. The light should be easily accessible from the bed and sufficiently bright if it is to be used for reading.

Art Deco, steel and glass bedside table lamp

Contemporary bedside table lamp

Japanese-style, ceramic and silk bedside table lamp

Contemporary bedside table lamp

Tiffany-style bedside table lamp

Iron-based standard lamp

Contemporary bedside table lamp

Whether your preference is for a traditional look, perhaps with an antique bed draped with an heirloom quilt, or you favour the pared-down minimalism of a Japanese-inspired room, the decorative scheme should be conducive to rest and relaxation, inspiring you to retreat there at the end of the day. The main item of furniture is undoubtedly the bed itself. You spend about a third of your life lying on it, so buy the best-quality mattress and base that you can afford. The style of bed – an elegant iron four-poster, say, or one with a handsome painted headboard – can also dictate the overall look of the room. Storage is another important factor – if you do not have enough, and in the right place, your bedroom will be hidden by clutter and you will not enjoy your peaceful haven.

▲ Cool blue walls complement the mellow tones of the floor and elegant bed, while elements of the decorative scheme are picked up in the pair of modern table lamps. The room's restful atmosphere is enhanced by the rug and crisp white bedlinen.

▲ With its imposing panelled headboard, this antique bed takes centre stage in a 16th-century country house with low, exposed beams and whitewashed walls. The cosy bedside lamps and cheerful bedspread help to dispel any hint of austerity.

◄ This bedroom in a suburban house built in the 1920s uses decorative flourishes such as the cherub motifs and dreamy muslin curtains to conjure up the style of an 18th-century boudoir.

► Pretty floral-patterned wallpaper makes a feature of the awkward proportions of an attic bedroom and creates a fresh backdrop for the feminine furniture and soft furnishings.

## STORAGE

Having enough space to store things so that they are not all piled in a messy heap on the floor will help you feel organized and will change the look of your bedroom. Think about what you will need to store and how much space you have. Decide whether you would prefer built-in units or freestanding pieces of furniture. Could some items, such as out-of-season clothing, be kept elsewhere? Explore the potential of any unused spaces – items that are not needed on a daily basis can be stored in baskets, boxes or crates under the bed. You may also need one or two flat surfaces such as a dressing table or a bedside table for a lamp or night-time reading.

▲ In a walk-in wardrobe leading off the bedroom, clothes are stored in a tower of pull-out crates, which are actually cardboard laundry boxes.

◀ Custom-built modular units provide capacious storage inside and ample surface space on top.

▼ Versatile, low-level storage in a children's room allows favourite items to be easily retrieved – and put away again at the end of the day. Here, shelves for books and toys and a chest of drawers for clothing have been customized with a cheerful blue paint.

## FURNITURE

The bed itself must be chosen with comfort firmly in mind, but you should also choose a framework that is in tune with your style. Think about how each item of furniture works with other pieces in the room in terms of size, materials and proportion – a small table next to a single bed, a larger chest of drawers at the side of a four-poster. Make sure you have enough room to move about and position storage where it is easily accessible and will open properly. Look at ways in which you can maximize the storage potential of a piece of furniture. You can double the amount of hanging space in a wardrobe, for instance, by adding another rail at a lower height.

◀ Crisp white and apple-green paintwork provides a perfect foil for the ornate wrought-iron bed. Other furniture has been kept to a minimum so that the bed is the room's main focus of attention. Picking up the Gothic theme, the Roman blind links the walls and bedlinen.

▼ Contemporary beech-wood furniture is given plenty of space to breathe in this well-proportioned room. Note the console table used as a dressing table and the freestanding, movable unit, which can be accessed from both sides.

## WALLS AND WINDOWS

The most dominant surfaces in any room are its walls, so the treatment you choose for them will set the scene for all the other elements. This is not the place to experiment with garish hues (no matter how fashionable) or clashing patterns. Instead, take advantage of the powerful influence colour has on mood by basing your scheme on one you really love, then finding a tone or shade of it that encourages serenity and relaxation: soft eau de nil rather than acid lime, subtle terracotta instead of fiery orange. Once you've established a colour theme, explore all the possible ways of interpreting it on your walls: as a plain paint finish, a textured or printed wallpaper, a layer of fabric, or a subtle decorative effect.

For the windows, choose a covering that provides privacy and reinforces the style you're trying to create: full-length curtains in a traditional room, for example, or sleek roller or venetian blinds in a contemporary one.

### FABRIC-COVERED WALLS

As a stylish alternative to paper or paint, try lining your bedroom walls with fabric. There are several ways to do this.

● Fix narrow timber battens top and bottom, seam your chosen material into the required width, stretch it taut and anchor it in place with a staple gun. For extra heat and sound insulation, line the walls with synthetic wadding first.

● Invest in a specialist track system that allows the fabric panels to be removed for washing and replaced quickly and easily.

● Gather your material gently onto curtain wire or rods at the top and bottom of each wall, or at the top only for a less formal effect.

◀ The dramatic arched window that dominates this ultra-feminine chamber has inspired a host of ingenious paint effects, from the blue colourwash on the walls to the trompe l'oeil moulding and the classical column on the projecting wall.

▶ Expanses of pale wall establish space and light as the principal design features of this cool bedroom. The sash window has been replaced with doors to the garden and a glazed area up to the original lintel, which admits daylight.

◀ Here, broad blue stripes establish a fresh seaside look and pull the pitched ceiling into scale with the rest of the room. The roughly plastered end wall cleverly suggests a chalky cliff face.

▶ Solid shutters block light well, take up little space, and suit the simple lines of this rustic bedroom perfectly. On the walls, a coat of paint in warm dusty rose sets off the natural wood..

▲ Avoid hanging elaborate, multi-coloured pictures on busily patterned walls. In this room, a set of simple framed prints sits elegantly against a traditional wallpaper design of subtle stylized blooms on a muted grey-green ground.

# PLANNING YOUR BATHROOM

## BATHROOM CHECKLIST

• How often is your bathroom used and at what time of the day?

• Could you install additional facilities elsewhere in the house – an *en-suite* shower in the bedroom, perhaps, or a separate toilet?

• Is the existing plumbing system adequate? Do you have enough hot water and at a high enough pressure?

• Would it make sense to relocate the bathroom to another room?

• How much storage space will you require?

• Would you like to install a new bathroom suite?

• What type of lighting do you need?

• Are there any special features, such as a new shower or a heated towel rail, that you would like to install?

• Does your bathroom have adequate heating and ventilation?

• Do you need to install a shaver socket?

• Do you need to make special provision for children or an elderly person?

• Would you prefer a separate bath and shower?

• In a large bathroom, could you move the bath into the empty space in the middle of the room, or even install a raised floor for a sunken bath?

Often tucked into a tiny, awkward space and feeling cramped and claustrophobic, many bathrooms are a long way from being the havens of function and relaxation that they should be. Further design challenges are posed by inadequate storage, lack of natural light and poor ventilation, making the bathroom one of the trickiest rooms in the whole house to get right.

Creating a bathroom that is right for you might mean overhauling the entire space – redesigning the original layout, installing a new suite or flooring. You might even decide to relocate to another room. Sometimes, though, you can give your bathroom a new lease of life by making just one or two changes. Inject some colour with a fresh coat of paint on the walls and some complementary tiles (see pp.154–155), replace the existing fittings and add some stylish accessories to give your bathroom an instant face-lift.

**CASE STUDY: A PLACE FOR EVERYTHING**

A functional, streamlined bathroom has been carved out of a narrow, awkwardly shaped space. The corner bath tucks neatly into the area in front of the window, while the washbasin unit features plenty of storage space, including drawers that allow you to see their contents at a glance. There is also plenty of surface room on either side of the basin, a useful feature that is often overlooked even in more spacious bathrooms. Boxing in the toilet cistern and pipework has created an additional surface on top. The neutral decorative scheme and simple blind help to create a light and airy atmosphere. The chrome fittings, glass shelf and large mirror also help to catch the light. Cheerful accessories bring welcome splashes of colour and help to enforce the mood of relaxation.

◄ Adding an internal window of glass bricks has helped to open up a small bathroom that gets no natural light.

► In a bathroom occupying what would have once been a bedroom, the bath takes centre stage. The position of the towel rail ensures that hot towels are easily accessible from the bath.

## BATHROOM PLAN

Maximizing all the available space, both horizontal and vertical, is the key to creating an efficient bathroom. With careful planning, a bath, shower and storage space can be tucked into the most compact space.

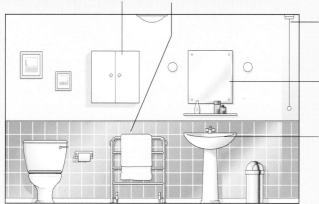

A central ceiling light provides overhead illumination. The bulb is enclosed for safety.

Power shower with a space-saving, inward-opening door made from shatter-proof glass. The controls are easily accessible and the shower head can be adjusted to suit the height of each user.

Ceramic tiles are used for the splashback, while an easy-to-wipe vinyl wallpaper has been used on the upper part of the wall.

A built-in floor-to-ceiling storage unit combines a lower cupboard for concealed storage and open shelving for items that are in regular use.

A compact bath with a non-slip surface tucks neatly between the shower and storage unit. A sturdy hand rail has been installed.

A lockable wall-mounted cabinet keeps medicines and other items well out of children's reach.

A heated towel rail means that warm towels are within easy reach of the bath and washbasin.

The main overhead light is operated by a pull-cord switch, which is conveniently situated next to the door.

Mirror with lights positioned on either side to illuminate all the planes of the face.

A deep, wide washbasin with mixer taps has been positioned so that there is plenty of space to manoeuvre. The shelf above keeps the edge of the basin clear of toiletries.

## ORGANIZING THE SPACE

● To position a washbasin at the right height, cup your hands together in front of you, with your arms extended towards the floor and your shoulders straight. The height from the floor to your hands is the correct position for the plug hole.

● A bath requires clearance equal to about its width.

● There should be a 200-mm (8-in) gap between the rim of the toilet seat and a wall or other obstacle.

● Curved baths and corner washbasins are designed to fit into dead spaces and awkwardly shaped rooms. Wall-hung lavatories and basins free up valuable floor space.

**Washbasin**
Make sure that there is enough space in front and at the sides so that you can wash in comfort.

# BATHROOM STYLE

## TAPS

If you don't want to rip out an existing suite, you can update your bath or washbasin with new modern or reproduction taps available in a range of styles and finishes.

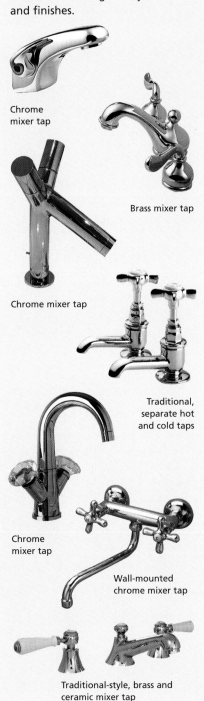

Chrome
mixer tap

Brass mixer tap

Chrome mixer tap

Traditional,
separate hot
and cold taps

Chrome
mixer tap

Wall-mounted
chrome mixer tap

Traditional-style, brass and
ceramic mixer tap

Enhancing the perception of space and light is a consideration in any decorating decision. Many bathrooms have no natural light, so you might consider adding an internal window or skylight, or even replacing a non-load-bearing wall with glass bricks. Reflective paint finishes, such as oil-based gloss or eggshell paint in cool, receding tones of aqua blue, green or lilac will help to make a small, dingy bathroom appear brighter. You can also inject light with mirrors, ceramic tiles, chrome fittings and other shiny surfaces.

▲ Suggesting purity and cleanliness, a white scheme enhances the sense of airiness in a sunny bathroom, occupying what would originally have been a bedroom. Simple pieces of furniture dispel any hint of the sterility that can be associated with all-white bathrooms.

▶ The combination of brick trellis, slate, glass, terracotta and cool white cotton at the main window brings interesting tonal and textural variation to a serene Mediterranean bathroom, while vibrant colour is provided by the red geraniums.

## WALLS AND FLOORS

Practicality is the key when you are choosing wallcoverings and flooring for your bathroom. Wall treatments should be easy to clean and able to withstand the hot, steamy atmosphere. Paint is the easiest and most affordable option, but you must use a silk or eggshell finish rather than matt emulsion to withstand the condensation. Ceramic, glass or mosaic tiles provide a good waterproof surface for walls, or they can be used in smaller amounts as splashbacks around the bath and washbasin. Tongue-and-groove panelling is another good-looking choice and can be painted or treated with polyurethane varnish, while bare plaster sealed with a matt varnish has a warm, rustic quality.

For floors, choose moisture-proof materials, such as cork or cushioned vinyl, rather than jute-backed carpet, which can quickly show up water marks and may rot if allowed to get wet. Some synthetic, foam-backed carpets and carpet tiles are specifically intended for bathroom use, but make sure that they can be lifted up easily to dry if necessary. A non-slip rug or bathmat placed next to the bath or shower will provide warmth underfoot and help to absorb any splashes.

▲ Although expensive, marble is a cool, sumptuous and hardwearing material. In this pared-down bathroom, the marble bath and floor blend seamlessly together.

▶ Blue and white is a classic colour combination for a bathroom. Here, a swimming-pool look is achieved by using small mosaic tiles on the floor and on the wall behind the walk-in shower. Although the bathroom is tucked into a small space with no windows, ceiling-recessed halogen spotlights, a clear shower screen and plenty of reflective surfaces ensure that the room feels bright and welcoming.

▲ Durable, water-proof and warm underfoot, linoleum is available in sheet or tile form and in a host of colours and patterns. The colours of this geometric design have been chosen to complement the old-fashioned bath.

## STORAGE

Every bathroom, regardless of its proportions, will function more smoothly and be more relaxing to be in if there is adequate storage for toiletries and other items. Things that are used on a daily basis should be kept close to where they are needed on a stable surface so they won't topple over and spill. A built-in cupboard on the walls or under the washbasin will keep clutter out of sight, but some open storage, such as shelves or even a freestanding table, is also useful and can be used to display a collection of pretty bottles, ornaments or plants. A mirrored bathroom cabinet near the washbasin is another practical option. Available in a range of styles and materials, some cabinets have additional features such as a fluorescent light or a small heater behind the mirror that prevents condensation from forming on it. Drawers are useful, as they allow you to see the contents easily. Hazardous substances, such as medicine and disinfectant, should be stored well out of the reach of children, preferably in a cupboard with a child-proof catch or lock.

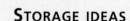

◀ Floor-to-ceiling open storage featuring glass shelving makes good use of space in a compact bathroom. Other paraphernalia is swallowed up by the capacious mirrored cabinet.

▲ A built-in storage unit featuring cupboards and drawers uses up every inch of dead space under the washbasin.

### STORAGE IDEAS

● Look for washbasins that feature integral storage. Some have drawers, a towel rail and plenty of surface space on top.

● Built-in bathroom furniture conceals unsightly plumbing and provides useful storage.

● Organize bathroom toiletries in a rack hooked on to a shower door.

● A slimline, mirror-fronted wall cabinet will swallow up plenty of bathroom clutter.

● Look out for compact units that double up as a laundry basket and storage for towels.

● Fix clothes hooks or a wire storage rack to the door.

# FIXTURES

Bathroom fixtures come in a huge range of styles and finishes to suit every taste and budget. There is also a wide choice of fixtures that have been specifically designed to fit into small or awkwardly shaped rooms. If you are combining a bath and shower, you should choose a wide, flat-bottomed bath with a non-slip surface; a glass bath screen must be shatter-proof. Otherwise, attractive plastic shower curtains are widely available and can be wiped down or replaced easily. A wall-mounted chrome towel rail combines function with good looks.

▶ Compact matching basins can be a worthwhile addition in a busy household. A large mirror, such as the one shown here, serves both a practical and an aesthetic role in a bathroom. Lights, with their bulbs enclosed and operated by a pull cord, should be positioned either side of a mirror over a washbasin so that they illuminate all the planes of the face.

◀ A lovely old roll-top bath with claw feet, an antique chair and tongue-and-groove panelling combine in an elegant period bathroom. If you can't find original fixtures and fittings, there are good reproductions on the market. A shelf and panelling can be used to hide the plumbing runs.

▲ You can give your bathroom an instant facelift with colourful accessories that help to create a visual link with the overall scheme. Here, towels and other finishing touches have been carefully chosen to pick out the zingy colours of the wall tiles and cabinet.

# HALLS AND STAIRCASES

## DOOR FURNITURE

Update a well-worn door with a choice of traditional or modern door fittings.

Plastic pull-down handle and key plate

Chrome and brushed aluminium pull-down handle

Classic brass pull-down handle and key plate

Modern steel and plastic pull-down handle

Brass pull-down handle

Steel and plastic door pull

Chrome knob

Brass knob

Pewter knob

Pewter knob

Wood and steel knob and key plate

Classic brass door plate

Classic brass door pull

As the main artery of a home and usually the first thing you see on entering, a hallway can set the tone and atmosphere for the rest of the house. Assess the impact your hallway makes by looking at it from different angles – from the front door, from the top of the stairs – and at different times of the day. Decide whether it is warm and inviting or cold and unwelcoming. Does the decorative scheme tie in with the rooms leading off it, or does the space feel disconnected from the rest of the house?

Are there any interesting decorative features on which you can capitalize – an appealing archway or balustrade, perhaps, or wood panelling, fretwork or cornicing? Elements such as these can make eye-catching focal points and can often provide inspiration for the whole scheme. Where halls flow into open-plan living spaces, it might be sensible to carry colour through. However, as halls are spaces to pass through, rather than linger in, you can use stronger colours than you might in other areas of your home.

◄ The tiled floor is in keeping with the period feel of this Victorian hallway, but carpet is a safer and less noisy choice for the stairs. The sunny half-landing with its uncurtained sash window serves as a pleasant stopping point when you are going up or down the stairs.

► A light, simple decorative scheme helps to open up a small, windowless hallway and ensures that the elegant spiral staircase is the main focus of attention. Note how the framed pictures pick out the wood of the banister and have been carefully arranged to follow the curve of the staircase.

◀ With a table and chairs, welcoming table lamps, and flowers and paintings lining the way, this wide galleried hallway leads you from the outside world into the main area of the house.

▲ Continuing the same colour scheme and flooring in the rooms leading off the hall helps to create a visual link between the different areas of the house, ensuring that there are no jarring contrasts.

Removing some of the doors has also helped to open up the space, making the rooms an extension of the hall. The shiny chrome coatstand is a lighter, stylish alternative to a wooden version.

## STAIRCASES

● Hard floor surfaces are durable and relatively easy to keep clean, but they can be noisy. Polished wood stairs can be slippery, and can be especially dangerous in homes where there are children or elderly people.

● Carpet is soft underfoot and has sound- and heat-insulating properties, but make sure that it is designed for heavy-duty traffic and is firmly fixed to the stairs. Carpet can also quickly show up marks, so avoid very pale colours; a softly patterned carpet will show up less dirt than a plain one.

● Light the top and bottom of the stairs for safety.

● Changing levels with a single step can be dangerous. Two steps are safer. Consider changing the colour or texture of the flooring to help the eye to notice the difference. Where three or more stairs are required, there should be a handrail for safety.

● Do not position uplighters on a staircase or lower landing, where the source of light would cause dangerous glare.

# PLANNING YOUR HOME OFFICE

## HOME OFFICE CHECKLIST

● Will you be working at home on a regular basis? What sort of work will you be carrying out?

● How many desks or work surfaces are you likely to need? Do you have to stack a lot of material before filing it away? Would it help to have a spare surface for any work in progress?

● When are you most likely to be working?

● How do you work? Are you messy or tidy?

● How do you see your work progressing in the next couple of years?

● What special equipment and storage requirements will you need, now and in the future?

● Will you need to install an additional phone line, extra sockets or more lighting?

● Will you be sharing your workspace with other members of the family?

● Would you prefer a noise-free environment away from household disturbances, or would it be helpful to be close to the kitchen, nursery or front door?

● Do you expect to have regular visitors?

● Is it possible to set aside a separate room, or will you have to adapt part of an existing one?

● Are there any underused spaces that can be used – a basement or attic, perhaps, or even a landing?

Once you have assessed your requirements, you need to organize your space for maximum comfort and efficiency. Try to choose a spot that is quiet, with enough room to house your equipment and storage, as well as your desk and chair. If you can set up an office in a separate, dedicated room, it is a good idea to accommodate an additional work surface. It's also a bonus to have somewhere that gets plenty of natural light, although you will still need to provide sufficient artificial lighting. In dual-purpose rooms, where an office is tucked into the corner of a bedroom, for example, a screen will help to separate the two areas. Items that are in constant use need to be easily accessible from your desk, and for every item of furniture always allow enough space for convenient use and clearance.

**CASE STUDY: ATTIC ROOM**

A compact but ergonomically sound home office has been tucked into an awkward space under the eaves. The desk, which has been custom-built to fit the full width of the attic, offers a good, deep work surface on top and plenty of legroom underneath. Instead of built-in drawers, sleek box files store office paraphernalia and fit neatly under the sloping ceiling. Dormer windows have been added to allow natural light to flood into the room, while a wall-mounted spotlight provides additional light for evening work.

## ORGANIZING YOUR SPACE

Once you have assessed your priorities, you need to design a practical and comfortable working area. With thought, this is possible in even the most confined space and need not be prohibitively expensive. Create a floor plan of the space, indicating where all the main pieces of furniture are to go (see pp.74–75). You should also mark on your plan such things as light fittings and power points, and indicate the position of windows, doors and wall-fixed items such as cupboards and shelves. Arrange storage so that frequently used items are easily accessible, and remember to allow at least 1 m (3 ft) in front of a filing cabinet or shelves for easy access.

## YOUR HOME OFFICE

Plan your office so that it meets all your needs and is safe and efficient to use.

Place a noticeboard in easy sight of your desk for notes and messages.

Uplighters provide wide-angle light that reflects off the ceiling.

Sockets are required for all your equipment.

A desk lamp is a vital part of your equipment. Make sure the light does not reflect off your screen.

Place your telephone to the left of your keyboard if you are right-handed and to the right if you are left-handed.

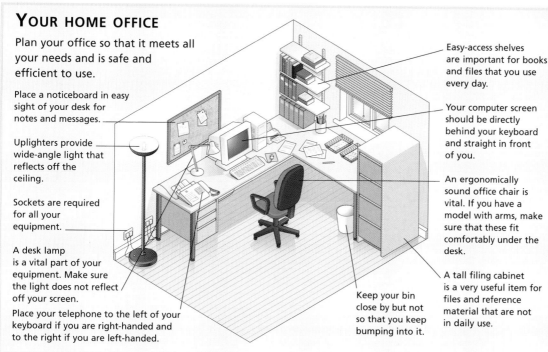

Easy-access shelves are important for books and files that you use every day.

Your computer screen should be directly behind your keyboard and straight in front of you.

An ergonomically sound office chair is vital. If you have a model with arms, make sure that these fit comfortably under the desk.

A tall filing cabinet is a very useful item for files and reference material that are not in daily use.

Keep your bin close by but not so that you keep bumping into it.

▲ The desk in this stylish, sun-filled home office has been correctly positioned at a right angle to avoid glare, while an Anglepoise lamp provides good task lighting on darker days. As the desk has no integral drawers, day-to-day storage is housed in the portable deep boxes on the floor.

## WORKING IN COMFORT

Paying attention to the ergonomics of your home office will help to ensure your long-term comfort, health and productivity.

● Invest in a good adjustable chair that will support your lower back. For stability choose a model with five legs.

● For easy access, allow at least 1m (3ft) between your chair and a wall or piece of furniture so that you can get in and out easily.

● The height of a work surface should be between 58–71 cm (23–28 in). If you use a computer, make sure the desk is deep enough for both keyboard and monitor to be in front of you rather than to one side, which can cause neck strain.

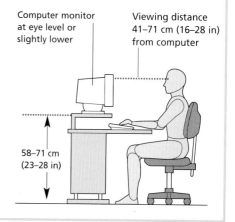

Computer monitor at eye level or slightly lower

Viewing distance 41–71 cm (16–28 in) from computer

58–71 cm (23–28 in)

# HOME OFFICE STYLE

## STORAGE

Office furniture suppliers are a good source of flexible storage for a home office. You can change the colour of pieces such as a filing cabinet with car-spray paint.

Filing cabinet

Desk storage unit

Lockable filing cabinet

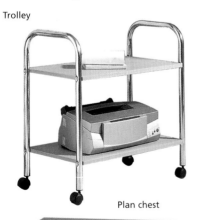

Trolley

Plan chest

The way your home office looks and the impression it creates is an important consideration. You need to strike the right balance between comfort and practicality: garish colours and fussy furnishings are not conducive to hours of concentrated work, but nor do you want to reproduce the grey functionality of a corporate office. For walls and ceilings, neutrals and shades such as soft greens or pale blues are easy on the eye and will complement traditional and modern office furniture. Choose a plain, hard-wearing surface such as wood or flat-pile carpet for the floorcovering. You can personalize your space and inject splashes of more vibrant colour with stylish storage and accessories or an eye-catching rug.

◀ The storage requirements in this well-organized home office have been cleverly thought through. Papers and other office paraphernalia are swallowed up by box files that have been chosen to match the calm, neutral tones of the room. An aluminium bin houses rolls of oversized papers.

▲ This compact cabinet has been custom-made to house a mini office, complete with computer, fax machine and plenty of storage space. Even a waste-paper bin has been tucked inside. At the end of the day, the keyboard tray slides away and the doors are closed to conceal the contents.

▲ In an office set up in a separate building in the garden, splashes of a favourite colour provide inspiration during the working day. The pedestal unit can be wheeled out to provide an additional surface.

◀ A home office set in an alcove under the stairs has been arranged to maximize space. The strong shade of blue helps to define the office area, while complementing the pistachio-and-white scheme. Colour-coordinated accessories complete the look.

# UTILITY ROOMS

## USEFUL STORAGE

There are plenty of attractive and sensible storage options available, including modular shelving, which allows you to add to it as your needs change.

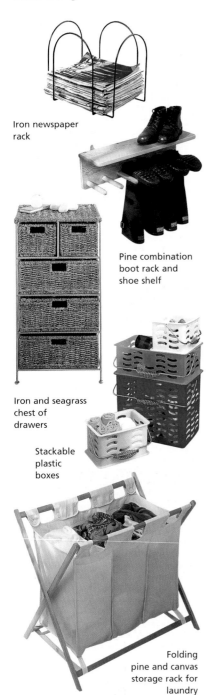

Iron newspaper rack

Pine combination boot rack and shoe shelf

Iron and seagrass chest of drawers

Stackable plastic boxes

Folding pine and canvas storage rack for laundry

I f there is no obvious place for a utility room, explore the potential of underused areas such as a cellar or shed. A cool, dry garage could be the ideal place to store wine, comestibles bought in bulk, recycling boxes or even out-of-season clothes. If you are altering the layout of your home, dividing a bedroom into a bathroom and a utility/laundry room is a useful arrangement. If your utility room is on the ground floor, an adjoining "mud" room allows you to keep dirty shoes and outdoor items separate from cleaner, indoor items.

▲ Sometimes a utility area can share quarters with other activities. Here, a quiet corner of a study is used as a place for ironing. The large wicker baskets, which allow air to circulate, and the gingham-covered ironing board blend with the rustic style of the room.

▶ Open storage allows you to find things easily and reach them right away. Industrial-style shelving such as this can be adjusted to accommodate different-sized items. The ironing board is mounted on wall brackets, keeping it away from the floor where it could easily topple over.

◀ Having a separate space where you can attend to the laundry or store household items, such as a vacuum cleaner, ironing board and cleaning products, can be an invaluable addition to a busy household, helping to take the strain off the kitchen and keeping other areas of the house free from clutter. This well-organized laundry room features plenty of closed storage, with a large surface on top for folding clothes, a double sink with wall-mounted faucets, and an overhead drying rack.

▼ Laundry facilities are housed in a compact cupboard, built to ceiling height to provide space for storing towels or clothes on top. When not in use, the stacked washing and drying machines are hidden from view by the door.

## SAFETY

● Never attempt to reroute wiring or install plumbing yourself. Always call in a professional electrician or plumber.

● Electric sockets should be positioned well away from water.

● Make sure that plenty of cool air can circulate around electrical appliances.

● An iron should have a separate, easily accessible socket positioned at the same height as the ironing board to make sure wires don't trail and that the plug can be easily disconnected when not in use.

● Floors must be level and structurally sound to carry the weight of heavy appliances such as washing machines or freezers.

● Store hazardous items, such as tools, detergents and cleaning products, well out of the reach of children, ideally in a locked cupboard. For extra safety, you could install a lock on the utility room door itself.

# TOOLS, MATERIALS AND TECHNIQUES

ARMED WITH FRESH INSPIRATION for transforming your home and with a clearer idea of the style you would like to achieve, you are now ready to put your ideas into practice. This part of the book will guide you through all the important stages of home decorating, showing you how to tackle essential techniques such as painting, wallpapering and tiling. Illustrated with clear photographs and accompanied by easy-to-follow instructions and expert advice, there are also step-by-steps covering everything from colourwashing and laying vinyl tiles to making your own roller blind or loose cover. Directory spreads give a summary of each of the projects, highlighting the tools that will be required and offering guidance on how long the work will take and the level of skill required.

Covering painting, wallpapering, tiling, flooring, working with wood and soft furnishings, this chapter gives advice on preparation and planning for each task to ensure that projects run smoothly and successfully.

# PAINTING DIRECTORY

## PAINTING: PREPARATION AND PLANNING

**SKILL LEVEL** Low
**TIME FRAME** 1 day per room
**SPECIAL TOOLS** Electric sander
**SEE PAGES** 120–121

Preparing and planning for any painting project is vital for ensuring that the finish is hard-wearing and attractive. Preparation is always the least appealing part of any do-it-yourself project, but it is essential and it must be looked on as part of the project. In most cases where a painting project does not live up to expectations, it is the result of poor planning and preparation. It is important to plan the order of the work before you start decorating. This way you can plan efficiently and make use of any labour-saving devices, such as electric sanders, to speed up preparation time.

You need to make sure that paint cannot splash or be sprayed on to areas that are not supposed to be painted. To prevent this, remove as much of the furniture as

possible from the room. Any furniture that has to stay should be covered with dust sheets. Carpets should be taken up or covered with dust sheets. Make sure that the dust sheets extend right to the edge of the floor, taping them down if necessary.

Fill any holes or cracks with one of the many types of filler that are widely available and wash down all the surfaces – this may need to be done before and after filling – to remove any impurities that could react with the paint.

If there are any stubborn stains or marks that cannot be removed, cover them with a proprietary stain blocking spray or paint to stop the marks bleeding through the the new paint finish.

## PAINTING SEQUENCE

**SKILL LEVEL** Low
**TIME FRAME** 1 day (depending on room size)
**SPECIAL TOOLS** None
**SEE PAGES** 122–123

When painting a room, the wall surfaces need to be

prepared first (see pp.120–121), then you have to plan the order of painting. You can save time, and achieve a better finish, by sticking to a simple order of work. Begin by tackling the larger room surfaces – the walls and the ceiling. Once these have been painted, you can turn your attention to the smaller, more ornate surfaces, including the doors, windows and any mouldings such as skirting boards, decorative rails and architraves.

Always start at the top of the room and work down because, no matter how careful you are, some overspray is inevitable and this will always fall towards the lower surfaces. By working from the top down, any overspray is covered over during paint application. It is also far easier to paint clear defining lines between wooden features and walls and ceilings if the wooden features are painted last.

As well as following the correct order for the room as a whole, there is a specific order of work for features such as doors and windows to

make sure that no sections are missed during the application of each coat of paint. It also helps to achieve a good finish with the different sections or parts of the door or window clearly defined.

## PAINTING AWKWARD PLACES

**SKILL LEVEL** Low to medium
**TIME FRAME** Dependent on the size of the job
**SPECIAL TOOLS** Extension pole, radiator roller, paint shield
**SEE PAGES** 124-125

Inevitably, not all areas in a room are easy to reach or gain access to. This means you have to devise various mechanisms and techniques to overcome this. To paint awkward areas successfully, you need to improve the access and make sure that you have the correct equipment and tools for the job, ones that are designed to deal with detailed or precision painting.

Many access problems are due to height, either of walls, ceilings or windows, so you

Paintbrushes

Soft-bristle brush

Masking tape

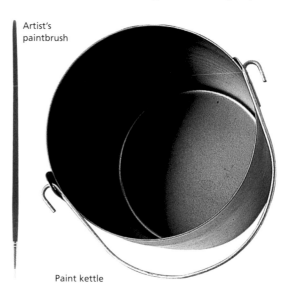

Artist's paintbrush

Paint kettle

may need to use a ladder or stepladder to deal with these situations. There are also various tools that can help, such as extension poles. These can be attached to paint rollers in order to gain access to high areas while you remain standing on the floor.

If you are unable to remove the radiators in a room before painting, a radiator roller is ideal for painting the wall surface behind them.

Another labour-saving device that helps improve accuracy and detail is a paint shield. This is a particularly useful tool when you are painting next to glass, as any paint overspill will go on to the shield, not the glass. This can save a considerable amount of time that would otherwise be spent removing paint from the glass.

## PAINTING FURNITURE

**SKILL LEVEL** Low to medium
**TIME FRAME** 2 hours
**SPECIAL TOOLS** Stamps
**SEE PAGES** 126–127

The same rules as for painting walls and woodwork apply to painting furniture, the only difference being that the project is on a much smaller scale. It is still important to stick to an order of work and ensure that the item of furniture receives the correct number of coats of paint in order to achieve the best possible paint finish.

It is also just as important to prepare well so that paint is applied to a smooth surface, and one that will accept paint readily. This often means removing all traces of previous coatings, especially if the furniture has been waxed or varnished.

The choice of paint colour may be linked to other areas of the room, making furniture painting an ideal way of integrating the items into the room scheme as a whole.

Stamps can be used to create a decorative embellishment and give greater interest to the finished effect. The painted effect on the furniture can also be aged or distressed to give it a more lived-in look. The painted finish should then be protected with wax or a coat of varnish.

To maintain a smart finish on furniture that receives a fair amount of wear and tear, such as kitchen chairs, it is a good idea to apply a further coat of wax or varnish to the surface from to time.

## METALLIC PAINT CRAFTS: ANTIQUE METAL

**SKILL LEVEL** Low to medium
**TIME FRAME** 2 hours, not including drying time
**SPECIAL TOOLS** None
**SEE PAGE** 128

The development of metallic paints has opened up a new area of decorative painting techniques. This type of paint can be used to change the appearance of household objects completely, although the cost of metallic paints means that it is more economical to use them on small items or to highlight small features on large items than to use them across wide open surface areas, such as walls and ceilings.

A metallic finish may be left as plain metal or a further effect can be created by adding a craquelure finish to give it a more distressed appearance. The craquelure finish is enhanced by painting on burnt umber to highlight the cracks in the finished surface. When applying burnt umber to the craquelure, take care to wipe away any excess colour before it dries, so the burnt umber is left only in the cracks in the finish.

## METALLIC PAINT CRAFTS: VERDIGRIS

**SKILL LEVEL** Low to medium
**TIME FRAME** 4 hours for average size of room, not including drying time
**SPECIAL TOOLS** Stencil brushes
**SEE PAGE** 129

Verdigris is different from most metallic paint effects in that the appearance that you are trying to recreate is the effect of oxidized, or weathered, metal rather than shiny, polished metal. This aged effect is particularly well suited to ornamental or strongly moulded features such as a cornice. By using a number of different coats of glaze, applied in the correct order, you can produce a verdigris effect that looks like the genuine deterioration of copper, brass or bronze. Many manufacturers supply the different paint colours required for this finish in kit form. Alternatively, you can mix your own colours by using normal acrylic glaze and standard colourizers. If you are mixing your own colours, it is worth looking at a picture of verdigris in order to achieve an accurate match of the different shades and tones of the real thing.

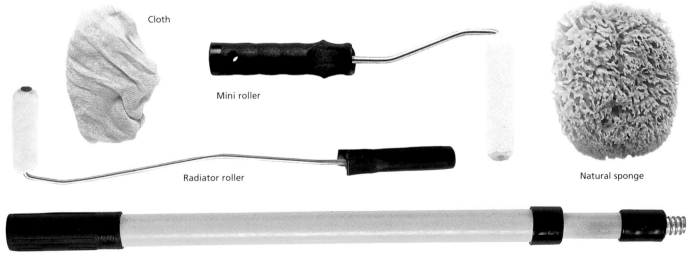

Cloth

Mini roller

Radiator roller

Natural sponge

Extension pole

## STENCILLING WALLS AND FLOORS

**SKILL LEVEL** Low to medium
**TIME FRAME** 1 day for average size of room
**SPECIAL TOOLS** Wax pencil, craft knife, stencil brushes
**SEE PAGES** 130–131

Using stencils on both the walls and floors in a room is a simple way of producing a well-integrated scheme. Much of the pleasure of stencilling can be derived from making your own stencils. This can be done by simply drawing a design on to a sheet of acetate, using a wax pencil. You can then cut out the design with a craft knife to give you a stencil. Border stencils are particularly effective used around the lower levels of walls or the perimeter of floors, where they can act as a frame for other decoration in the room. There are any number of combinations of stencil and pattern you can use on walls and floors, and you can use one or more colours. It is worth experimenting with various colours on some scrap paper so that you are sure of your choice before you start on the wall or floor surface.

## STENCILLING FURNITURE

**SKILL LEVEL** Low to medium
**TIME FRAME** ½ to 1 day
**SPECIAL TOOLS** Stencil brushes, artist's paintbrush
**SEE PAGES** 132–133

A furniture stencilling project needs to be approached in much the same way as you would any other painting job. Surfaces must be well prepared and the correct number of coats of paint must be applied to give a sound base for the stencils. Only then you can think about applying your stencil design.

Many manufacturers produce groups of stencils that are designed to be used together to form an overall stencil picture or pattern. However, there is a certain amount of flexibility in this design idea – you can either follow the manufacturer's instructions exactly, or you can vary them to add your own personal touch. Whatever choice you make, it is important to take time to position the stencils before applying the paint and pay careful attention to detail. Using colour with a greater intensity in particular places on the stencil can create a more three-dimensional effect, and employing an artist's paintbrush for fine detailing can be very effective.

## COLOURWASHING WALLS

**SKILL LEVEL** Low
**TIME FRAME** 1 day for an average-size room
**SPECIAL TOOLS** Badger-hair or soft-bristle brush
**SEE PAGE** 134

Colourwashing is a relatively simple paint effect, using a tinted glaze to produce a restful and textured colour tint on a wall surface. Texture is created by the way in which the glaze is applied, and its coarseness depends on how much you soften this application. Colourwashing requires a light-coloured base coat of emulsion paint, which works as the background for the glaze. It is a particularly good paint finish for rough or uneven wall surfaces, as the colour tends to be picked up more clearly within the grainy texture of such walls. To increase the depth of this effect, you can apply more than one coat of colourwash.

## COLOUR RUBBING WOOD

**SKILL LEVEL** Low
**TIME FRAME** 1 day for woodwork in an average-size room
**SPECIAL TOOLS** None
**SEE PAGE** 135

This paint effect is similar to colourwashing, except that colour rubbing is done on wooden surfaces. Diluted emulsion paint or a tinted glaze is applied to bare wooden surfaces, allowing the grain of the wood to pick up the pigment of the glaze. In this way, a stained wood appearance is achieved, with the grain highlighted in your chosen colour.

When colour rubbing items such as decorative wooden rails, try and colour rub them before fixing them to the wall, if possible, because this makes the decoration much easier. Once decorated, use bonding adhesive to attach the items, so no mechanical fixings are required, which might spoil the effect. Colour rubbing is a particularly good paint effect to use in combination with colourwashing, as the two together provide a well-integrated decorative scheme.

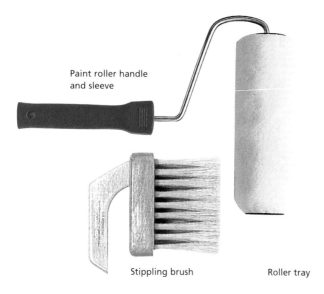

Paint roller handle and sleeve

Stippling brush

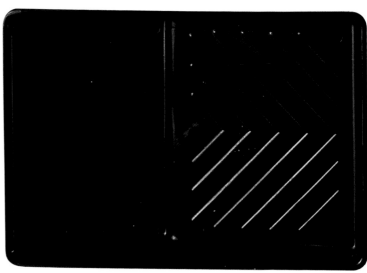

Roller tray

## MARBLING

**SKILL LEVEL** Medium to high
**TIME FRAME** 1 to 2 days for an average-size room
**SPECIAL TOOLS** Stippling brush, soft-bristle brush, artist's paintbrush
**SEE PAGES** 136–137

Marbling is quite a difficult paint effect to achieve. However, with practice, it can be used to produce highly decorative finishes throughout your home. It is important to follow the step-by-step instructions carefully. Never be tempted to skip any of the steps, otherwise you will not produce an authentic marbled finish. Before attempting a large area, it is best to master the technique on a slightly less ambitious project.

As with many paint effects, it is very useful to have an extra pair of hands to help with marbling – if the glaze dries before you have time to apply the marbling effect, you may have to start the process all over again.

You need to use several types of brush to produce a marbled effect, so make sure you have them all to hand before you start on the project.

## RAGGING AND RAG ROLLING

**SKILL LEVEL** Low to medium
**TIME FRAME** 1 day for an average-size room
**SPECIAL TOOLS** Cotton rags
**SEE PAGES** 138–139

Like most paint effects, ragging and rag rolling use a tinted glaze. The glaze may be applied with rags or it may be painted on the wall with a paintbrush before the rag is applied to the surface to create patterns or impressions.

Although both ragging and rag rolling are created with the same tool – rags – the two effects are markedly different. Ragging alone provides a highly textured paint finish, whereas rag rolling turns this finish into a more directional effect. Excellent striped patterns can be made on wall surfaces by rag rolling. Areas are masked off before the glaze is applied. The masking is then removed to reveal the striped pattern. The masking technique illustrated on p.139 demonstrates just one example of this design idea. The same principle can be applied in various other ways to produce all kinds of very individual finishes.

## STIPPLING

**SKILL LEVEL** Low to medium
**TIME FRAME** 1 day for an average-size room
**SPECIAL TOOLS** Stippling brushes
**SEE PAGES** 140–141

Stippling is a simple textured paint effect produced by using a specially designed brush to make small impressions in a glazed surface. It can mimic the textured look of velvet. More than one colour can be used on a wall surface – they can be blended or changed according to personal choice.

Patience is required in order to achieve an even finish when applying a stippling brush. Corners need particular care; the easiest way is to use a smaller stippling brush to get right into the corner junction.

## CREATING DÉCOUPAGE

**SKILL LEVEL** Low to medium
**TIME FRAME** 2 to 4 hours (depending on project size)
**SPECIAL TOOLS** None
**SEE PAGES** 142–143

Although not strictly a paint technique, découpage wall effects tend to require a painted background in order to show them off to their best advantage. You can add your own completely individual touch to a room's decoration with découpage. Fix your design on the wall with spray adhesive, then cover the design with several coats of varnish to protect it. Or, instead of using spray adhesive, stick the designs on the wall with a standard wallpaper paste made up in a diluted consistency (similar to the mixture required for hanging lining paper).

As well as creating designs on walls, you can use the découpage technique on items of furniture. This is an especially attractive option if you want to link the pattern or design on the wall surfaces with the furnishings in the room to integrate the whole room scheme. For example, it can be very effective to copy the design used on wall surfaces on to the top of a coffee table. If you do this, it is worth considering covering the design on the table top with a sheet of glass to give the découpage finish added protection. If you do use a sheet of glass, make sure that it has a bevelled edge so that it is not sharp to the touch.

Sanding block

Cartridge gun

Abrasive paper

Electric sander

Stippling brushes

# PAINTING: PREPARATION AND PLANNING

**YOU WILL NEED**

**Masking up**
Fabric dust sheet
Low-tack masking tape
Plastic bags

**Filling and sanding**
Utility knife
Filling knife
Electric sander or medium-grade abrasive paper

**Washing down**
Mild detergent solution
Rubber gloves
Bucket and sponge

**Flexible filling**
Cartridge gun

**Staining**
Brush (if required)

**MATERIALS**

**Filling and sanding**
All-purpose filler

**Flexible filling**
Tube of flexible filler

**Staining**
Proprietary stain sealer

With all painting projects, it is vital to take time to prepare and plan the procedures so that you achieve the best possible finish. Although preparation and planning are undoubtedly the least interesting aspects of decorating, they are the processes that frequently make the biggest contribution to the quality of the end result. As well as preparing the surfaces you wish to paint, it is equally important to protect those surfaces that you want to keep free from paint. The room needs to be cleared of as much furniture and soft furnishings as possible, and items that cannot be moved need to be covered with dust sheets or masked to protect them from splashes of paint.

A poor finish on a newly painted surface can be the result of various factors, but in the majority of cases it is due to lack of filling and sanding, or inadequate cleaning down of the surfaces before starting to paint. Dirt and grime cannot simply be covered over with a coat of paint, as they will always bleed through the paintwork eventually and spoil the finish. Washing down walls and woodwork will ensure that you have a sound surface for painting before you begin.

Another consideration is whether any major construction work needs to be carried out before you paint. Any rerouting of pipes or cables is better done before you start to redecorate, as this type of work will leave patches on the walls that will need redecoration.

In the same way, decide whether pictures or shelves will be staying in the same place on the wall. If they are going to be moved, take them down, remove any fixings from the wall surface and fill the holes as necessary before you start painting. The shelves or pictures can then be repositioned once the decorating is finished.

## MASKING UP

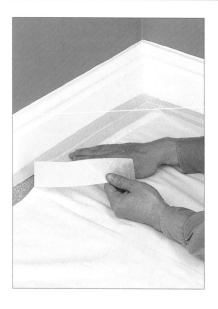

**1** If carpets have to remain down during decoration, ensure that they are well covered with dust sheets. It is even worth securing the dust sheets to the skirting boards by using masking tape around the edge of the room, so that there is no danger of the sheets creeping away from the walls.

**2** You should mask light fittings before painting near them, but first turn off the electricity at the mains. Ceiling spotlights can often be lowered and covered; mask them in a plastic bag while you are painting. Remove door handles, or mask them and other fittings, such as electrical points, using masking tape.

## FILLING AND SANDING

**1** All small holes and cracks in wall surfaces should be filled with an all-purpose filler. Cut away the crumbly edges of wall cracks using a utility knife. Dust out any loose material and wet the crack and edges with some water applied with an old paintbrush.

**2** Mix up some all-purpose filler to a smooth but firm consistency. Load the filler on to a filling knife and apply it to the crack. The flexibility of the knife blade should allow you to press the filler firmly into the crack. Do it as neatly as possible to reduce the amount of sanding needed once the filler has dried.

**3** When the filler is dry, sand the area to a smooth finish. A hand-held electric sander is ideal for this purpose, making the job much faster. For deep holes in the wall surface, you may find that you need more than one application of filler.

## WASHING DOWN

All surfaces must be washed down before painting. This can be done before or after filling. Use a mild detergent solution to remove any dirt or grime from the surface. After this, wash down and rinse the surfaces with clean, warm water.

## FLEXIBLE FILLING

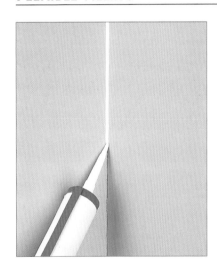

Where cracks have appeared in corners, it is best to use a flexible filler rather than an all-purpose one. Use a cartridge gun to apply the filler (which comes in a tube) to the crack. Smooth the filler with a wet fingertip before it dries, as you cannot sand this type of filler.

## STAINING

Occasionally you will come across areas or stains on the wall surface that do not disappear during the washing down. These must be sealed before painting, or they may bleed through the new paint. Spray or brush on a proprietary sealer in these areas to neutralize the stain.

# PAINTING SEQUENCE

Keeping to a specific order of work when painting a room helps to ensure the best use of both time and energy. As a rule, work from the top down, painting the ceiling and wall surfaces before moving on to the other surfaces such as doors, windows and skirting board. This is because it is much easier to cut-in a straight line along woodwork edges at the junction they make with ceilings or walls rather than cutting in the other way around.

In order to get a really good finish on your painted surface, always allow enough drying time between the coats of paint. When painting doors and windows, try to stick to a regimented order, particularly when you are applying two or more coats of paint – you do not want to risk missing any areas because you cannot remember, or cannot see, which ones have been painted several times and which still require another coat.

## ROOM ORDER OF WORK

One of the most important reasons for beginning at the top of a room and working down is to avoid repeating work because of paint splashes. By painting the ceiling first, especially if you are using a roller, any paint that falls on adjacent surfaces can be painted over when you reach those surfaces. If you work the other way around and finish the lower levels first, you risk spilling paint on the finished areas when you paint the ceiling, which could ruin the finish on the lower levels. A good order of work avoids this problem. The diagram on the right shows the sort of features that will need painting in a typical room.

### HELPFUL HINTS

When estimating the quantity of paint needed for a job, always refer to the manufacturer's guidelines on the side of the tin. Unsealed surfaces such as new plaster will require more paint to cover them than repainting a painted surface. The first coat of paint on a surface will use more than the second or subsequent coats. The amount will also vary according to the type of paint you are using. As a rule, water-based or acrylic paints will go much further than oil-based ones.

**1** Begin with the ceiling. If using a roller, begin along one side of the ceiling and work to the opposite side. Cut in (paint into the angle) with a paintbrush around the edge.

**2** Continue on to the coving or cornice. Cut in precisely on the top edge along the ceiling; the lower edge can overlap on to the wall.

**3**, **4** and **5** Once the ceiling is done, work down on to the walls. Cut in a precise line with the wall and coving base and overlap on to dado rail, skirting board and architrave.

**6,7** and **8** Paint the rails and skirting board, working down the wall surface. Cut in at the junction with the wall surface.

**9** Paint doors and windows. Cut in around the junctions of architrave and window frame with the wall.

**10** If required, turn your attention to the floor surface last of all.

## How to paint a panel door

Panel doors are a common door design and, as with other surfaces, it is important to follow a strict order of work when painting them so that all areas are painted with the correct number of coats of paint and look as good as possible when finished. Remove the door handles or any other door furniture before you start painting so that you do not need to cut in around them. This also gives you the opportunity to give them a clean before you reposition them on the door after the paint has dried. The order illustrated in this diagram helps to ensure that all the separate components that make up the door structure are well defined and painted in a way that shows off this type of detailing. As you progress across the door surface, keep checking for runs or drips of paint, especially at the corners of the panels. Brush them out as necessary.

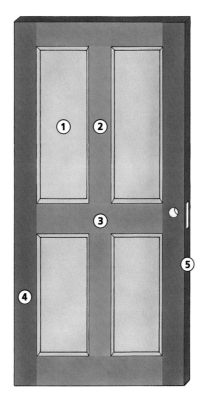

**1** Start by painting the panels, working from the top down. Paint the panel mouldings at this stage. Some doors may have more than the four panels shown here. Simply begin at the top levels and work down.

**2** Continue on to the central vertical stiles, thus linking the panels.

**3** Carry on to the horizontal rails, working from the top down, therefore finishing the central area of the door.

**4** Finish the face of the door by painting the two outer stiles.

**5** Finish by painting the top and side edge of the door, as required. Once these are painted, you can paint the door frame.

## How to paint a casement window

Windows require even greater precision than doors because there needs to be a well-defined dividing line between the rebates and the glass surface. The best plan is to divide the window into sections. Start each section with the rebates next to the glass, and gradually work away to the outer areas of the window frame.

### Helpful hints

● There are various tools, such as paint shields (see p.125), that aim to make painting windows easier. There are also brushes that have angled heads, which make it easier to paint window rebates because the shape allows better access into the corner of the rebates next to the glass.

● If any paint does splash on to the window surface, allow it to dry and then remove it with the aid of a specially designed window scraper.

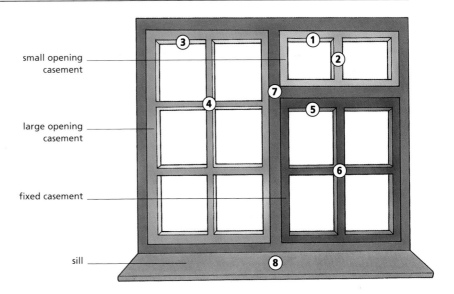

small opening casement

large opening casement

fixed casement

sill

**1** and **2** Start with the rebates on the small opening casement window, then paint the rails.

**3** and **4** Paint the rebates, then the rails on the large opening casement window.

**5** and **6** Paint the rebates, then the rails on the fixed casement.

**7** Paint the main frame.

**8** Before painting the sill, wipe with a cloth dampened with white spirit.

# PAINTING AWKWARD PLACES

**YOU WILL NEED**
......................................................
Extension pole and brush
with extended handle
Scrap cloth and masking
tape
Radiator brush, cardboard
and low-tack masking tape
Thin cardboard or paint
shield
Small paintbrush
Artist's paintbrush

Not all surfaces are easy to paint, either because of limited access or a problem with the actual surface itself. Many of these problems can be overcome by simply applying a very methodical approach to your work. However, there are also a variety of different tools available that can help to deal with restricted access and unusual surfaces. It is also worth considering using products that can speed up work, such as items that will shield or protect areas that you do not wish to come in contact with the paint. You should try to plan ahead of time so that you'll have on hand any of the devices that will help to tackle your project.

## DEALING WITH HEIGHT

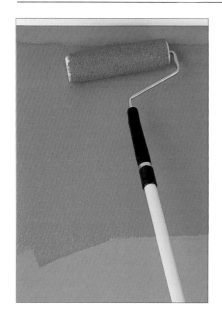

**1** Extension poles are an ideal labour-saving device, as they eliminate the need for a ladder when you have to paint ceilings or the top area of wall surfaces. Before buying an extension pole, ensure that its joining mechanism is compatible with the roller frame you are using for painting.

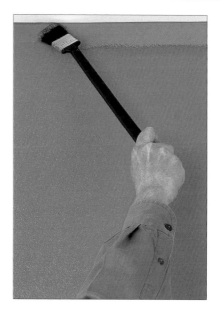

**2** Once the top area of a wall has been rolled, it is still necessary to finish off around the edge – known as "cutting in". Brushes that have extended angled heads are ideal for this purpose, as you can continue to paint while still standing at floor level.

## PROTECTING WALLS

In particularly high areas, such as stairwells, you will almost certainly need to use a ladder to gain access to the higher points. Protect wall surfaces from the top edges of the ladder by binding them with cloth and securing them in place with masking tape.

## HELPFUL HINTS

Ladder technology has now reached the stage where it is no longer necessary to purchase a number of separate ladders for different uses. For exteriors you may still need to use longer extension ladders, but for interiors you can now buy combination ladders that are specially designed to fold into step-ladders, normal extension ladders or even working platforms. It is always worth spending a little extra money on these items to ensure good quality, and the time-saving, cost and space-saving benefits will far outweigh the burden of the initial investment.

## RADIATORS

1 Ideally, radiators should be removed so that you can decorate behind them, but this does require plumbing knowledge. Also, in many cases, the radiator may be too awkward to move. In these instances, use a custom-made radiator roller to paint the wall surface behind it.

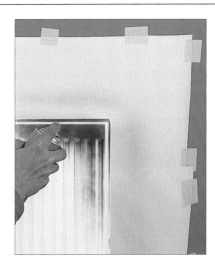

2 Make sure that the radiator is turned off before you start painting it. Aerosol paints are quick and easy to use on radiators, but be sure to wear a respirator mask, and protect the wall from any overspray by taping an oversize sheet of cardboard behind it.

## SHIELDING TIPS

Speed up the painting of pipes that are next to the wall by using a piece of cardboard to protect the wall surface. As you move along the pipe, move the cardboard with one hand and apply the paint with the other.

Windows are always time-consuming to paint, mainly because it is necessary to cut in neatly around the edge of the glass. Speed up the process by using a paint shield, which should be held at the rebate/glass junction, so that any overspill goes on to the shield rather than the glass.

## DEALING WITH DETAIL

1 Picking out any particular details in architectural features within a room, such as the detail found in a cornice or coving, can take a long time. Speed up the painting process by using the base coat or undercoat as a background colour for all additional colours used.

2 Use a small artist's paintbrush to paint in the detailed features, completing one colour at a time as you progress across the moulded surface. This type of painting does take time, but the attractive finish is certainly well worth all the effort.

# PAINTING FURNITURE

## YOU WILL NEED

Coarse- and fine-grade
abrasive paper
Cloth
Paintbrush
Stamp(s)
Stamp roller
Fine-grade wire wool

## MATERIALS

Emulsion paint
Stamp paint
Clear wax

A coat of paint is a simple way of reviving an old piece of furniture or providing an alternative effect for a new one. There are a number of options available . Depending on the look you want, these range from using a number of coats of paint to produce a precise and new looking finish, to achieving a more distressed appearance by masking and/or sanding the chair between coats. In this example, the distressed look has been used to revive an old painted chair.

Stamps can be used as an additional embellishment to give a decorative finish. Choosing coloursand the stamp design is a matter of personal preference, but always bear in mind the colour scheme in the room where the piece of furniture will be placed. It is very easy to get carried away with stamps and overdo their use, so try to refrain from covering the whole chair with stamps – using a simple design and pattern often produces the best result on furniture.

*Painting furniture is a perfect way of softening a room's colour scheme and integrating chairs and other items into the overall design.*

**1** Sand the whole chair completely with coarse-grade abrasive paper, then with a finer grade. This removes any flaky or loose old paint layers and provides a key for the application of new paint. Wipe the chair down with a damp, clean cloth to remove any dust from the surface.

**2** Working from the top down, apply a coat of emulsion paint to all parts of the chair, ensuring a good, even coverage. Once the first coat has dried, apply a second coat to even out the finish. During the application, keep checking your work to ensure that there are no runs in the paint finish, and brush them out, if necessary.

**3** Apply stamp paint to the stamp using a roller. Ensure that the whole face of the stamp is covered with an even coat of paint. Before applying the stamp to the chair, test the impression on a scrap piece of paper to check that the paint is evenly distributed.

**4** Position the face of the stamp in the desired position on the chair surface. Apply steady, even, downward pressure, taking care not to allow the face of the stamp to move across the surface of the furniture and thus risk smudging the image.

**5** Remove the stamp from the surface with a perfect vertical action to avoid any smudging. Re-apply paint to the stamp before applying the stamp once again to the next position on the furniture. Build up your own pattern or design, varying the size of the stamp, if required, as shown in this example.

**6** Once the stamp paint has dried, use a piece of fine-grade abrasive paper to gently distress areas on the chair. Pay particular attention to the edges and high points in the moulded areas of the furniture, as these would be the places that would naturally wear first over time.

**7** Finally, with some fine-grade wire wool, apply a coat of clear wax to the furniture surface to protect the finish. This will also rub away a little more paint, including some of the stamped areas, which will add to the overall distressed effect.

## NAUTICAL THEME

Furniture that has been personalized with a decorative paint finish can become the starting point for a room scheme, as in this spacious kitchen, where the colours of the wood-topped table are echoed elsewhere (see p.67). The table base was given several coats of soft green paint to create a distressed look and then a stamp was used to add the fish motif.

# METALLIC PAINT CRAFTS: ANTIQUE METAL

**YOU WILL NEED**

Paintbrush
Cloth

**MATERIALS**

Metallic paint
Craquelure (base coat and top coat)
Burnt umber (available at artist's supply shops)
Varnish (optional)

Applying a metallic finish to various household objects is a simple way of completely revamping an item, giving it a new look and texture. This look may be enhanced further by ageing the metallic effect by painting it with craquelure to create a distressed or antique appearance.

Metallic paints are now more widely available, and the latest types can provide an increasingly more realistic metallic effect to items made of other materials. There is a good selection of colours, or "metals", to choose from, catering for all kinds of personal preference. In this example, a pewter effect has been chosen to change the appearance of a simple terracotta pot. However, equally impressive finishes may be achieved in such colours as gold, brass or copper, again with a craquelure effect added to produce the "aged", or antique, appearance.

**1** Apply an even coat of the metallic paint to the terracotta pot with a paintbrush. Check the manufacturer's guidelines for the particular paint you are using, but generally only one coat is required, as metallic finishes tend to have excellent covering properties.

**2** Once the metallic paint has dried, apply one layer of craquelure base coat to the pot, following the manufacturer's guidelines. Make sure that it is well brushed out with no drips or runs in its surface. The initial milky coating will eventually dry to a slightly sticky but clear finish.

**3** Apply one layer of craquelure top coat, again using a paintbrush, and ensure that the entire pot surface is covered. As the top coat dries, small cracks will begin to appear in its surface. The thicker the layer of top coat applied, the deeper the cracks will be.

**4** To highlight the cracks in the finish, rub over the pot surface with a rag that has been dipped in a small amount of burnt umber. The burnt umber becomes stuck in the cracks that have been created by the craquelure finish and provides the final antique effect. Varnish the pot, if required.

# METALLIC PAINT CRAFTS: VERDIGRIS

**YOU WILL NEED**

Stencil brushes
Paint brush
Cloth

**MATERIALS**

Emulsion paint
Acrylic glaze
Colourizers

Verdigris is a crystallized substance that forms on copper, brass or bronze surfaces, caused by the action of acid breaking down the surface. However, the characteristic shades of green produced by verdigris can be replicated on all sorts of other surfaces to give a highly decorative "aged" finish. Reproducing this effect on interior surfaces is very effective, particularly when applied to surfaces that have a relatively intricate or ornate make-up, such as the cornice around a room. To produce a good verdigris effect, you will need to mix up glaze mixtures in two or three shades of green by mixing acrylic glaze and colourizers, following the manufacturer's instructions. Some manufacturers produce specific verdigris kits, eliminating the need for you to do your own mixing. The different shades are then applied to the surface one at a time.

**1** Apply an emulsion base coat to the cornice and allow it to dry. Using a large stencil brush, apply the palest of the green mixes to the cornice. Try to get the bristles into most areas of the design without saturating the surface with colour.

**2** Before the green dries, wipe over the cornice surface using a slightly dampened cloth. This removes some of the paint from the cornice high points while leaving a much greater concentration of the paint in the lower depressions of the moulding.

**3** Add the second, much darker, green to the cornice, again using the large stencil brush (after cleaning it), but concentrating efforts on the high points of the moulding in the cornice. Once this has dried, use a smaller stencil brush to add a slightly darker green to these "high" areas. Leave this to dry.

**4** Finally, dilute the darkest green mix with some more glaze to make it a much lighter colour and a more transparent consistency. Apply a coat of this diluted glaze over the entire cornice. This helps the "aged" effect while also filling in any areas where the base coat may still be showing through.

# STENCILLING WALLS AND FLOORS

## YOU WILL NEED

Paper
Pencil
Cutting board
Acetate
Wax pencil
Craft knife
Tape measure
Stencil
Paintbrush
Masking tape
Stencil brushes

## MATERIALS

Stencil paint
Emulsion paint
Varnish (optional)

*Ethnic designs always make effective stencil finishes, with subtle colour variations adding to the finished look of the stencilled wall or floor.*

Stencilling is a versatile decorative effect for bringing colour and pattern to all kinds of surfaces. The technique is the same whatever the surface being stencilled, whether it be walls, floors or items of furniture (see pp.132–133). There is a wide range of manufactured stencil designs to choose from, or it can be very rewarding to make your own, and add a more individual touch to the stencilled surface. Stencils can be made from pieces of thin cardboard or acetate. Acetate stencils last longer and are easier to clean than stencils made of cardboard.

## MAKING A STENCIL

**1** Draw your design on a piece of paper, ensuring that the outline is clearly defined. For the less artistically inclined, a picture can be traced rather than drawn, but it is worth noting that it is often the simplest designs that are the most effective.

**2** Transfer the design to a piece of acetate and use a wax pencil to trace the picture on to the acetate. Place the acetate on a cutting board and cut out the traced design with a craft knife, following the design lines very carefully.

# USING A STENCIL

**1** Adding a background colour to a stencil design can enhance the finished effect. In this case, a border stencil is being used to run around the perimeter of the floor in the room. Measure the width of the stencil to calculate the correct positioning on the floor.

**2** Transfer the width measurement to the floor, then mask off this area around the floor perimeter. Using a small paintbrush, apply emulsion paint as a background colour in the masked-off area, taking care not to let any brush strokes extend on to the main part of the floor.

**3** Once the painting is complete, remove the masking tape to reveal a perfect painted border around the room. If there are any areas where paint has seeped under the tape, they can be sanded back to the floor colour so that the lines of the border are kept sharp and precise.

**4** Apply the stencil over the painted border, using a stencil brush to paint the design. Remove excess paint from the bristles before application, and keep the brush perpendicular to the floor at all times while stencilling, "pouncing" the brush up and down. Move the stencil along to continue around the whole room.

**5** The same border design may be applied to the walls, if wished. In this case, a home-made stencil has been used to highlight just the corners in the room. To create a more three-dimensional effect, apply the colour more densely around the edge of the pattern.

**6** The home-made design may also be used to embellish the floor finish and link the two designs. Wash the stencils in warm water from time to time to remove any excess paint. This ensures that a neat finish is achieved with each new application of the stencil. Once the paint is dry, apply a coat of varnish to protect, if you wish.

# STENCILLING FURNITURE

**YOU WILL NEED**

Abrasive paper
Cloth
Paintbrush
Stencil set
Masking tape
Large stencil brush
Small stencil brush or artist's
paintbrush

**MATERIALS**

White emulsion paint
Acrylic glaze
Colourizers
Stencil paints

*A simple piece of furniture, such as a small, plain chest of drawers, can be given an elaborate decorative effect with a series of striking individual stencils that create a well-coordinated theme.*

S tencils are a good way to add a decorative edge to simple pieces of furniture. Stencil designs can be as simple or as intricate as you want. They can be applied to older pieces of furniture to add interest or to disguise a worn surface. Alternatively, as in this example, a new, but unfinished, chest of drawers can be painted and customized by a stencil pattern of your choice to make a highly decorative piece of furniture.

1 Lightly sand the chest to smooth any rough areas, then wipe it down with a damp cloth to remove any dust and debris from the surface. Pay particular attention to the drawer faces and top and sides of the chest, because this is where the stencils will be positioned.

2 Remove the drawers. Paint the chest with a base coat of white emulsion paint, then paint the drawers separately. If the wood is particularly resinous, it is advisable to prime it first, but in most cases a standard emulsion paint will act as an adequate primer for the acrylic glaze.

**3** Mix up two glazes, adding colourizer as needed. In this example, acrylic glaze has been tinted to produce a pale green and a mid-blue. Apply a coat of the pale green to the outside of the chest, applying the glaze evenly to produce an overall but semi-transparent finish.

**4** Apply the pale-green glaze to four of the drawers, and use the blue glaze on the other four. The sides of the drawers and their edges must be painted. The inside of the drawers can be painted with glaze, or not, as you wish.

**5** Decide on an overall design for stencilling the chest and begin with one drawer. Place it on its back so that the face of the drawer is facing upwards. Stick the required stencil on to the drawer face, using some masking tape to hold it in position.

**6** Begin to apply the stencil paint, using a large stencil brush for the larger areas of the pattern. Always keep the stencil brush perpendicular to the drawer face, "pouncing" it in an up-and-down motion, and remove excess paint from the bristles on a scrap piece of paper before applying it.

**7** Clean brushes regularly, ensuring that different coloured areas of the design are not contaminated by paint from other areas. For the more detailed work, and specifically for highlighting, as shown here, use a small stencil brush or even the end bristles of a small artist's paintbrush.

**8** Once each design is complete, carefully remove the stencil and continue on to another drawer or part of the chest. Build up your designs until all the stencilling is done. Once the paint has dried, the chest can be given a coat of varnish for added protection before it is used.

# COLOURWASHING WALLS

**YOU WILL NEED**

Large paintbrush
Badger-hair or soft-bristle
brush

**MATERIALS**

Emulsion paint
Acrylic glaze
Colourizers
Varnish (optional)

Colourwashing is one of the easiest paint effects to achieve. Strokes made by the bristles of the brush create a textured finish that combines with the colour of the base coat to form a three-dimensional, semi-transparent finish. The intensity of the effect depends on the base-coat colour and the number of glaze coats applied.

*Combining colourwashing on the walls and colour rubbing on the woodwork is a dramatic way of using two paint effects in one room.*

**1** Apply an emulsion base coat to the wall surface and allow it to dry. In this example, a pale blue has been used. Apply glaze to the wall surface, spreading it evenly with a large, relatively coarse-bristled brush. Move the brush in all directions across the wall surface.

**2** Use a badger-hair or other soft-bristle brush to take the harshness out of the brush strokes and blend the glaze colour across the surface of the wall. Use very light strokes in all directions, ensuring that the bristles of the brush barely touch the wall surface.

**3** Once this coat has dried, apply a second, slightly darker coat of glaze and, again, use the badger-hair brush across the wall surface. Further coats of glaze may be added, and softened, to create greater depth and dimension in the finish. Seal the wall surface with a coat of varnish, if you wish.

## CREATING MOOD

Colourwashing is a subtle paint effect, but it can have a great impact in terms of adding warmth to a room. Colourwashed walls make an excellent backdrop for the other features in a room. To give the illusion of a Mediterranean courtyard, a colourwash of faded terracotta has been applied to roughly plastered walls (see p.23).

# COLOUR RUBBING WOOD

**YOU WILL NEED**

Paintbrush
Cloth
Clear wax
Cartridge gun
Pencil
Spirit level

**MATERIALS**

Acrylic glaze
Colourizers
Bonding adhesive

Colour rubbing is a similar effect to colourwashing, except that once the colour has been applied to a surface, it is rubbed away. The effect is similar because the glaze provides an allover effect that has no particular pattern but simply highlights different areas in a random fashion. Although colour rubbing can be used on wall surfaces, the term generally applies to a finish for wood surfaces. The procedure involves tinting a bare wood surface, which highlights the grain and provides a very decorative stained appearance to the wood. The best effect is achieved on a wood that has a relatively prominent grain, as this gives a greater variation in colour and a more defined finish. An emulsion base coat is not required – the acrylic glaze is mixed to the colour of your choice with one or more colourizers, and then it is painted straight on to the wooden surface.

**1** Mix the glaze with the colourizer of your choice and apply it directly on to the surface of the wood with a paintbrush, covering it evenly. Here, a dado rail is being coated. Where possible, colour rub items before they are attached to the wall, as this makes it easier to achieve a neat edge once in position.

**2** Before the glaze dries, use a clean cloth to rub over the rail length, removing excess glaze from its surface. The glaze left on the wood will become ingrained in the surface and highlight the grain of the wood. Once dry, rub a coat of clear wax over the rail to provide a decorative and protective coat.

**3** Rather than nailing the dado rail to the wall surface and running the risk of ruining the colour-rubbed effect, use a proprietary bonding adhesive. This is usually supplied in a tube that fits into a cartridge gun and is easy to apply to the back of the dado rail.

**4** To act as a guideline, draw a pencil line on the wall surface, along the top of the spirit level. Press the rail in place. Remove any excess adhesive from around the edge of the rail with a damp cloth before the adhesive has time to dry.

# MARBLING

**YOU WILL NEED**

Paintbrushes
Stippling brush
Soft-bristle brush
Artist's paintbrush
Fine-grade abrasive paper

**MATERIALS**

White emulsion paint
Acrylic glaze
Colourizers
Raw umber
Lacquer

Marbling is one of the more difficult paint effects to achieve with any high degree of authenticity – it is almost like painting a picture and does require some practice before trying it on the wall surfaces.

One of the benefits of practising a marbling effect is that it allows you to experiment with different colours and designs before committing them to the wall. You can practise varying the intensities of the colours and the number, angle and prominence of the veining in the marble until you achieve an attractive finish that fits into the colour scheme of the room you want to decorate.

Depending on your level of skill, the finish can be applied to entire wall surfaces, although maintaining an even effect over large areas is difficult. The easier option is to decorate smaller areas, such as the panels below a dado rail. Whichever option you choose, a well-executed marble effect provides a stunning addition to the decoration in a room.

It is often easier if two people work together – one can apply the glaze while the other uses the various tools needed to produce the marbled finish, each concentrating on their own particular tasks in order to maintain a consistent finish.

*Marbling is a good mood-creating finish for walls – its appearance can vary according to the light source in a room and its intensity.*

**1** Apply a white emulsion base coat to your surface and allow it to dry. Then apply two different coloured glazes using a 25-mm- (1-in-) wide brush. Apply the glazes in random strokes that fall in a similar direction, leaving the base coat showing in some areas.

**2** While the paint is still wet, use a stippling brush across the glazed surface, pressing the tips of the bristles into the glaze and allowing them to blend the two glazes into each other. Allow the stippling brush to spread the colour on to the unglazed white areas, so the whole surface has a stippled glaze finish.

**3** Take a soft-bristle brush and gently draw the bristles across the glaze surface, removing any harsh brush marks from the glazed effect. First, draw the brush across the direction in which the glaze was initially applied; then draw it in the same direction in which the glaze was applied.

**4** Use an artist's paintbrush to apply thin veins of raw umber in the glaze surface. Rotate the brush between thumb and index finger as you draw it across the glaze. Try to keep the veins running across the wall in the same direction as the initial glaze application.

**5** Again, take the soft-bristle brush and draw it over the vein surfaces, blending them into the overall effect. Initially, work the brush gently against the vein direction, then apply the brush in the same direction as the veins to produce the most authentic effect.

**6** Once the glaze and raw umber have dried, sand the wall surface gently with fine-grade abrasive paper. Take care not to make scratches in the wall surface. The function of the sanding is to flatten the finish and raise a little dust on the surface without damaging the effect.

**7** Do not remove the dust with a cloth – instead apply a coat of lacquer directly on to the wall. Allow it to dry, sand again, and apply another coat. This alternate sanding and lacquering provides the final marble effect, softening the marbling and giving a very solid-looking, flat finish.

### HELPFUL HINTS

● Because marble is a naturally occurring substance, it is important to try to mimic its appearance as accurately as possible for an authentic. look. It is very difficult to produce a perfect replica, but a picture or a piece of marble will help your efforts. A piece of natural marble will also provide a good guide for the colour you use.

● A marbling paint effect does not have to be restricted to walls. The finish can be used on other items that look as if they might have been made from marble, such as coffee-table tops, lamp bases or shelves.

# RAGGING AND RAG ROLLING

**YOU WILL NEED**

Protective gloves
Paintbrush
Paint kettle
Cotton rags

**Masking options**

Masking tape

**MATERIALS**

Emulsion paint
Acrylic glaze
Colourizers

*A ragged paint effect, whether completely random or more directional as shown here, creates a strong, dramatic look on wall surfaces.*

Using cloths or rags to create paint effects is a popular way of adding a textured finish to wall surfaces. The two main techniques are ragging on – this involves applying glaze to the wall with the rag – and ragging off, where the glaze is brushed on to the wall and impressions are made in its surface with the rag. A third method, rag rolling, involves brushing the glaze on to the wall, then rolling rags down the wall surface in one direction. Using masking tape with rag rolling produces a flowing, striped effect.

## RAGGING ON

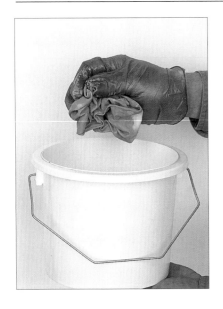

**1** It is advisable to wear gloves for all ragging, otherwise cleaning your hands can be a lengthy job. Apply a base coat of emulsion paint to the wall surface and allow it to dry. Mix the glaze and colourizers. Dampen a rag and, holding it in a crumpled position, dip it into the glaze. Squeeze out the rag to remove excess glaze.

**2** Apply the rag to the wall surface, still holding it in a crumpled ball in your hand. After each impression, alter your hand and wrist angle to create a random rather than uniform pattern. Once the impressions start to become less defined, reload the rag with more glaze.

## RAGGING OFF

**1** Apply a base coat of emulsion paint to the wall surface and allow it to dry. Apply glaze to the wall surface, using a large paintbrush. Ensure that the entire base coat is covered, working in areas of 1 sq m (1 sq yd) at a time, or the glaze may dry out before you create a ragged effect.

**2** With a crumpled, dampened rag, create impressions on the glazed surface by pressing the rag into it. After each impression, change your hand and wrist angle. When the rag is clogged with glaze, wash it thoroughly in clean water. Continue the process over the entire glazed surface.

## RAG ROLLING

**1** Cut up a number of rags into squares of 25 cm (10 in) and roll them up into sausage-shape cylinders. For each rag, fold in both ends to make the rolls a uniform length and ensure that there are no frayed pieces of material.

**2** Apply the glaze as in step 1 of Ragging off. Dampen the cylindrical rags and roll them down the glazed surface in as vertical a direction as possible. After each run, slightly overlap the next roll on to the previous impression. Clean or change rags once they become clogged with glaze.

## MASKING OPTIONS

**1** Use masking tape to divide up the wall surface into a vertically striped design. Apply glaze between the masked-off areas. Then roll the rags down between the masked-off areas, making sure that the rag length does not extend beyond the tape guidelines.

**2** Once the rag-rolled impression has been made, remove the masking tape on either side to reveal a patterned stripe. Continue applying the striped effect to the other areas on your wall surface, as required.

# STIPPLING

**YOU WILL NEED**
...........................................................
Paintbrush
Stippling brushes
Cloth

**MATERIALS**
...........................................................
Acrylic glaze
Colourizers
Varnish or glaze coat

Stippling is a subtle paint effect that breaks up the finish on a wall surface to give a more textured look than that produced by flat paint colours. As with most paint effects, glaze is used to produce the finish, so the texture of the stippling is slightly translucent. Stippling is not difficult, but great patience is required while using the stippling brush across the entire wall surface – any missed areas will show up and ruin the effect. In terms of colour, it is always best to apply a coat of light emulsion paint before the glaze, because this provides the most suitable background for showing off the texture. Walls can be stippled with a single colour, or, as in this case, two colours can be used and blended into one another to give an unusual decorative effect. The stippling technique can also be used to create random stripes on the wall surface, or to colour the edges or corners of the room a slightly different shade than the central wall areas.

*A stippled textured finish on the walls provides a mellow, warming backdrop for the overall decorative scheme of a room.*

**1** Apply glaze to the wall surface, ensuring a good even coverage. The brush marks can be either left going in random directions, or, once the surface is covered, you can use some light strokes with the brush to "lay off" the glaze in a vertical direction, so that all brush marks are pointing one way.

**2** Use a large stippling brush across the glaze surface, "pouncing" it in an up-and-down motion, allowing the extreme ends of the bristles to press into the wet glaze surface. After each impression, move along to the next area, shifting your wrist position slightly in order to apply random brush impressions.

**3** As you progress across the wall surface, use a cloth to remove excess glaze from the bristle ends after every few applications of the brush. Failure to do so will cause the bristles to become clogged with glaze, which will smudge and affect the stipple finish.

**4** If using two colours, apply the second color once you have stippled one section. Apply the colour up to the first colour, leaving a small gap between them where the basecoat on the wall surface will continue to show.

**5** Stipple the second colour using the same technique as for the first one. If using the same stippling brush, clean it very thoroughly before using it for the second colour; otherwise, the first colour will contaminate the second glaze and take away from the effect.

**6** At the dividing line between the two colours, use the stippling brush to blend along the junction. The subtlety of this joint depends on how much glaze you applied to the wall and the amount of white you left showing between the two colors when applying the glaze.

**7** Deal with corners using a smaller stippling brush, which is designed precisely for this purpose and makes access into these junctions much easier. Once stippling is complete, allow it to dry thoroughly before applying two coats of varnish or a protective glaze coat.

## HELPFUL HINTS

● When stippling, apply glaze to the wall in areas of 1 sq m (1 sq yd) at a time; if you do a larger area, you risk the glaze drying out before you apply the effect.

● Use silk emulsion paint as a base coat. The glaze takes longer to dry on this type of surface than on matte finishes, giving you a longer working time on the glaze.

● Build up depth of colour and texture by applying more than one stipple coat. Applying a slightly darker shade over a lighter one will produce a more three-dimensional finish.

# CREATING DÉCOUPAGE

### YOU WILL NEED

Thin cardboard
Pencil
Cutting board
Craft knife
Straight edge
Spirit level
Cloth

### MATERIALS

Photocopied musical score
Spray adhesive

*The musical theme of this découpage provides a decorative, framed picture effect on a plain wall surface.*

Découpage literally means to "cut up", and it is a way of producing a decorative collage effect on walls and furniture (or even household items such as vases, trinket boxes and table mats) by cutting out paper images and sticking them on to the chosen surface. All kinds of things can be used for this technique, such as old wallpaper motifs, photocopies of your favourite pictures or old writing scripts. In this example, a musical score has been photocopied, then the centre portion has been removed and a large musical note has been cut from it. The musical note has then been stuck on to a white surface surrounded by the border of the black-and-white photocopied score. If preferred, it can be stuck straight on to the wall. Although a musical theme has been used here, you can adapt this idea to many other subjects. Framed cut-outs of vegetables and fruit, for example, make an excellent picture for a kitchen wall, or use fish or seashells in a bathroom.

**1** Draw a musical note with a pencil on a piece of thin cardboard. If you are not confident enough to do this freehand, photocopy a picture of a note and enlarge it to the size that you want for your project.

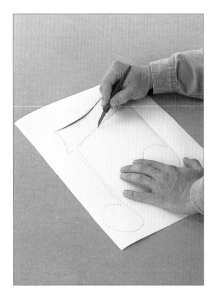

**2** On a cutting board, cut around the edge of the note, using a sharp craft knife, to separate the note from the main body of the cardboard. Take care when using a sharp craft knife and never position your free hand in front of the blade.

3 Position the note you have cut out in the centre of your photocopied musical score, trying to align it with the design. Measure a border or frame around the edge of the note and mark it with a pencil; cut around this line with the craft knife. Remove the centre of the photocopied score, leaving just an outer frame.

4 On the central cut-out portion of the photocopy, position the cut-out cardboard note once more. Using the craft knife, cut around the edge of it, until you are able to lift out a replica of the note design from the photocopied sheet.

5 Decide where you want to position your découpage on the wall. Use a spirit level and pencil to draw a guideline on the wall surface. This guideline should be to the width of the photocopy frame and it should be positioned where the bottom edge of the frame will sit.

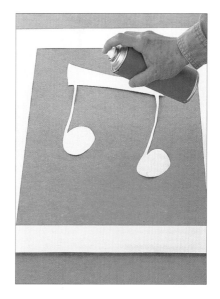

6 Using spray adhesive, spray the back of the photocopy frame and the back of the note cut from the photocopy. Follow the manufacturer's guidelines – most of them recommend leaving the spray to soak into the paper for a short while before applying it to the wall.

7 As soon as the adhesive is ready, stick the frame to the wall, following the pencil guideline marked on the wall. Stick the note in the centre of the frame to complete the picture. Using a slightly dampened clean cloth, flatten the design into place, removing any air bubbles from the paper surface.

## HELPFUL HINTS

● Instead of spray adhesive, ordinary wallpaper paste or slightly diluted PVA adhesive may be used to stick the designs to the wall. For the beginner, a PVA solution is often easier to use because the découpage image will take longer to dry on the wall surface than it will with a spray adhesive, which means that you can move the image around and re-position it if necessary before it dries fast to the wall.

● Once they are dry, découpage images can be protected with several coats of clear varnish.

# WALLPAPERING DIRECTORY

## WALLPAPERING: PREPARATION AND PLANNING

**SKILL LEVEL** Low
**TIME FRAME** ½ day for an average-size room
**SPECIAL TOOLS** None
**SEE PAGES** 146–147

In the same way that you need to prepare before painting any surfaces, preparation and planning are vital before you start wallpapering. Old layers of wallpaper should usually be removed, then the bare walls can be filled, sanded and sealed as required before lining paper and new wallpaper is applied. Take your time measuring up the room to decide on how much paper is needed and where in the room to start papering.

## WALLPAPERING A ROOM

**SKILL LEVEL** Low to medium
**TIME FRAME** 1 day for an average-size room
**SPECIAL TOOLS** Pasting brush and table, paper-hanging brush
**SEE PAGES** 148–149

Check whether the wallpaper is ready-pasted or if it requires pasting. Whichever type, the application technique is similar. When hanging wallpaper, you must begin from a totally vertical starting line and always butt-join lengths, trimming to fit at ceiling and skirting-board level with a utility knife. Have a good supply of knife blades, as they tend to become blunt very quickly.

## WALLPAPERING PANELS

**SKILL LEVEL** Low to medium
**TIME FRAME** 2 hours
**SPECIAL TOOLS** Metal ruler, pasting brush, paper-hanging brush
**SEE PAGES** 150–151

Making panels out of wallpaper creates an effective decoration for the walls, especially when a border is applied around the perimeter of the panels. Precise pattern matching and accurate application techniques are necessary to create a good effect. Take time to plan the

panel size so you achieve a balanced effect on the wall surface. Be sure to choose wallpaper and borders with suitable designs for this technique, as the borders will require mitre joins at each of the corners.

## USING BORDERS AND FRIEZES

**SKILL LEVEL** Low to medium
**TIME FRAME** 2 hours for an average-size room
**SPECIAL TOOLS** Pasting brush, paper-hanging brush
**SEE PAGES** 152–153

Borders and friezes may be hung at any level on the wall. Take care to ensure that patterns are matched in corners and that the border is level. Some borders and friezes are self-adhesive; others require pasting. Use border adhesive for borders that need pasting before applying them. If you use wallpaper paste, the edges of the border or frieze may lift away from the wall surface after a relatively short time. Border adhesive is much

stronger and creates a more secure bond between border and wall. When applying a border, don't make the common mistake of forgetting to keep both the border and the wall surface clear of excess adhesive during and after the application process. Adhesive dries very quickly, so it is vital to have a bucket of clean water and a sponge ready at all times. As soon as a length has been hung, wipe off excess adhesive, paying particular attention to the border edges. Once adhesive has dried on a wall surface it is almost impossible to remove it, and characteristic shiny patches are left on the wall or border surface, which spoil the finished look. If, despite all your precautions, you do get a shiny area, it can can sometimes be improved by wiping the surface down with a mild detergent solution, followed by rinsing with clean warm water. If the border has been applied over a painted surface rather than wallpaper, it may be possible to paint over any shiny areas with the wall colour, but take care that no paint spills.

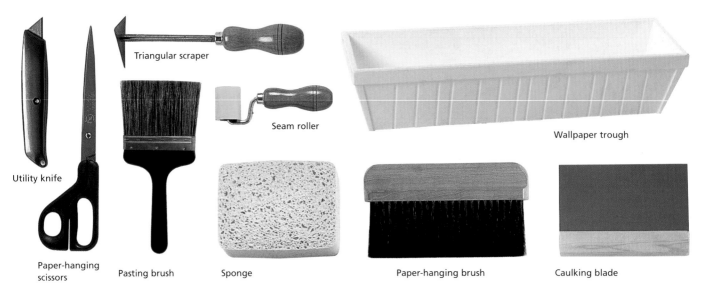

Triangular scraper

Seam roller

Wallpaper trough

Utility knife

Paper-hanging scissors

Pasting brush

Sponge

Paper-hanging brush

Caulking blade

# TILING DIRECTORY

## TILING A WALL

**SKILL LEVEL** Low to medium
**TIME FRAME** 2 to 4 hours for
an average-size wall
**SPECIAL TOOLS** Adhesive
spreader, platform tile cutter,
grout spreader, grout shaper
**SEE PAGES** 154–155

Tiling is straightforward as
long as you build up the
design from a solid and level
starting point. Wooden
battens are generally required
to give a sound base. Plan
carefully and make accurate
cuts to deal with the edges of
the design. Good grouting will
add the necessary final touch.

## USING DIFFERENT PATTERNS AND DESIGNS

**SKILL LEVEL** Low to medium
**TIME FRAME** 2 to 4 hours for
an average-size wall
**SPECIAL TOOLS** Adhesive
spreader, platform tile cutter,
grout spreader, torpedo level
**SEE PAGES** 156–157

The basic tiling technique can
be adjusted to deal with tiles
of different sizes and patterns
in order to produce any
number of unusual finishes.
Experiment with different
designs by laying out the tiles
dry before actually applying
them to the wall.

## TILING A SPLASHBACK

**SKILL LEVEL** Low to medium
**TIME FRAME** 2 hours
**SPECIAL TOOLS** Adhesive
spreader, platform tile cutter,
grout spreader
**SEE PAGES** 158–159

Splashbacks are areas that are
nearly always tiled, and offer
an opportunity to create some
interesting design elements to
make a feature of what is
basically a very practical area
of wall space. For greater
impact, you can then apply
border tiles around the edge.
Always make sure that you
make a good seal with silicone
sealant at the junction
between the bottom row of
tiles and the basin. Create a
guideline with masking tape
before applying the sealant so
that a neat silicone bead is
achieved along the junction.

## BLENDING SHEET MOSAICS

**SKILL LEVEL** Low to medium
**TIME FRAME** ½ day for an
average-size room
**SPECIAL TOOLS** Adhesive
spreader, mini roller, grout
spreader
**SEE PAGES** 160–161

Sheets of mosaic tiles provide
all the practical advantages of
normal tiles but create a
different look. The sheets are
backed with netting and can
be cut up or used in their
entirety, so are relatively quick
to use. They can also be used
in small areas unsuitable for
larger tiles. Different coloured
sheets can be blended to
create further interest. A mini
roller is good for ensuring
that mosaic tiles are fixed
firmly on the wall.

## MAKING A MOSAIC TABLE TOP

**SKILL LEVEL** Low to medium
**TIME FRAME** ½ to 1 day
**SPECIAL TOOLS** Platform tile
cutter, grout spreader
**SEE PAGES** 162–163

Creating a mosaic pattern on
the top of an old table is the
perfect way to revamp it.
Mosaic tiles offer many design
options, allowing you to show
off your own ideas to their
full potential. Although a
circular table has been used in
the example on pp.162-163,
there is no reason why designs
cannot be successfully applied
to tables of other shapes and
sizes. Square or rectangular
tables, in fact, are often easier
because there is no need to
make a compass for marking
the circular guidelines when
planning the design. Old tiles
can be used as the raw
material for making your own
mosaic tiles. Simply cut them
to the required size with a
platform tile cutter. Plan your
design before you start
applying the tiles. As with all
tiling projects, grouting is
necessary to make the tiled
finish waterproof. The
finished design can be further
embellished by using a
coloured grout, rather than a
plain white one. Coloured
grout is readily available in
most DIY outlets and offers
the opportunity to experiment
with your mosaic finish.

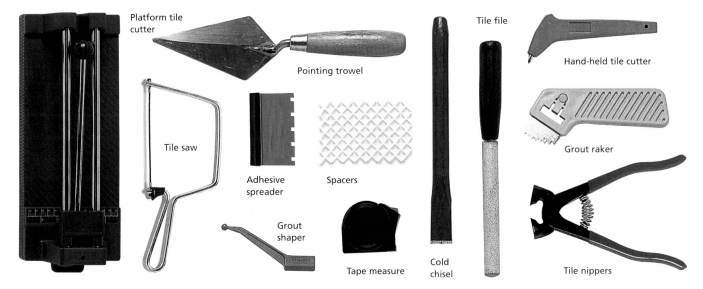

Platform tile cutter

Pointing trowel

Tile saw

Adhesive spreader

Spacers

Grout shaper

Tape measure

Cold chisel

Tile file

Hand-held tile cutter

Grout raker

Tile nippers

# WALLPAPERING: PREPARATION AND PLANNING

**YOU WILL NEED**

Bucket of hot water
Scraper or filling knife
Medium-grade abrasive paper
Large paintbrush or pasting brush
Tape measure

**MATERIALS**

PVA glue

Preparation and planning is as important for wallpapering as for any other home improvement task. Wallpaper must be hung on a well-prepared and stable surface, otherwise it will not adhere properly and the desired effect will be ruined. Most mistakes are made by papering over old wallpaper surfaces. This can be achieved with some success as long as the old wallpaper is stuck down securely – often a situation that is not apparent until the new wallpaper is applied, so it is always risky to try. It is better to strip old wallpaper from the walls. This can be done with a wallpaper stripper; however, in many cases, traditional soaking methods, as shown below, are just as quick if there are only one or two layers of paper on the wall. The next steps are to measure up the room for the new wall covering and to decide on the best place to start wallpapering.

**1** The top layer of some types of wallpaper can be easily removed while dry. Try pulling away this layer by lifting from the bottom corners of the lengths and progressing up across the wall surface. You may be surprised at how much paper will come away before any soaking is necessary.

**2** Once as much of the top layer has been removed as possible, soak the remaining backing paper on the wall surface with hot water. You can use cold water, but hot water will usually lift the paper more effectively and make it much easier to strip – a scraper or a filling knife are ideal for removing it.

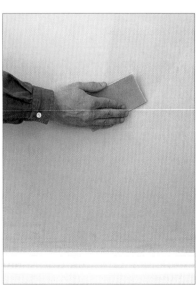

**3** Once all the paper has been removed, allow the wall surface to dry out completely. Sand the walls to remove any small remaining scraps of paper and any rough areas on the surface that might otherwise show through the new wallpaper once it has been applied to the wall.

**4** Wash down the wall surface, allow it to dry and then apply a coat of PVA solution (five parts water to one of PVA glue). This will seal and stabilize the surface, ensuring that the wallpaper will adhere to the wall. Line the walls with lining paper if this is recommended in the guidelines for your chosen wallpaper.

## MEASURING UP AND WHERE TO START

Before you begin wallpapering, you will need to decide how many rolls of paper you require to complete the room. The diagram below illustrates the best way to measure up and calculate your requirements. Wallpaper can be expensive, so it is important to be as accurate as possible. However, it is better to have one roll too many rather than being one roll short. If you have to buy an extra roll at a later date, you may not get the same batch number as the original rolls and you may end up with slight colour variations in the wall finish. Also, if you have a little wallpaper left over, you are prepared for any future repairs to the wallpaper surface that may be necessary. When deciding on the best place to start papering in a room, there are few hard and fast rules. The most important points to consider are also shown in the diagram below.

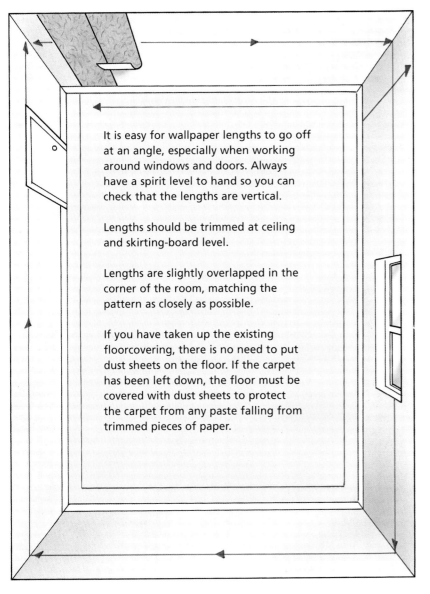

It is easy for wallpaper lengths to go off at an angle, especially when working around windows and doors. Always have a spirit level to hand so you can check that the lengths are vertical.

Lengths should be trimmed at ceiling and skirting-board level.

Lengths are slightly overlapped in the corner of the room, matching the pattern as closely as possible.

If you have taken up the existing floorcovering, there is no need to put dust sheets on the floor. If the carpet has been left down, the floor must be covered with dust sheets to protect the carpet from any paste falling from trimmed pieces of paper.

### HELPFUL HINTS

● If you line the walls before wallpapering, use the same technique for measuring up as you used for wallpaper, but don't add any extra for pattern repeat – just excess for trimming. Hang lining paper as you would wallpaper, but hang it horizontally.

● The quality of the finish you achieve with wallpaper will depend on the lining paper you use. Lining a wall with thin lining paper will not give as smooth a surface as one lined with thicker paper.

#### ➡ Measuring up

Measure around the perimeter of your room and multiply the entire distance by the height to which you want the wallpaper to reach. This gives the wall surface area. Divide into this figure the surface area of one roll of the wallpaper you are going to use. This will give you the number of rolls required.

Papers with a large repeat pattern tend to produce more waste than those with a small repeat pattern. If the paper has a large repeat pattern, add the repeat figure on to that of the room height before you start to work out the surface area. Include the doors and windows in your calculations – treating them as part of the wall surface allows for unavoidable wastage when trimming wallaper lengths to size.

#### ➡ Where to start

The first length must be hung precisely vertical and in a position where there are no wall obstacles that require trimming around. In a relatively square, obstacle-free room, begin close to a corner. Continue wallpapering around the room, finishing in the corner. Wallpaper lengths can then be slightly overlapped at the corner junction. In rooms with prominent features, such as a chimney breast, and where the wallpaper pattern design is large, it is better to start in the middle of the chimney breast so that you can centralize the wallpaper pattern on the middle and provide a balanced effect in the room.

# WALLPAPERING A ROOM

## YOU WILL NEED

**Pasting up**
Pasting table
Pasting brush

**Ready-pasted paper**
Wallpaper trough and water

**Hanging paper**
Pencil
Tape measure
Spirit level
Paper-hanging brush
Utility knife or
paper-hanging scissors
Sponge

## MATERIALS

Wallpaper
Paste

## SEE ALSO

Wallpapering: preparation
and planning pp.146–147
Using borders and friezes
pp.152–153

*Wallpaper is a very popular form of decoration because it is a simple way to add colour and pattern to what would otherwise be plain wall surfaces.*

Wallpapering is a straightforward decorative technique, as long as you take time to plan thoroughly (see pp.146–147) and follow a few simple rules. Always read the wallpaper manufacturer's guidelines; these will explain how the paste should be applied to the paper, and give any special instructions for handling your chosen wallpaper. The manufacturer's guidelines will also recommend whether the walls should be lined first. If in any doubt, lining the walls in the same way as wallpaper, but horizontally, is always the best course of action to follow.

## PASTING UP

For papers that need pasting, mix up some wallpaper paste according to the weight of paper you are using, following the manufacturer's guidelines. Apply the paste to lengths of wallpaper cut with paper-hanging scissors, working it from the centre of the length outwards, ensuring even and total coverage.

## READY-PASTED PAPER

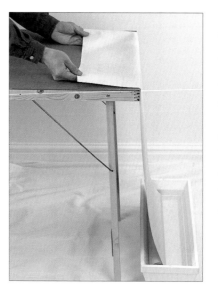

Ready-pasted paper requires no mixing of paste and simply needs a wallpaper trough filled with cold water. Roll up the cut lengths and soak them in the water before pulling them up on to the pasting table. The water activates the dried paste that has been impregnated into the back of the wallpaper.

# HANGING PAPER

**1** Whichever type of paper is being used, the method of applying it to the wall is the same. At your starting point (see pp.146–147), draw a vertical pencil line on the wall. Apply the first length of paper, using this guideline along one edge of the length. Allow an overlap on to the ceiling.

**2** Use a paper-hanging brush to smooth the wallpaper into the wall/ceiling junction, ensuring it is firmly stuck in position on the wall. Allow the bristles of the brush to create a crease in the paper all the way along the junction, to provide a guideline for trimming purposes.

**3** With the top section of paper in position, work down the length of the wallpaper, using the paper-hanging brush to smooth it in position and remove air bubbles from below the paper surface. Work from the centre of the length outwards to the sides.

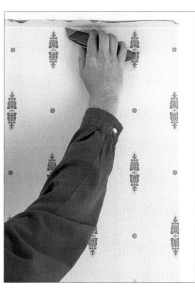

**4** Once the length has been secured in position at the bottom level, usually next to the skirting board, the paper can be trimmed. Use a utility knife or paper-hanging scissors to cut along the creased guideline at ceiling level. Trim in the same way at the junction of the wall and skirting board.

**5** Continue papering, butt-joining subsequent lengths as you progress across the wall surface. Use the paper-hanging brush to smooth along the joins, ensuring that the pattern matches as precisely as possible. Remove any excess paste on the wallpaper with a clean damp sponge.

## HELPFUL HINTS

When cutting the lengths of wallpaper to size, you should take into account the size of the pattern repeat. Most manufacturers state the size on the label on the roll of wallpaper, but it is always a good idea to measure it yourself to be as precise as possible. When cutting lengths to size, the size of the pattern must be added to the height requirement of a length. This allows for adjustment on the wall in order to match the pattern. Look out for "drop pattern" designs, where a pattern drops down from one length to another – these require a further allowance on the length.

# WALLPAPERING PANELS

## YOU WILL NEED

Tape measure
Straight edge and pencil
Utility knife
Cutting board
Spirit level
Pasting brush
Paper-hanging brush
Sponge

## MATERIALS

Wallpaper and border
Paste

*As well as being an attractive feature in its own right, a panel may act as a background for items such as paintings or mirrors.*

Using lengths of wallpaper to create panels is an alternative but highly effective way of decorating wall surfaces. The technique is not difficult, but it is essential to plan how to use the particular wallpaper design to achieve a balanced effect and to measure very accurately. It is also important to choose a border for the panel's frame that will complement the design on the wallpaper panel. Some manufacturers supply borders that are made to match particular papers, but not all are suitable for panelling. The border has to be mitred and joined to go around the panel corners, and the pattern on the border itself must be suitable for this procedure. Strong geometric border designs are often unsuitable, as cutting through the design at a 45-degree angle for each corner would provide a disjointed finish. Choose instead a border design that has flowing patterns, with areas that can be mitred to give precisely joining corners for the panel effect, or busy floral designs where any inconsistencies in the pattern match will not be noticed. Unless you are going to create particularly small panels, it will be necessary to join at least two pieces of wallpaper to make up the central panel size. Cut the panels down to size before applying them to the wall so that the patterns can be aligned and the correct length chosen.

**1** Cut wallpaper lengths to slightly larger than the panel requirement; place them side by side (dry) on a table top or other flat surface. Position a piece of border to provide a guide for the panel size, then use a pencil and straight edge to mark the panel size on top of the paper lengths.

**2** Place one of the paper lengths on a cutting board to prevent marks or grooves on any other surfaces. Using a utility knife and the straight edge, cut along the pencil guidelines. Repeat the procedure with the other paper lengths.

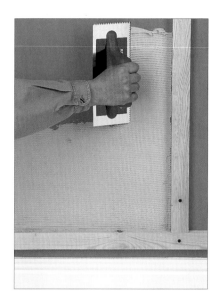

**3** Using a notched spreader, apply tile adhesive to the wall surface, starting at a bottom corner. The teeth of the spreader ensure that the adhesive is spread evenly. Cover an area of 1 sq m (1 sq yd) at a time, otherwise the adhesive will dry out before you have time to apply the tiles.

**4** Apply the tiles, using the bottom batten as an initial guide. Position tile spacers between the tiles to keep the gap between each tile consistent. Continue adding tiles along the length of the wall, and gradually build up the rows on the wall.

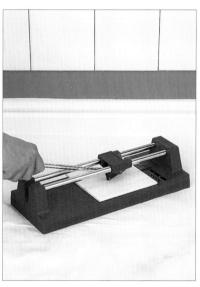

**5** Once the main body of tiles has dried (normally about 24 hours), remove the battens; cut and apply any tiles that are needed to fill the gaps. For each tile, measure and mark it with a wax pencil, score the tile in the platform tile cutter and snap it in the tool. Apply adhesive to the back of the tile; position it on the wall.

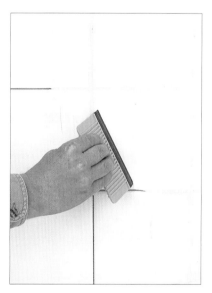

**6** Once all the cut tiles have been positioned, allow the surface to dry for 24 hours. Mix the grout and press it in position between the tiles, using a grout spreader. Work across the tile surface in all directions, forcing the grout into place.

**7** Wipe away excess grout from the tile surface with a damp sponge. Use a grout shaper or small dowel to shape each joint, making a perfect, slightly concave finish in the grout joints between each tile. Once the grout has dried, polish the tiles with a clean dry cloth to remove any cloudy grout residue from the surface of the tiles.

## USE OF COLOUR

It can be very effective to mix two different colours to achieve an interesting decorative pattern. Combining dark colours with white tiles in a chequerboard design adds interest to the wall surfaces in this contemporary bathroom (see p.21). Similar tiles have also been used on the floor to create a well-integrated colour scheme throughout the room.

# USING DIFFERENT PATTERNS AND DESIGNS

## YOU WILL NEED

Graph paper
Pencil
Wooden battens
Spirit level
Tape measure
Adhesive spreader
Platform tile cutter
Wax pencil
Grout spreader
Sponge
Cloth
Diamonds
Torpedo level

## MATERIALS

Tiles
Tile adhesive
Grout

## SEE ALSO

Tiling a wall pp.154–155

*Using tiles of varying sizes and patterns can enhance the different areas and features in a room as it does in this kitchen.*

Although tiles can be used in lots of simple designs with great effect, it is also possible to experiment with size, colour and the way in which the actual tiles are applied to the wall surface to achieve a more ambitious finished look. There are any number of different patterns that can be made using this approach, and such finishes can cover entire wall surfaces or be incorporated into a larger design. It is always worth laying out tiles dry on a flat surface and experimenting before committing to a finished design.

## PLANNING

When using different colours and sizes of tile, it is sensible to draw a scaled-down picture of your proposed design. This gives you a better guide as to what the finish will look like and makes it much easier to estimate the tile requirements and the quantities needed.

## HELPFUL HINTS

● When choosing different tiles to use in the same design, take care to ensure that the depth of the tiles is the same. Different manufacturers make tiles with varying thicknesses, and trying to combine them in a design while producing a flush finished surface is very difficult because adhesive layers will need to be constantly adjusted during application.

● Some tiles have straight, square edges and corners, whereas others have more undulating or slightly rustic-looking edges, and combining these types can also be difficult. When using hand-made tiles, or ones that have that effect, use a strong adhesive that does not require spacers, as slightly random spacing can be interesting.

## VARYING SIZE

**1** Combining large tiles with smaller ones provides an effective finish. Choose the smaller tiles so that a grouping (four in this design) will equal the size of one of the larger ones. Use a batten support to act as a guideline for the first tiles (see p.154).

**2** Build up the design in rows, alternating groups of four tiles between each of the larger ones. Using different colours for the various sizes will emphasize the effect being created. It can be further enhanced by changing colours within each size category.

## DIAMONDS

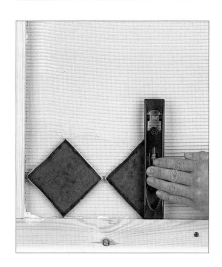

**1** A diamond design involves rotating tiles 45 degrees from a standard position, so that they are aligned and positioned using the corners of tiles to create the level guideline. Use a torpedo level to establish the first positions of the bottom row of tiles.

**2** Continue to add tiles, building up the design and varying colours, as you wish. When using tiles with undulating edges – without spacers – stand back from the wall from time to time to make sure that a balanced diamond design is being achieved; adjust the tiles if necessary.

## RANDOM COLOURS

**1** Using a number of different colours in a simple standard tile design can be a very effective way of providing a decorative tile finish. Begin in the normal way and add tiles in rows or blocks of four, mixing the colours as required.

**2** Continue to build up the design, following no particular sequence of colours, so that a random effect is achieved. A good number for this finish is three to four colours. Whether these colours complement each other or provide a contrast is a matter of personal choice.

# TILING A SPLASHBACK

## YOU WILL NEED

Tape measure
Pencil
Spirit level
Adhesive spreader
Platform tile cutter
Spirit level
Grout spreader
Sponge
Cloth
Cartridge gun
Masking tape

## MATERIALS

Tiles
Tile adhesive
Grout
Silicone sealant

## SEE ALSO

Tiling a wall pp.154–155

*A splashback with a geometric pattern offers an interesting finish for a practical area.*

The area directly behind and above a basin or sink always requires protection from water overspray. The most effective way of protecting this area is to apply a tiled splashback, so that any overspray can be wiped away easily. As long as the basin or sink is level on the wall surface, it is usually possible to use its back edge as the support for the first row of tiles in your design.

The splashback will be much more attractive if you can plan your design so that only full tiles are used, with no cuts or other interruptions. You can use border tiles around the edge of the main body of tiles to frame the finish. Any size of tile can be used for the main body of the design. However, larger tiles reduce the number of grout joins, which will extend the life of the splashback because grout is the first area of a splashback to deteriorate – so the fewer grout joins there are, the less refurbishment will be required. Because splashbacks are small in size and do not need a great many tiles, this is a good opportunity to spend a little more money on the tiles you choose. This small extravagance can make a significant difference to the final finish, providing a practical feature that is also decorative.

**1** Tile a splashback from the centre outwards so that the design is centred. Begin by finding the central point along the back edge of the basin. Position a spirit level vertically at the central point and draw a guideline along it with a pencil.

**2** When dealing with relatively small areas of tiles, it can be easier to apply adhesive directly to the back of the tiles before positioning them on the wall, rather than the usual technique of applying adhesive to the wall.

**3** Apply the first tile to the splashback area, aligning the vertical edge precisely with the pencil guideline. Press the tile on to the wall surface to create a good bond between the tile and the wall.

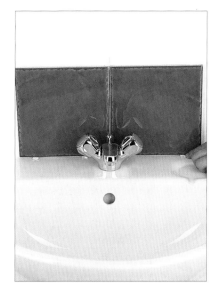

**4** Apply the next tile on the other side of the pencil guideline, working towards the opposite edge of the basin. Again, ensure that it is precisely positioned, and use spacers to maintain a consistent gap between tiles and between the bottom layer of tiles and the basin. Continue applying all the main body of tiles.

**5** In this particular design, a border is being used around the edge of the main body of tiles. Apply the border tiles, being sure to use spacers in the normal way in order to maintain an even gap between the large tiles and the border sections. Again, apply the adhesive to the back of the tiles.

**6** It may be necessary to cut some border tiles to fit precisely around the main tile design edge. In this case, the square design of the border tiles lends itself to being cut into the required sections to make a continuous border pattern. Plan ahead to place cut tiles in the least obvious position.

**7** After applying all the tiles, allow the adhesive to dry for 24 hours. Grout the entire splashback (see p.155). Once the grout has dried, wipe off any residue. Using a cartridge gun, seal the junction between the bottom row of tiles and basin with silicone sealant. For a neat finish, first apply strips of masking tape alongside the junction.

**8** Once the sealant has been applied, remove the tape before it dries, revealing a perfectly neat silicone bead along the tile/basin junction. Allow the sealant to dry for 24 hours before you begin using the basin.

# BLENDING SHEET MOSAICS

## YOU WILL NEED

Utility knife
Wax pencil
Wooden battens
Tape measure
Spirit level
Pencil
Adhesive spreader
Mini roller
Grout spreader
Sponge
Cloth

## MATERIALS

Mosaic tiles
Tile adhesive
Grout

## SEE ALSO

Tiling a wall pp.154–155

*Mosaic tiles allow you to produce complex designs to create a highly decorative look.*

S caled-down tiles – sheet mosaics – provide an effective alternative to large or standard-size tiles. Mosaics provide a completely different look from conventional tiles, and their size produces a finely detailed surface that

is highly decorative but still hard-wearing. Mosaic tiles can be applied in large blocks of continuous colour, borders can run through them or two different colours can be blended together to create a merging pattern between the tiles. This is effective when entire walls are covered with tiles or where a slightly more random, colourful finish is desired.

Because the tiles are small, they are attached to sheets of backing so that a large number can be applied at one time. Single tiles or strips of tiles can be cut away from the backing for smaller areas of tiles or to create a random effect. Even when the finish is random, careful planning needs to take place to achieve a satisfying finish, and it is a good idea to lay out the blocks of tiles on the floor before applying them to the wall. If tiling a large area, use a tile gauge (see step 1, p.154).

**1** Before fixing the mosaic sheets to the wall, decide on the way in which two joining sheets will be divided. Place them on a flat surface or cutting board, as it will be necessary to cut through some of the netting, allowing one sheet to overlap on to the other.

**2** On each row of tiles in the overlapping section, cut through both tile layers with a utility knife. To create random lengths of mosaic tiles, trim away up to five tiles or as few as one tile in some rows, and any number between these two in the other rows.

**3** Remove the excess tiles and allow the cut rows to interlock on the flat surface. This gives an initial pattern that can then be altered by exchanging tiles of each colour within the main body of the sheets. Decide where you want single mosaic tiles on the sheets, and mark the position of each one with a wax pencil.

**4** Apply the first tile sheet to the wall, using a batten to support the first layer of tiles in the usual way. A mini roller is the ideal tool for flattening the tiles in position, helping them to adhere firmly and evenly to the wall.

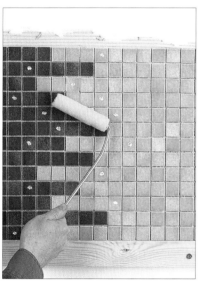

**5** Apply the second colour of tiles, interlocking them with the first colour, as planned. Again use the mini roller to flatten the tiles in position, paying particular attention to the join between the two colours to ensure that the rows of each colour are neatly aligned.

**6** Before the adhesive dries, use a utility knife to cut out the marked tiles from the design. This procedure is better done at this stage rather than when the tiles were laid out flat – if cut into numerous different sections at that stage, the mosaic sheets would be more difficult to handle.

**7** Position the single mosaic tiles of the opposite colours in the appropriate cut holes in the design layout. Continue to add sheets of tiles, following this random design, until the pattern is complete. Once the adhesive has dried, grout in the usual way (see p.155).

## SURFACE COMBINATIONS

The swimming-pool effect created by mosaic tiles works particularly well in a bathroom, where they can introduce interesting variations of colour and texture that will lift the whole atmosphere of the space. In the small bathroom featured on p.101, wall-to-ceiling mosaic tiles are combined with a wall of glass bricks.

# MAKING A MOSAIC TABLE TOP

**YOU WILL NEED**

Screwdriver
Abrasive paper
Cloth
Pencil
String
Felt-tip pen or wax pencil
Tape measure
Platform tile cutter
Adhesive spreader
Tile nippers
Grout spreader

**MATERIALS**

Tiles
Tile adhesive
Tile grout
Polish

*Creating a mosaic on a table top is a very decorative and effective way of adding interest to an old occasional table that is in need of some refurbishment.*

Special mosaic tiles can be bought for making mosaics – pick ones of similar depth so that you produce a flat mosaic finish, rather than one with an uneven surface. Alternatively, you can make your own from standard-size tiles – breaking them into irregular pieces or, as shown in the example below, cutting them all to the same size to produce a more uniform pattern. Depending on your artistic skills, mosaic tiles can be used to create intricate patterns such as on the table top above. However, simple designs such as the concentric circle pattern below can also work very well.

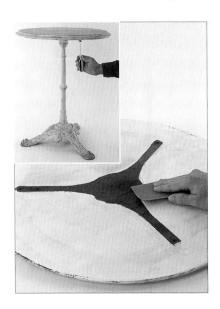

**1** In this example, the table has a better bevelled edge if it is turned over. Unscrew the table top, and sand the side you wish to tile, removing any rough areas from the surface. Clean it with a damp cloth to remove any dust.

**2** Decide how many circles or bands of mosaic tiles you want. Attach some string to a pencil and use it as a compass to draw circular guidelines on the table surface. At the required distances, simply anchor the string in the centre of the table with one finger, while drawing the pencil guideline with the other hand.

3 Cut a piece of MDF to the height for the bookcase and equal to the depth of the battens. Holding the MDF and a shelf support upright in position against the battens, mark the required position for the upright on the MDF with a pencil. You'll need two uprights on each side of the alcove, 5 cm (2 in) from the edge.

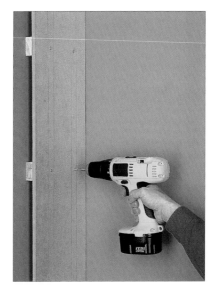

4 Remove the shelf support upright and drill pilot holes through the MDF and into the battens. These holes should be inside the bounds of the guidelines for the shelf support uprights, so that, once the uprights themselves are fixed in place, the MDF fixings will be hidden from view, creating a neat finish.

5 Screw the uprights in place, using a spirit level to check that they are precisely vertical. Normal woodscrews or those supplied with the uprights will be adequate for fixing purposes, as the screws should extend only as far as the batten and not into the wall behind.

6 Cut an architrave to fit around the edge of the bookcase and nail it in position, allowing the fixings to go into the ends of the alcove battens. If the bookcase requires a top edge of architrave, it will be necessary to batten and apply MDF to the top of the architrave in the same way as for the sides.

7 The shelf support uprights will normally come supplied with pegs, which are inserted into the uprights to bear the weight of the shelves. Because this design is adjustable, it means that you can change the shelf height whenever your collection of books or other items dictates.

8 Finally, cut MDF shelves to size and position them on the pegs. Once you are happy with the fit, the bookcase can be painted. It is easier to paint the shelves out of situ before you place them in their final position.

# MAKING BATTEN SHELVING

## YOU WILL NEED

Pencil
Tape measure
Spirit level
Mitre saw
Panel saw
Power drill and screwdriver
and drill bits
Hammer

## MATERIALS

MDF (medium-density
fibreboard)
Wood batten
Prepared softwood strip
Woodscrews
Wall plugs (if required)
Nails

*Batten shelving is simple in design, but it provides effective storage while still retaining a keen decorative edge. In this dining room (featured on p.85), batten shelving used for storage and display has been installed in the alcoves on either side of the fireplace.*

Batten shelving makes an effective storage system that is inexpensive and relatively straightforward to construct. As with all shelving mechanisms, it is crucial to make sure that both shelves and supports are fixed precisely level, as any inaccuracies are always accentuated once the shelves are in place. The side and back walls of an alcove provide substantial support for shelves, making them suitable for bearing heavy objects such as large books. In this example, 5 5x2.5 cm (2 5x1 in) battens have been used as the supports, but the size can be varied according to the width of the shelves and the weight that they will support.

1 Use a pencil and a spirit level to mark where you want to place the shelves on the wall. Use these guidelines to position the supporting battens. You will not be able to make any adjustments, so take time to decide exactly where you want to position the shelves.

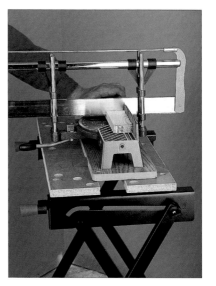

2 Cut battens to size using a mitre saw, as shown here, or a panel saw. It is easier to cut accurately with a mitre saw, and this ensures that the joins between sections of batten will be neater. Drill a pilot hole 25mm (1 in) from both ends of each batten.

**3** Position the short battens on the sides of the alcove, using the pencil guidelines to position them accurately. Use a torpedo level to ensure they are level. Mark the positions of the wall plugs with an bradawl and drill holes. Insert the wall plugs and screw the battens in place.

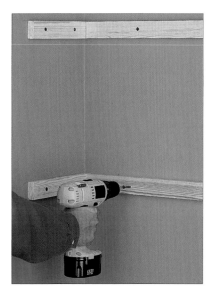

**4** Check that the heights of corresponding battens on the opposite side of the alcove are exactly the same. Once the side battens are in place, cut lengths of batten for the back wall of the alcove and position them in the same way. Again, remember to check the level before fixing them permanently.

**5** Measure the size for each shelf individually, taking care to measure the width at both the back and front edges of the battens. Alcoves are rarely completely square, and careful measuring is required to produce a good fit.

**6** Once the shelves are cut from the MDF, they can be left free fitting. However, for added strength, they are best nailed or screwed in position by fixing through the top of the shelves, down into the battens below the shelves.

**7** To finish off the front of the shelves, fix lengths of prepared softwood whose dimensions are equal to the height of the battens plus the thickness of the MDF. The wood will cover the front of the shelving, giving a neat finish. Punch in the nail heads before decorating.

## HELPFUL HINTS

Where alcoves are not completely square, it is always difficult to cut shelves precisely so that they fit tight up against the wall junctions. Where there is any gap between the shelf and the wall, it can be filled with flexible filler or decorator's caulk. For this particular job, these are better than all-purpose filler because they can cope more effectively with any shelf movement once the shelves have been painted and are in use. An all-purpose filler is less tolerant of movement and is more likely to crack along the junctions, spoiling the finished look of the shelves.

# ASSEMBLING READY-MADE SHELVING

**YOU WILL NEED**

Spirit level
Pencil
Bradawl
Power drill and screwdriver
and drill bits

**MATERIALS**

Ready-made shelving system
Woodscrews
Wall plugs (if required)

*Adjustable ready-made shelves are the ideal choice for fitting into a space with a sloping ceiling, as the shelf edges can be positioned to follow the angle of the slope.*

There are a variety of ready-made shelving systems available that are based on a design of attaching adjustable rails to the walls, to which brackets are then attached at the desired heights to support shelves. Because they are so easy to adjust, these systems are perfect for fitting shelving into awkward areas such as a space under a sloping ceiling. They can also be used in more traditional ways to form standard shelving stacks or as single shelves on a wall surface.

As with all shelving systems, it is vital to make sure that the bracket supports are positioned precisely level, otherwise the shelves will slope and look unsightly.

**1** Use a spirit level and pencil to draw precise vertical guidelines on the wall. These lines should be the exact length of the rails you are using. Manufacturers will generally provide guidelines on how far apart the rails should be positioned for the shelves you are using.

**2** Hold a rail in position on the first pencil guideline and use a bradawl to mark the wall surface through the screw holes in the rail. You can try using a pencil for this purpose, but generally the screw hole will not allow the pencil head to go through the hole.

**3** Remove the rail from its position on the wall and drill holes into the wall at the marked-off positions along the line. Make sure that the drill bit size is equal to that of the wall plugs you are using. Once the holes have been drilled, insert wall plugs as required.

**4** Reposition the rail, aligning the screw holes with the plugged holes on the wall surface, and screw the rail in place. As you screw the rail in position, hold a spirit level to the side of the rail to ensure that it is still vertical.

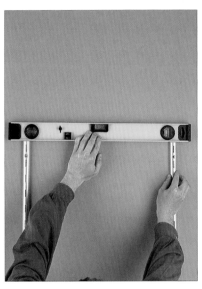

**5** Hold the next rail on the next pencil guideline and double check its position by holding a spirit level across the top of the two rails to make sure that they are exactly level. Mark, drill and plug the required holes before screwing the second rail in place.

**6** Attach the shelf brackets to the adjustable rails in the positions required for your desired shelf heights. Designs vary slightly between manufacturers, but generally each bracket has two to four protrusions along the back edge that simply clip into the rails.

**7** Once the shelves are positioned on the brackets, they can be secured in place with grub screws. If using glass shelves, as shown here, stick protective pads to the top of the brackets, followed by adhesive pads to hold the shelves in place.

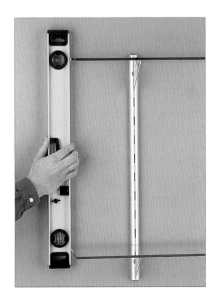

**8** Place the shelves in position on the brackets and use a spirit level to ensure that the shelf edges align vertically. You can adjust the height of a shelf by simply repositioning the brackets it sits on.

# INSTALLING SHELVES WITH HIDDEN SUPPORTS

## YOU WILL NEED

Tape measure
Pencil
Spirit level
Electric drill and drill bits,
including screwdriver bits

**Resin fixing system**
Workbench

## MATERIALS

Ready-made shelving system

**Bracket system**
Woodscrews
Wall plugs

**Resin fixing system**
Resin
Threaded rod

*Shelves hung with hidden supports provide a neat storage solution for a home office in a visible location.*

Although shelves have a clear, practical function, there are ways of designing or decorating them so that they can become an attractive part of a room's decorative scheme and layout. One way of improving the appearance of shelving is to try to hide the way in which the shelves are attached to the wall – in many cases the actual hardware detracts from the aesthetics of the system. Two methods are demonstrated here, one using hidden brackets and the other a resin fastening technique on a simple shelf.

## BRACKET SYSTEM

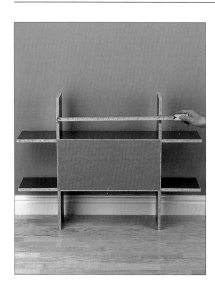

**1** Many ready-made shelving systems have hidden brackets positioned on their backs, but it is still necessary to transfer this measurement to the wall surface. Use a tape measure to find the distance between the brackets, taking care to measure precisely from the centre of one to the centre of the other.

**2** Transfer this measurement to the wall surface as accurately as possible. Make two small crosses on the wall surface to mark their positions. Use a spirit level to check that the marks are horizontal. If you draw a line, this can be touched in with some paint before the shelving is hung.

3 Drill into the wall at the marked points and insert the wall plugs into the drilled holes. Insert screws into the wall plugs far enough into the wall to provide a solid load-bearing fixture, but with the heads of the screws extending out far enough to be housed in the brackets on the back of the shelving system.

4 Hang the shelving system in place, hooking the brackets over the screwheads. The accuracy of the measurement will show here, because anything that is less than perfect will not allow the brackets to hook over the screws and fit snugly in place.

## RESIN SYSTEM

1 For a single wooden shelf, measure and draw a level line on the wall surface that is slightly shorter than the shelf width. At each end of the line, drill a hole large enough to take a threaded rod and far enough in to be two-thirds the depth of the shelf. Inject proprietary resin into the drilled holes.

2 Cut two lengths of threaded rod to one and one-third times the depth of the shelf. Insert each rod into a hole, allowing half of its length to protrude. Use a spirit level to make sure that the rods protrude horizontally from the wall. Allow the resin to dry, which will secure the rods firmly in place.

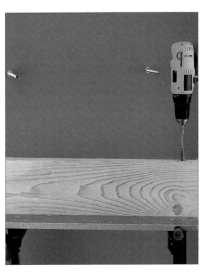

3 Clamp the shelf upright in a workbench, with its back edge on top. Drill two holes in the back edge of the shelf, corresponding to the distance between the rods in the wall. Each hole should be the same diameter as a rod and the depth should be equal to two-thirds the depth of the shelf.

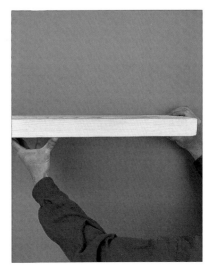

4 To hang the shelf on the wall, position it so that the threaded rods in the wall slide into the drilled holes on the back of the shelf. For a stronger hold, apply resin to the holes in the back of the shelf before hanging it on the wall. The result is a simple shelf with no visible hardware to spoil it.

# MAKING CORNER SHELVING

## YOU WILL NEED

Drawing pin
String
Pencil
Metal ruler
Jigsaw or panel saw
Dust mask
Router
Power drill and screwdriver
and drill bits
Torpedo level

## MATERIALS

MDF (medium-density
fibreboard)
Woodscrews
Wall plugs (if required)

*Corner shelving makes a compact storage system that is ideal where there is limited space.*

C orners are often under-used when it comes to space management in the home, but they are ideal areas for storage systems. Corner shelving and cupboards can be bought ready-made, but there are lots of situations where it may be necessary to build your own shelving system to fit a particular space, or simply to provide an

individual design that will enhance the room's decorative scheme. The rounded design of this shelving system can counteract a corner's angularity and provide a larger surface area than shelves with straight edges across the corner, thus creating more space.

The two sides and shelves are cut from a circle, but you'll need to buy a square of MDF (medium-density fibreboard). To calculate the size required, measure from the corner along one wall as far as you want the deeper, bottom shelf to extend. Double this measurement and add 5 cm (2 in) for trimming. This is the measurement for each side of the square of MDF.

You can use a router, a type of cutting tool, to make curved edges on shelves. Follow the manufacturer's safety guidelines and, before routing the edges of new shelves, practise the technique on scrap pieces of MDF – it can take time to get used to a router.

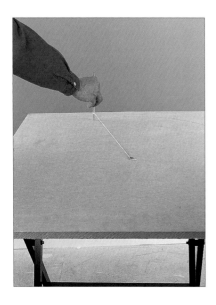

**1** Attach a pencil to one end of the string, pin the opposite end to the piece of MDF and draw a circular guideline on the MDF surface. The exact size of the guideline depends on your particular shelving requirements, but in the example shown here, the length of string is 40 cm (16 in).

**2** Using a metal ruler, divide the circle into quarters. These sections will be used to create the sides and shelves of the shelving system, so it is important that they are equal otherwise the finished shelving system will not be balanced on the wall.

**3** Cut around the edge of the circular guideline with a jigsaw. A panel saw can be used, but a power tool is more accurate. When cutting MDF, always wear a dust mask to avoid inhaling any of the dust created by the sawing.

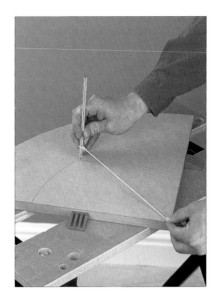

**4** Cut the circle into four quarters. On one section use the pencil and a shorter piece of string – a piece 25 cm (10 in) is used here – to draw another pencil guideline. This will be the smaller of the two shelves. Cut around this guideline with the jigsaw.

**5** Wearing the dust mask, rout the curved edge of the other three quarters, using a side cutter blade to give a moulded finish. Do not allow the router to extend all the way to the end of each curved edge – these areas must be left square-edged to give a good finish.

**6** Screw the three larger sections of MDF together, drilling pilot holes before adding the screws (see Helpful hints). The screws go through the first section, with one-third of their length entering the second piece. By fixing from the back of the shelving, the screws will not be visible when the system is complete.

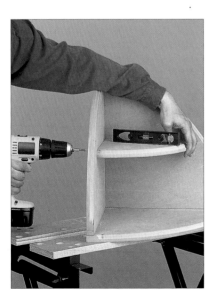

**7** Drill more pilot holes for the screws for the smallest of the four sections and fix it in position to provide the second shelf. Hold a torpedo level on top of the smaller shelf to ensure that it is precisely positioned and both the shelves are level.

## HELPFUL HINTS

● To achieve neat joints when joining the three larger sections together, you may need to readjust the exact position where the routed edges finish. You may also want to trim the back edge of one of the sections to ensure a tight and accurate fit, depending on your initial measurements. Try to keep a flexible approach in terms of fitting this system together.

● Once complete, the shelving system can be painted. After the paint is dry, screw the system into the wall using standard woodscrews and wall plugs.

# UPDATING A CUPBOARD

**YOU WILL NEED**

Screwdriver
All-purpose filler
Cloth
Medium-grade abrasive paper
Fretwork panel (design or pattern of your choice)
Mitre saw
Cordless powerdrill and drill bits

**MATERIALS**

All-purpose primer
Emulsion paint
Aerosol paint
Moulding
Double-sided self-adhesive tape

*Masking cupboard door fronts to help create individual designs is an effective way of transforming their appearance. Here, doors have been painted with a dark blue base colour, then low-tack masking tape has been used to mask off all sides of selected areas. These areas have been painted a paler blue before removing the tape.*

When you want a change of style or design, replacing cupboards can be an expensive option, and it can be far more economical simply to revamp the existing cupboard system. The internal sections of cupboards are generally hidden from view, so, from an aesthetic point of view, it is only the cupboard faces that need changing. Simple options include replacing the handles, adding trims or mouldings and a general paint overhaul to transform their look. In the example below, all of these ideas are used on a cupboard door from a basic kitchen unit. A bought fretwork panel is used as a stencil to create an intricate painted design on the door, illustrating how a complete change of style can be achieved without replacing the door.

1 Unscrew the cupboard door from the kitchen unit. Take off any hinges and remove the handle. Most handles are secured in position with screws inserted from the inside surface of the door. Lay the door front-side down to gain access to the screw heads.

2 Turn the door right-side up and fill the old handle holes. Once the filler is dry, sand it down along with the rest of the door face. For a melamine door surface, such as the one shown here, use an all-purpose primer to prepare the sanded surface for painting, following the manufacturer's instructions for use.

**3** Paint the face of the door with a base coat. Emulsion paint may be used, or you can use an oil-based alternative. The advantage of emulsion paint is that it dries quickly, letting you apply two coats to the door surface on the same day.

**4** Take your chosen fretwork panel and use it as a stencil on the door surface. Place it in position on the door face, making sure that it is aligned precisely with the door edges. Shake the aerosol paint can before applying two light coats of paint across the fretwork and door surface.

**5** Carefully remove the fretwork panel, lifting it upwards rather than sideways to avoid smudging the paint. The fretwork panel can be reused.

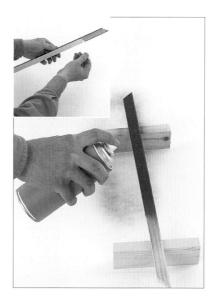

**6** Cut lengths of moulding the height and width of the cupboard door. Mitre the ends so they will join in each corner on the door face. Paint each section with the aerosol. When dry, apply double-sided self-adhesive tape to the back of each moulding. Peel away the second strip to secure it to the door.

**7** Press each of the mouldings in position on the edge of the door face, ensuring that the mitred joins match precisely for a neat finish. Once applied, there is a short period of time when you can adjust the mouldings, before the adhesive hardens and secures them permanently.

**8** Mark the position of the new door handles on the door face, then drill holes and secure them in place. Reattach the hinges, and screw the door back in position on the kitchen unit.

# MAKING A BASIC PICTURE FRAME

### YOU WILL NEED

Tape measure
Scissors or craft knife and
metal rule
Pencil
Mount cutter or
bevel cutter
Mitre saw
Staple gun
Pin hammer
Bradawl

### MATERIALS

Mounting card
Frame moulding
Wood glue
Staples
Picture glass
Masking tape
Nails
Backing card or board
Screw-in eyes
String or cord

*A light-coloured picture frame sits well against a dramatic wall colour such as this, producing a harmonious and coordinated effect.*

P ictures, paintings and prints are an important decorative feature in most homes, covering the walls to a larger or smaller degree, according to personal preference. Most of these are framed in some way or another, and it

is well worth knowing how to frame pictures yourself so that you can avoid the added expense of having it done professionally.

In the example shown below, a print has been framed using mounting card and an outer frame of wooden moulding. There is plenty of choice with these two items – different qualities and colours of mounting card are available as well as numerous types of moulding to make the frame. This means you can choose something that not only sets off the picture attractively but also complements the rest of the decor in the room. These choices are even more important if you are planning to hang a series or group of pictures on a wall. Because they will make a forceful visual impact on the room decoration, it is vital to consider the frame design and mounting card colour before you begin.

**1** Measure the exact size of the picture you want to frame, using a tape measure. If the picture has any roughened edges that need to be trimmed or you want to cut down its size, do this before you take the measurements, using scissors or a craft knife alongside a metal rule.

**2** Using a sharp pencil, mark out the dimensions of the picture as accurately as possible in the centre of a piece of mounting card. Cut out this central square using a mount or bevel cutter, making sure that your cuts are as precise as possible. Lift out the central cut-out area.

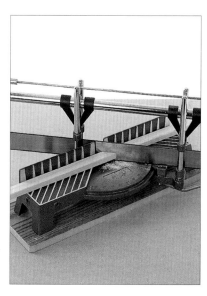

3 Measure the outer edges of the mounting board; these will be the inside dimensions of the frame. Cut four pieces of wooden moulding to these dimensions, using a mitre saw to mitre each end. Make sure you mitre the ends in the right direction, with the outside edge extending beyond your measurement.

4 Apply a small amount of wood glue to each mitred end of the pieces of wooden moulding; join them together to form the frame. To strengthen the frame, use a staple gun to add two staples at each mitred corner. Make sure they are on the back of the frame, where they will be hidden. Leave the wood glue to dry.

5 Ask a glazier to cut a piece of picture glass to fit your frame. Insert it into the frame, so that it rests precisely on the moulding ledge. Insert the mounting board into the back of the frame, ensuring that the fit is tight. Carefully trim the board if it is too tight; if it is too loose, cut a new mounting board to fit the frame.

6 Secure the picture or print in place on the back of the mounting card, using masking tape. This can be slightly tricky, as you must make sure that the picture is precisely positioned so that when viewed from the front it fills the "window" in the mounting card.

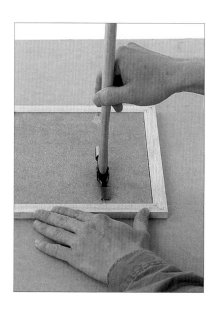

7 Cut a piece of backing card or board to size, and fit it into the back of the frame, covering over the mounting card and picture. Secure it in position by tacking it in place with a few small nails around the internal edge of the picture frame.

8 Tape over the join between the frame and the backing board, then fix a hanging system for the picture. Use a bradawl to make pilot holes in the back of the frame, then screw in the eyes and attach some string or cord between them. The picture is now ready to be hung.

# GILDING A FRAME

**YOU WILL NEED**
..................................................
Paintbrushes
Small artist's paintbrush
Cloth

**MATERIALS**
..................................................
Emulsion paint
Metal size
Metal laef
Raw umber

*A gilded frame offers classical elegance and style in any room scheme. It may be used as part of the overall room design or can stand alone as a decorative feature in its own right.*

Old wooden frames can often benefit from a revamp of some kind. This may simply involve a new coat of paint, but there are other options available such as the gilding effect shown here.

In bygone years, gilding was always carried out with real gold leaf, but nowadays you can buy substitutes, such as Dutch metal, which is sold in sheets and gives the same effect at a fraction of the cost. It is applied over a coat of Dutch metal size, which bonds the Dutch metal to the surface. For an antiqued effect, the finish can be aged slightly by rubbing some raw umber into the moulding on the frame after it has been gilded.

1 To enliven the gilded effect, it is best to apply the Dutch metal over a coloured basecoat. Both dark and pale colours work well – in this case a deep red emulsion paint is applied to the frame. Apply the paint with a small paintbrush, ensuring that the paint gets into all the moulded areas of the frame.

2 Once the basecoat has dried, apply a coat of size to the area that you are going to gild first. It is a good idea to gild one width or length at a time, so only apply size along one length at a time.

**3** Let the size dry so that it is tacky to the touch. This normally becomes apparent when the size loses its initial milky colour and becomes transparent. Lay a sheet of Dutch metal on the frame, pulling away the backing paper, if any, once it is in position (not all metal leaf comes with backing paper).

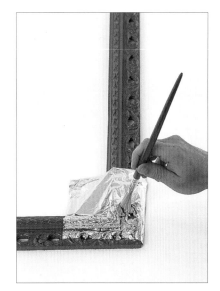

**4** Use a small clean artist's paintbrush to gently brush and push the leaf on to the frame surface. The tacky nature of the size makes the metal bond to its surface. The ornate nature of the frame means that some areas will be left without metal in place. These can be filled in later or left alone to give a more worn or aged look.

**5** Take the excess from each sheet as it is applied and use it to fill in other areas as required. The level of gap-filling in the moulding is a matter of personal preference and depends on how much of the basecoat you want to be visible in the finished frame.

**6** Once the entire frame has been gilded, you may find small, loose flakes of Dutch metal attached to the frame. These unfixed areas can simply be brushed away with a clean, dry soft-bristled paintbrush.

**7** To finish, dip a cloth in a little raw umber and rub it across the surface of the frame, pushing the colour into all the intricate areas in the moulding of the frame. This helps to create an aged antique effect.

## COORDINATING FRAMES

Pictures create a homely, welcoming atmosphere (see p.107). Although the pictures themselves provide the focal points on the wall, the frames are often used as a design link. A series of similar coloured frames with different styles of pictures make a striking feature without detracting from the coordinated feel of the overall decor.

# CLADDING WALLS WITH TONGUE AND GROOVE

## YOU WILL NEED

Tape measure
Pencil
Spirit level
Power drill and screwdriver
and drill bits
Hammer
Nail punch

## MATERIALS

Wooden battens
Concrete anchor screws or
woodscrews and wall plugs
Tongue-and-groove boards
Nails
Bonding adhesive
Moulding
Skirting board

*A tongue-and-groove effect in pastel colours brings a relaxed, calm atmosphere to a room.*

Tongue and groove is a traditional form of wall cladding that is equally at home in modern house design. It is highly decorative and also hard-wearing, able to withstand the knocks and scrapes of everyday living with more success than painted or papered walls. Tongue and groove is mainly used up to dado level on a wall surface, but it can also be effective covering an entire wall or a ceiling. It is a most versatile form of panelling that can be used to extremely good effect in any room in the home.

The decorative options for tongue and groove are numerous, with some people preferring to keep the natural wood look, while others opt for stains, paint or even special paint effects. All of these can be considered according to your own decorating scheme.

Much of tongue and groove's decorative exterior is left unscathed by the technique in which it is fixed to the wall surface, with all the fixings invisible to the naked eye. This "secret" nailing method, shown below, is the best technique for applying this type of finish. Tongue-and-groove cladding should be applied over a batten framework, and this is the first step you will need to complete before the boards can be applied.

**1** To fit a tongue-and-groove dado 1 m (3 ft 3 in) high, you will need to fix at least three battens to the wall. Use a tape measure and pencil to mark up the wall surface for a central batten and a top batten. The first batten will be fixed at floor level.

**2** At the marks, use a spirit level to draw level lines across the wall surface. These lines will act as guidelines for positioning the wall battens. Make sure that they are exactly level, so that the finished panelling will be precisely aligned.

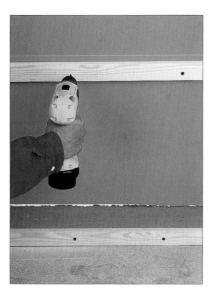

**3** Drill pilot holes and attach the battens following the pencil guidelines made in step 2. Join separate lengths as necessary, depending on the width of your wall and the length of the battens you are using. You can use concrete anchor screws, as shown here, or plugs and normal screws can be used with equal effect.

**4** Cut the boards to exactly the same height, from floor level up to the top edge of the top batten. The boards are initially fitted together by hand, interlocking the groove of one board with the tongue of the previous one.

**5** Once a board is interlocked, nail through the tongues at a 45 degree angle, into the batten below. Use a nail punch to knock the head of the nail well in. Do this on each of the three battens to secure the board in place. As each new board is fixed in place, it should cover the previous fixing.

**6** To finish the top edge of the tongue and groove, some sort of dado rail is required. In this case, a further length of batten that has been cut to fit is attached along the top edge of the top batten and the top edge of the tongue-and-groove boarding.

**7** Finally, a moulding can be applied to the front edge of this batten for a perfect finish. Use a bonding adhesive to stick it in place so that the invisible fixing theme is continued. Complete the look by applying skirting board to the base of the panelling.

## TILE ALTERNATIVE

Tongue and groove is a good alternative to tiles in a bathroom. Tiles and tongue and groove can also be used together very effectively, as shown here (see p.14), to produce an unusual combination of finishes. Wooden panelling that is likely to get splashed with water should be coated with an oil-based finish for extra damp-proof protection.

# CLADDING WALLS WITH PANELS

**YOU WILL NEED**

Tape measure
Panel saw
Cartridge gun
Spirit level
Mitre saw

**MATERIALS**

Panelling system
Bonding adhesive

**SEE ALSO**

Cladding walls with tongue
and groove pp.182–183

*Panelling may be applied on one level, or it can be used to climb stairwells with equally good results. Matching the finish with other features, such as doors, links room layout and panel design.*

Fielded panelling offers a slightly different effect from tongue and groove, but it has equally decorative appeal. Traditionally, it was made by craftsmen over a considerable period of time. Nowadays, there are various proprietary systems that enable the home improvement enthusiast to achieve the same effect. The panelling is supplied as a kit, which is assembled as you position it on the wall surface. This means that most of the fitting work has been eliminated and the task is little more than a straightforward process of adding factory-made panels to the wall in the correct order. There is no need to fix a batten framework to the wall before you begin.

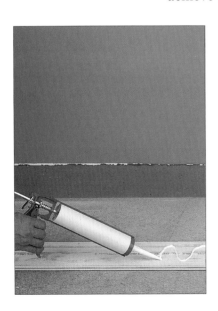

1 In order to use the complete system, it is necessary to take the old skirting board off the wall. The new skirting board sections should be cut to the correct length before they are attached to the wall with bonding adhesive, rather than nails. The panels are designed to slot into this skirting board.

2 Position the new skirting board, pressing it into place on the wall surface. Use a spirit level to make sure the top edge is straight, because floors are not always completely level. If necessary, make a slight adjustment to the skirting board to ensure that its top edge is level on all the walls.

3 To attach the panels to the wall, apply bonding adhesive to them along those sections of the panel that will come into immediate contact with the wall surface when it is fitted to the wall.

4 Position the panel on the top edge of the skirting board, pressing it in place so that the adhesive creates a good bond with the wall surface. As long as the skirting has been positioned level, it follows that the panels will also be correctly positioned.

5 To join panels, most of these panelling systems use joining strips between the panels. Apply adhesive along the back of the strip and position it next to the previously applied panel. The edge of the strip should join with the panel using a tongue-and-groove interlocking system.

6 Continue to add panels and strips along the wall surface as required, cutting down final panels to fit tightly into the room corners. Mitre the ends of the dado rail so that it will join snugly between lengths in the room corners.

7 Apply adhesive to the back of the dado rail and position it along the top level of the panelling. Once all the adhesive has dried, check for any small gaps or cracks between panel sections and fill these before decorating. The panelling can now be decorated as desired.

## HELPFUL HINTS

● Decide where to start in a particular room to avoid cuts going through panels and spoiling the look. Starting on either side of a door will give a balanced effect.

● Try to have a join at the bottom of a stairway so that half panels can be used to make the stepped ascent.

● If it is inevitable that some unsightly cuts will be required, try to plan it so that these areas are positioned in one of the less conspicuous parts of the room, or where they will be hidden by furniture.

# FLOORING DIRECTORY

## FLOORS: MEASURING UP A ROOM

**SKILL LEVEL** Low
**TIME FRAME** ½ day for an average-size room
**SPECIAL TOOLS** None
**SEE PAGES** 190–191

Measuring up a room before laying any type of flooring is an essential part of a flooring task. You need to do this in order to ensure that you purchase the correct amount of floorcovering and any other materials. The other essential is that the floor must be properly prepared. This preparation varies according to the type of floor and the covering that is going to be laid. Concrete floors require levelling, whereas wooden floors may need the addition of a plywood or hardboard layer to provide a good base for the new flooring.

There is always a right and a wrong place to start when laying a floor, particularly when dealing with any type of tiled flooring. These pages give guidelines on where to start tiling a floor, showing you how to find the centre of the room and how to plan your designs from this point. Achieving the correct balance for full tiles and cut tiles in a room is important for the look of the finished design. It is also worth remembering that although some rooms are relatively square in shape, others have awkward angles or features, such as alcoves, and your calculations – especially for tiling – need to be adjusted to take this into account. A practical thought process is required to break the room shape down into square components so that you can work out an order of work in the usual way.

Flooring is expensive to buy and it can never be emphasized enough that the planning process, if carried out correctly, will eliminate costly mistakes. Cutting a sheet of vinyl too small or beginning to tile a floor in the wrong place are both courses of action that will be very difficult to rectify. Therefore, it is worth taking the time to check and double check all your measurements and your planning strategy before you start laying a floor.

## LAYING VINYL TILES

**SKILL LEVEL** Low to medium
**TIME FRAME** 1 day for an average-size room
**SPECIAL TOOLS** Chalk line, adhesive spreader, metal ruler
**SEE PAGES** 192–193

Vinyl tiles can be laid on a concrete screed as long as it is completely dry, or they can be laid on sound subfloors such as plywood or hardboard. They may also be laid on chipboard. It is vital that the surface is totally flat so that good adhesion is achieved. Traditionally, tiles are laid with all the joints aligned across the floor surface, but a brick bond pattern can be used for a different effect.

Whichever pattern you choose to use, planning is essential in order to ensure that you start tiling in the correct place in the room (see pp.190–191). A chalk line is the best tool to use for finding the centre of the room, then all the measurements can be planned from this point. Vinyl tiles can usually be cut successfully with a utility knife, but because blades become blunt quickly, you need to make sure that you have a large enough supply at hand to finish the job. It is also essential to have a metal ruler and a cutting board for making the required cuts as accurately as possible – edges that are not straight will be noticeable on the finished floor. Wipe away any excess adhesive from the tile surfaces as you proceed, so it does not harden and spoil the surface.

## LAYING SHEET VINYL

**SKILL LEVEL** High
**TIME FRAME** 1 day for an average-size room
**SPECIAL TOOLS** None
**SEE PAGES** 194–195

Although vinyl tiles and sheet vinyl are constructed from the same material, this is where the similarity ends. The techniques required to lay the two types of floorcovering are different. As with vinyl tiles, the subfloor should be a concrete screed, plywood or hardboard, but whereas tiles are placed one at a time to cover the floor, with sheet

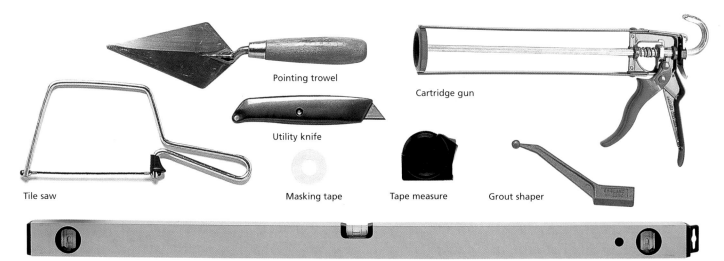

Pointing trowel

Cartridge gun

Utility knife

Tile saw

Masking tape

Tape measure

Grout shaper

Spirit level

vinyl the whole floor is generally covered with one piece of vinyl sheeting, except where the floor is so large that you need to join one or more sheets. This means that the sheet must be accurately trimmed to ensure a good fit.

It is a good idea to make a template of the floor you are going to cover, as this will make the fitting process easier. Although professional floor layers are unlikely to use this technique, it is by far the best option for the home improvement enthusiast. Take your time to make an accurate template on paper, and take care when transferring it to the vinyl. Make sure that a balanced effect will be achieved once the vinyl is fitted, particularly with vinyls that have any sort of directional pattern. Sheet vinyl can be stuck down around the edges with adhesive, but this is not usually essential except where two pieces are being joined. Also, if you do need to join two pieces of sheet vinyl, the join will always look neater if you can place two factory-cut edges next to each other, rather than edges that you have cut yourself with a utility knife, so always try to follow the former option.

## LAYING FOAM-BACKED CARPET

**SKILL LEVEL** Low to medium
**TIME FRAME** ½ day for an average-size room
**SPECIAL TOOLS** Bolster chisel
**SEE PAGES** 196–197

Foam-backed carpet is much easier to lay than hessian-backed alternatives. However, traditionalists would say that there is a large difference in the quality of the two finishes. Although this is true to a certain extent, in recent years foam-backed carpets have increased in quality while still remaining a cheaper option to hessian-backed carpets. In addition, with foam-backed carpets there is no need to lay underlay, which saves on the cost. However, foam-backed carpets must be laid on sound floor surfaces, because they tend to be relatively thin and even slight imperfections underneath the carpet will show up and increase the wear in these uneven areas.

Double-sided adhesive tape is used to secure the carpet around the perimeter of the room. In larger rooms where joins are required, double-sided tape may be used underneath any joining seams. The carpet must be

trimmed to roughly the right size before it is laid in the room and then cut more exactly to the precise dimensions of the room. A utility knife is the ideal tool for cutting the foam-backed carpet to the correct size.

## LAYING HESSIAN-BACKED CARPET

**SKILL LEVEL** Medium
**TIME FRAME** ½ to 1 day for an average-size room
**SPECIAL TOOLS** Knee kicker, bolster chisel
**SEE PAGES** 198–199

Hessian-backed carpet requires more time and effort to lay than foam-backed equivalents. as it is necessary to fix gripper strips and lay underlay first. Another drawback is that hessian-backed carpets are more difficult to lay. However, the result is a more cushioned effect than that achieved with foam-backed carpet.

Remember that the quality of the finish underfoot will depend on the quality of the carpet and the depth of the underlay. The best effect will be achieved if good quality materials are used. Wool carpet with a high percentage

of natural fibre retains it shape better than carpet with a higher man-made content.

Once the preparation has been done and the carpet has been put down, it is necessary to use a knee kicker to put the carpet under slight tension as it is fitted over and behind the gripper strips around the perimeter of the room. Because you are able to stretch the carpet slightly, the cuts around the edge of the room may be neatened to a certain degree during the fitting process.

At entrances to the room, there needs to be something to differentiate between the floorcovering in one room and that in the next. If the same carpet continues into the next room, this shouldn't be a problem. If it doesn't, it will be necessary to fix some sort of threshold strip so that a neat join can be made between the different types of floorcoverings. Choose the threshold strips carefully to ensure that you have the right one, and pick a finish that suits the room decoration. For example, metal threshold strips, such as those finished in a chrome effect, are ideal in some room situations, while hardwood threshold strips are more appropriate in others.

Cold chisel

Tile file

Sponge

Grout spreader

Tile spacers

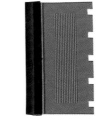

Small notched adhesive spreader

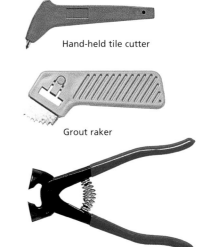

Hand-held tile cutter

Grout raker

Tile nippers

## LAYING CORK TILES

**SKILL LEVEL** Low to medium
**TIME FRAME** 1 day for an average-size room
**SPECIAL TOOLS** Adhesive spreader, rolling pin
**SEE PAGES** 200–201

Planning the layout is essential when laying cork tiles. This means you need to find the centre of the room and work back from this point to find the appropriate starting position (see pp.190–191). Rather than using traditional brown cork tiles, a coloured variety has been used, giving the opportunity to introduce more of a pattern to the floorcovering. The tiles are cut with a utility knife, using a cutting board and a metal ruler for precision. A good tip is to roll an ordinary household rolling pin over the tiles to improve the adhesion between the tiles and the subfloor and to ensure that the tiles are laid completely flat. The type of cork tile illustrated on these pages does not require sealing once laid, but some types of cork tile will need coats of varnish or sealer once the surface of the floor is complete and the adhesive has dried.

## LAYING CERAMIC TILES

**SKILL LEVEL** Medium
**TIME FRAME** 1 to 1½ days for an average-size room
**SPECIAL TOOLS** Adhesive spreader, platform tile cutter
**SEE PAGES** 202–203

Ceramic tiles are heavier than vinyl or cork tiles and require a slightly different laying technique. They can be laid on a concrete screed subfloor or on wooden floors, as long as plywood has been laid to ensure that the surface is flat and that there is no flexibility or movement in the floor surface.

Planning for the positioning of ceramic tiles is similar to vinyl or cork tiles, but a different adhesive is required. It is a good idea to nail a temporary batten into the floor along the starting line for the design, as this provides a solid support for positioning the first row of tiles. Spacers are required to maintain an even distance between the tiles. Any tile cuts should be made with a robust platform tile cutter that can deal with the thickness and strength of ceramic floor tiles.

Ceramic tiles will also need grouting after they are laid because most of them are laid with gaps between the joints, unlike soft tiles, such as vinyl and cork, which tend to be butted tightly together at each joint. The neatness and general appearance of the surface depends on the quality of the grouting. This final stage is crucial to the overall finish of the tiles.

## LAYING A NATURAL SLATE FLOOR

**SKILL LEVEL** Medium to high
**TIME FRAME** 1 to 1½ days for an average-size room
**SPECIAL TOOLS** Adhesive spreader, platform tile cutter
**SEE PAGES** 204–205

Laying natural slate floors involves many of the processes described for laying ceramic tiles, but a few refinements are necessary to deal with slight variations in the tile make-up and structure. Slate tiles may not have the uniform shape or depth of ceramic tiles, in which case it becomes necessary to vary the thickness of the adhesive layer in order to make the floor as level as possible. These tiles have a more hand-made appearance, which lends itself to spacing the tiles by eye rather than using tile spacers when laying them.

Slate tiles are particularly hard and it is necessary to hire an electrically operated tile saw to cut them. These machines make cleaner, more accurate cuts than hand-operated tools, improving the tile finish, and they make it less likely that tiles will be broken when they are being cut. It is possible that your first job will have to be sealing the slate tiles to make sure that no dirt or excess adhesive becomes ingrained in the tile surfaces during the installation process.

## LAYING A LAMINATE WOODSTRIP FLOOR

**SKILL LEVEL** Low to medium
**TIME FRAME** ½ to 1 day for an average-size room
**SPECIAL TOOLS** Jemmy
**SEE PAGES** 206–207

Laminate wood floors are attractive, hard-wearing and

Floor sander

Cordless power drill

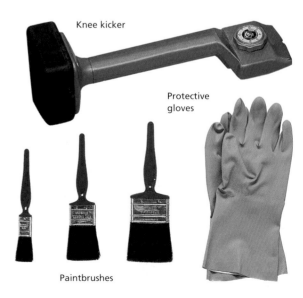

Knee kicker

Protective gloves

Paintbrushes

generally maintenance-free surfaces that look similar to natural floorboards that have been given a more polished appearance. These floors are mainly supplied in kit form nowadays, and are generally laid "floating" – there are no physical mechanisms joining the laminate floor to the subfloor below. A special underlay is generally laid on the subfloor before the laminate floor is put down.

Sections of laminate boards are joined together with clips or, as in this case, glued together with a tongue-and-groove mechanism. Cuts are usually required in the lengths of flooring to make it fit in the room, and a jemmy bar is used to join sections at the end of rows as you progress across the floor surface.

Spacers are used to maintain a gap around the edge of the room between the floor and walls. This gap acts as an expansion area once the floor is laid, so that any slight movement in the floor will be tolerated without distorting the laminate woodstrip flooring. This gap is usually covered over with moulding attached directly to the skirting board or base of the wall.

## PAINTING A FLOOR

**SKILL LEVEL** Low
**TIME FRAME** 1 day for an average-size room
**SPECIAL TOOLS** None
**SEE PAGES** 208–209

Painting floors is a simple and straightforward way of adding a decorative finish to bare floor areas, and one that can be achieved quickly. The best painted floor effects are generally created by painting floorboards, although other surfaces, such as concrete, chipboard and, in some cases, hardboard, can be painted. There are many different options when it comes to painting floors, just as when painting any surfaces in the home, and all should be considered in terms of the style and atmosphere you wish to convey.

In the example shown on pp.208–209, a pattern has been painted on floorboards to create an alternate colour effect across the floor surface. A bolster chisel has been used to create fake joints between the floorboards, which add to the overall effect and provide lines of division between the different paint colours. Remember that floors receive

a great deal of wear and tear, so bear this in mind when choosing between using standard floor paint (which will last longer) or other types of paint, such as emulsion paint, which will wear more quickly. In many cases, this sort of distressed, ageing appearance may be the look that you want.

## FINISHING WOOD FLOORING

**SKILL LEVEL** Low
**TIME FRAME** 2 days, sanding on the first day and finishing on the second
**SPECIAL TOOLS** Floor sander, edging sander, corner sander
**SEE PAGES** 210–211

If you wish to keep the natural grain effect of your floorboards, you can sand the floor back and stain or varnish it. Sanding a floor involves hiring a floor sander, edging sander and corner sander. It is a messy job, so be sure to mask or cover up areas as necessary.

Once the floor has been sanded, it can be finished with the desired natural wood finish. Traditional colours can be used, but manufacturers

now produce any number of colours, which can give a greater impact to a floor finish. For example, pale blues or greens provide an effective alternative when applied to light-coloured floorboards – this can also make it easier to plan your colour scheme and integrate floor and wall surfaces more convincingly.

Whichever finish you choose, remember that floors receive a lot of wear and tear. No matter how good the quality of the materials you use for your new floor, it will still be necessary to apply some sort of maintenance coat to the floor from time to time. This does not need to involve all areas of the floor, simply those that get the most use and are most likely to show signs of wear. When applying these maintenance coats, make sure that the floor has been cleaned thoroughly so you get the best adhesion possible between the new coat and the floor surface. This simple process also maintains the look of the floor without causing disruption to the household because there is no need to remove all the furniture from the room, eliminating the turmoil such events produce.

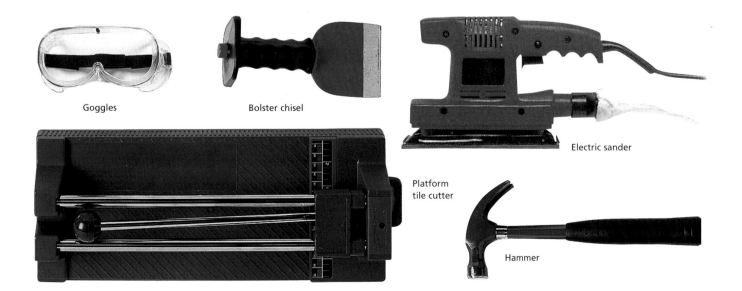

Goggles

Bolster chisel

Electric sander

Platform tile cutter

Hammer

# FLOORS: MEASURING UP A ROOM

**YOU WILL NEED**

**Filling concrete floors**
Trowel and bucket
Sand/cement mortar mix

**Laying plywood**
Plywood and nails
Hammer and panel saw

**Laying hardboard**
Hardboard and nails or
staples
Hammer or stapler
Utility knife

Measuring up a room for new flooring is a straightforward process and simply requires accurate measurements of the floor dimensions to calculate the surface area. From these measurements, you can estimate the quantity of material you need and purchase the floorcovering. Good preparation is essential for all flooring in order to produce a stable subfloor underneath the new floorcovering. The type of subfloor required depends on the flooring you are planning to use – whether it is vinyl, hard tiles or carpet (see pp. 192–207).

Whichever flooring you use, be sure to prepare it correctly, following the manufacturer's guidelines where necessary. The better the preparation, the easier it will be to lay your chosen floorcovering, and the longer the new floor will last after it has been laid.

## FILLING CONCRETE FLOORS

On a concrete floor, any holes or cracks must be filled prior to laying the floorcovering. A mixture of 5 parts sand to 1 part cement mortar mix is ideal for this. Press the mixture firmly into any holes or cracks and smooth it before it dries.

## LAYING PLYWOOD

Plywood must be laid over floorboards when a sound surface is required for hard tiles. It also acts as a good base for soft tiles, such as those made of cork or carpet. Nail the plywood down, making sure that it forms a rigid base. Take care to stagger the joins between sheets. Cut sheets with a saw to fit at the end of rows.

## LAYING HARDBOARD

Hardboard subfloors are used as a base for vinyl or carpet. They can either be stapled or nailed to existing floorboards. Stagger edges between sheets and make sure that the hardboard is laid smooth side up. Cut sheets to size with a utility knife to fit at the ends of rows.

## HELPFUL HINTS

● Use a panel saw to cut plywood, but use a utility knife for hardboard. Draw a pencil guideline on the hardboard and score it with the knife, then snap it along the guideline.

● When fixing either of these types of board with nails or staples, make sure that the fixings are long enough to penetrate securely into the floorboards, but are not so long that they extend below the floor level and risk damaging any cables or pipes running under the floor.

3 Tape the template on top of your vinyl, then cut around the edge of the template, leaving a 5 to 7.5 cm (2 to 3 in) excess. It may be easier to lay out the vinyl in a larger room, so it can be laid out flat. Protect the floor below the vinyl from the cutting blade of the utility knife, if this is necessary.

4 Remove the template and position the sheet of vinyl where it is to be laid, fitting it roughly in place and allowing the excess vinyl to extend up the wall slightly. Crease the vinyl into the junction of the skirting board and floor, then cut precisely along this guideline to fit the vinyl snugly against the skirting board.

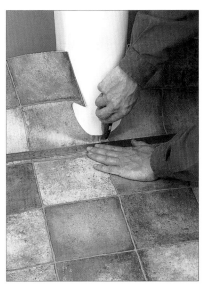

5 With obstacles such as basin pedestals, make a number of cuts in the excess vinyl areas at right angles to the pedestal profile. This will allow you to mould the vinyl edge around the pedestal to give you the required cutting line.

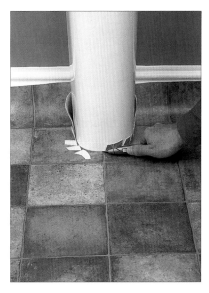

6 Crease the small cut areas of vinyl tightly into the junction at the bottom of the pedestal and use a utility knife to trim each section in turn. Once you have cut around the pedestal, continue cutting the straight skirting-board edge.

7 Where a join is required, try to ensure that you are matching two factory edges rather than cut ones, as you will get greater accuracy with the factory edges. (Make sure you match up any patterns if necessary.) Join the vinyl with a strip of adhesive laid under the edges of the vinyl; alternatively, use double-sided tape.

## HELPFUL HINTS

● Although it is not essential to glue down vinyl, especially the heavyweight types, adhesive can be used around the edge of the room to hold it securely in place. In the same way that it is used at a join (see step 7), apply a similar band around the edge of the room. Once you fit the vinyl, simply lift it back from the edges, apply adhesive and glue the vinyl down.

● Another area where adhesive will be required is stairways – the vinyl needs holding firmly in position to avoid the possibility of it slipping out of place.

# LAYING FOAM-BACKED CARPET

**YOU WILL NEED**

Utility knife
Bolster chisel

**MATERIALS**

Double-sided carpet tape
Foam-backed carpet

*Foam-backed carpets are an excellent choice for bedrooms, where it is likely that you will want to walk about barefoot and will appreciate comfort.*

T he benefits of fitted carpet include a comfortable floor with a soft texture underfoot and also improved soundproofing – qualities useful in most areas of the home. Carpeting generally sets the style of a room. Most carpets have either a foam or a hessian backing. Foam-backed carpet, normally thought of as the cheaper alternative to hessian-backed carpet (see pp.198–199), has the advantage that it is much easier to lay, and requires less floor preparation beforehand. Hessian-backed carpet tends to be better quality carpeting.

There is a wide range of foam-backed carpets available, and since these vary considerably in quality, the amount of money you want to spend will decide the quality and type of carpet you can lay.

Because these carpets have a cushioned foam backing, there is no need to put down underlay before fitting them. In years gone by, people often put down newspaper as a form of underlay, but modern carpet design makes this procedure unnecessary.

If you have wooden floorboards (which may be uneven), it is advisable to cover them with hardboard before laying the carpet, as this will prolong the life of foam-backed carpet. For techniques to prepare the floor, see pp.190–191.

**1** Place double-sided tape around the perimeter of the room, but do not remove the backing paper on the top side of the tape yet. The tape will hold the carpet in position after it has been laid.

**2** Unroll and roughly fit the foam-backed carpet, allowing an excess to extend up the walls. Push the carpet into position across and around the entire floor surface. Check that the whole floor area is covered before you proceed to the next stage.

**3** Smooth the carpet flat and trim it back to within 2.5 to 5 cm (1 to 2 in) of the skirting-board/floor junction, using a utility knife. Now lift the carpet back along one wall, remove the backing paper from the top side of the double-sided tape, then press the carpet in place.

**4** As you work your way around the perimeter of the room, smooth and stretch the carpet into all the wall/skirting-board junctions and corners. Press down firmly so that the carpet adheres properly to the double-sided tape.

**5** Give the edge of the carpet a final trim to ensure that its edge fits precisely in the skirting-board/floor junction. Trim the edges with a utility knife, taking care not to cut into the surface of the painted skirting board and damage it.

**6** Tidy up around the edges of the carpet to ensure there are no loose ends or ill-fitting areas. Then give the carpet a neat finish by using a bolster chisel to crease the carpet edge into the junction.

**7** In some cases it may be necessary to join sections of carpet, especially if it is being laid in a large room. Try to join along the factory edges of the carpet as you will get a more accurate join. Apply double-sided tape to the floor below the join, then remove the top backing paper and press the carpet along the join to fix in place.

## HELPFUL HINTS

Once the carpet has been laid, check all the way around the skirting-board floor junction. Carpet edges often fray if the cuts made when fitting are not totally clean. It is worthwhile going along each side of the carpet with a utility knife, trimming any areas where a thread has come loose, or dealing with any other imperfections that spoil the neat-looking finish. This doesn't apply to just foam-backed carpets – you should do the same with hessian-backed carpet. At the same time, you should also check that all the edges are stuck down securely.

# LAYING HESSIAN-BACKED CARPET

**YOU WILL NEED**

Hammer
Utility knife
Knee-kicker (hired)
Bolster chisel

**MATERIALS**

Gripper strips
Underlay
Hessian-backed carpet

*Using the same carpet throughout a number of rooms in the house helps to link colour schemes and provides continuity of style.*

Hessian-backed carpet is better quality and more hard-wearing than foam-backed alternatives, and these differences can usually be seen in the price. Even if you choose a relatively inexpensive hessian-backed carpet, you will still need underlay and gripper strips, which add to the cost. Once laid, however, this type of carpet provides many years of good service. Because underlay is used, it can be laid on most subfloors, including floorboards, chipboard, plywood, hardboard and concrete screeds.

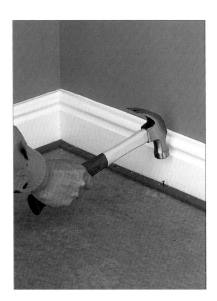

**1** Nail gripper strips along each wall of the room, and across the door opening. Leave a 5 mm (¼ in) gap between the strips and the skirting board. Take care not to damage the skirting board with the head of the hammer – it is easy to scuff the skirting-board surface.

**2** Roll out lengths of underlay across the floor, butt-joining them where necessary. Do not allow the underlay to extend over the top of the gripper strips – use a utility knife to trim it back flush with the inside edge of the strips.

**3** Lay out the carpet across the room surface, allowing the excess to extend up the walls. Using a utility knife, trim large excess amounts so that the carpet does not extend up the wall higher than the skirting board.

**4** Trim the carpet back into the skirting-board/floor junction, using a utility knife. Hessian-backed carpet can be fairly rigid and inflexible, so make sure that it is pushed tightly into the junction before you begin to trim it.

**5** A knee-kicker, which stretches the carpet, is required to lay hessian-backed carpet effectively. The teeth on the knee-kicker are adjusted according to the depth of pile of your carpet. A dial on top of the tool is turned to extend or reduce the protruding distance of the teeth.

**6** Work from the central areas of the carpet out towards each wall, gradually pushing and stretching the carpet towards the gripper strips and skirting board. Do not overstretch the carpet, but simply allow it to fit evenly and lie flat on the floor.

**7** At the skirting-board/floor junction, use a bolster chisel to push the edge of the carpet over and beyond the gripper strips to secure it in place. The teeth on the strips grab hold of the hessian backing and grip the carpet in position.

## DESIGN INFLUENCE

Carpeting is an important colour factor in a room. Because fitted carpets cover such a large surface area, they can be a major influence on the overall look (see p.99). Take the carpet colour into consideration at an early stage so you can coordinate it with the rest of the room. If you have a strong carpet colour, for instance, it may be best to have pale walls.

# LAYING CORK TILES

**YOU WILL NEED**

Chalk line
Tape measure
Pencil
Notched spreader
Rolling pin
Utility knife
Straight edge
Cutting board
Cloth

**MATERIALS**

Floor adhesive
Cork tiles

**SEE ALSO**

Floors: measuring up a room
pp.190–191

*The attractive natural appearance of cork tiles makes them an ideal choice for a stylish flooring – these tiles are also comfortable to walk on with bare feet and are easy to maintain.*

Cork tiles provide an easily cleaned and hard-wearing floor surface that is suitable for most rooms and hallways. The tiles are laid in a similar manner to vinyl tiles (see pp.192–193) and require a sound subfloor – hardboard or plywood are suitable choices. Cork tiles should not be laid directly on to floorboards.

The tiles are available in a range of styles; some have a sealed finish while others require sealing once they have been laid. The most traditional tiles are the natural cork colour, but some tile manufacturers offer a range of colours, giving you more options for the patterns and designs that you can create on your floor.

**1** Find the centre of the room by attaching and snapping a chalk line between opposite walls; plan your tile layout from this point. Use the diagram on p.191 as a guide to finding the starting position. It is a good idea to start by laying out the design dry – without adhesive – to help plan your layout.

**2** Make a pencil guideline along the back edge of the tiles nearest the wall (see step 3, p.193), before removing tiles. Starting in a corner, apply adhesive to the floor, using a notched spreader. Spread enough adhesive for several tiles at a time. (Make sure you can lay the tiles without standing on the adhesive.)

**3** Position the first tile in the corner, allowing it to bed down on to the adhesive layer. Take extra care when positioning this first tile so that it sits precisely along the pencil guidelines – this tile will be the one that ensures that the rest of the design is balanced.

**4** Build up the design in rows, aligning subsequent tiles accurately to ensure all joins are precise and butted together tightly. Use a rolling pin to run over the tile surface to make sure that the tiles are stuck down securely with no lifting edges.

**5** To fill in gaps around the edge, position the tile that requires cutting on top of the nearest full tile to that edge. Place another tile on top, but with its edge butted up against the skirting board. Use the top tile as a guide to draw a pencil cutting line along the surface of the middle tile.

**6** Using a utility knife and a straight edge, cut along this line. When cutting through tiles, place them on a cutting board so that you do not damage the floor below. Apply adhesive to the back of the tile before positioning it.

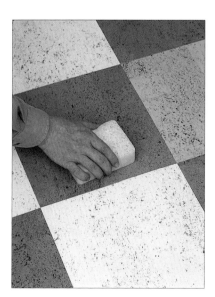

**7** Finally, clean the floor surface with a damp cloth to remove any excess adhesive. Depending on the tiles you have used, the floor may be ready for use, or a sealant coat may be needed. Follow the manufacturer's guidelines for cleaning and sealing.

### HELPFUL HINTS

● Most manufacturers advise that cork tiles be left for 24 hours in the room in which they are to be laid to acclimatize them to the room temperature.

● With untreated cork tiles, it is a good idea to apply a coat of sealant before they are laid. However careful you are, some adhesive inevitably gets on to the top of the tiles, and if they are not sealed, the adhesive can become ingrained in the cork and stain it. Further coats of sealant can be applied once the floor is laid.

# LAYING CERAMIC TILES

## YOU WILL NEED

Chalk line
Tape measure
Pencil
Wooden batten
Hammer
Notched spreader
Spirit level
Wax pencil
Platform tile cutter
Grout spreader
Sponge
Grout shaper or small
wooden dowel

## MATERIALS

Nails
Tiles
Tile adhesive
Grout

## SEE ALSO

Floors: measuring up a room
pp.190–191

*Ceramic floor tiles are hard-wearing and easy to clean, making them ideal for kitchens.*

Ceramic floor tiles are among the most hard-wearing of surfaces. They are available in a huge range of sizes, shapes and colours; some are plain, others are hand-painted. The quality differs considerably and it is essential to use tiles that are intended to be used on floors. You should also take into account the thickness of the tiles, and whether they might affect any doors opening into the room.

Ceramic floor tiles do not require treatment once they have been laid, other than grouting. It is important that ceramic floor tiles are laid on a firm base – concrete screeds are ideal, as is plywood, which gives an even cover to floorboards. Some manufacturers recommend using a flexible sheet sandwiched between adhesive layers before tile application (this is not always necessary); it is important to read the manufacturer's guidelines and follow any specific instructions when laying the tiles.

Take time to plan your strategy for application – mistakes are not easily rectified once the floor is finished. A good-quality platform tile cutter is necessary, as many floor tiles are thick and difficult to cut. In some cases, it may be necessary to hire a tile-cutting saw (see pp.204–205).

**1** Find the starting position for tiling by referring to the diagrams on p.191. It is a good idea to nail a temporary wooden batten in position here. You can then apply the first row of tiles, butting them up against this secure guide.

**2** Apply adhesive across the floor surface, working in manageable-size areas, about 1 m (1 yd) long and just wider than the tiles. Use a coarse-toothed notched spreader, as this provides an even coverage of adhesive with relatively deep channels, which will help to provide good adhesion between tiles and floor.

**3** Position the first tile, pressing it in position tight up against the supporting batten and using a slight twisting motion to ensure good adhesion. Be careful not to exaggerate any movement, as this can upset the consistent level of the adhesive.

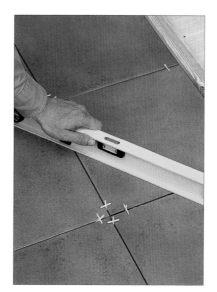

**4** Continue to apply tiles and position spacers between them to ensure the correct gap is maintained between all the tiles across the floor. Hold a spirit level across groups of tiles from time to time, to make sure that they are all sitting level.

**5** Once all the full tiles have been applied, allow the adhesive to dry before returning to cut tiles to fit around the perimeter of the room. One by one, carefully measure the size of cuts required, using a tape measure, and transfer this measurement to a full tile, drawing a guideline with a wax pencil.

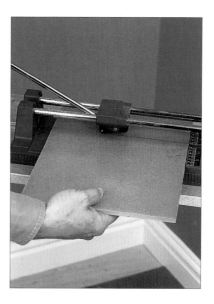

**6** Position the tile in the platform tile cutter and score along the guideline with the cutting wheel. Make one run with the wheel; apply enough pressure to scratch through the glazed surface of the tile and leave a clear scored line. Move the tile under the rails of the cutter; bring the arm down to snap the tile along the line.

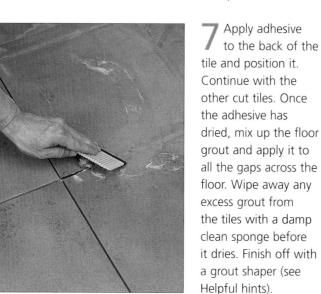

**7** Apply adhesive to the back of the tile and position it. Continue with the other cut tiles. Once the adhesive has dried, mix up the floor grout and apply it to all the gaps across the floor. Wipe away any excess grout from the tiles with a damp clean sponge before it dries. Finish off with a grout shaper (see Helpful hints).

## HELPFUL HINTS

● A new ceramic tile floor is set off to perfection by the grouting in the joints between tiles. Once grout has been applied, remove any excess with a damp clean sponge, then use a grout shaper to ensure that all the joints are smooth.

● If you do not have a grout shaper, a similar effect may be achieved by using the end of a cylindrical piece of wooden dowel – running the dowel along the grout joints makes a slightly concave finish of an even depth and gives the grout a neat, uniform finish across the tiled floor.

# LAYING A NATURAL SLATE FLOOR

## YOU WILL NEED

Paintbrush
Protective gloves
Notched spreader
Wooden batten
Spacers (optional)
Chalk line
Pencil
Tape measure
Spirit level
Tile-cutting saw (hired)
Safety goggles
Grout spreader
Sponge
Grout shaper or small
wooden dowel

## MATERIALS

Slate tiles
Proprietary sealer
Tile adhesive
Grout

## SEE ALSO

Floors: measuring up a room
pp.190–191

*The dusty tones of slate tiles have a natural elegance that helps to set off the other features in a room.*

Laying tiles that have a natural look or composition, such as slate tiles, requires some variation in technique compared to laying standard ceramic tiles. Although sizes tend to remain consistent, slate tiles often vary slightly in depth. The tile surface tends to be untreated when supplied, so it is necessary to add a finish to the tiles so that they can be cleaned once laid.

Slate tiles must be laid on a sound subfloor – a concrete screed is the ideal surface, but thick plywood is also acceptable as long as there is no "give" in the floor surface and it provides a completely rigid base. Obtain the starting position for tiling by referring to the diagrams on p.191, and adjust the tile position as required to produce balanced cuts around the edge of the room. Take care when handling slate tiles as they are easily chipped or damaged. Their strength and hard-wearing properties only come into effect once they are laid in adhesive and the grouting is complete.

**1** Before you begin to lay the tiles, seal their surfaces with a coat of proprietary sealer. In this way, they will be protected and any overspills of adhesive can be wiped away easily as you lay the floor, before they have a chance of becoming ingrained in the tile surfaces. Wear protective gloves while using the sealer.

**2** Find the centre of the room and lay the first row of tiles (see p.191), butting them up against a batten and applying tile adhesive to the floor – as shown in steps 1 and 2 on p.202. Using spacers is optional, as the slight variations in gaps between tiles adds to the natural look of this floor.

3 After every few tiles have been laid, place a spirit level across their surface to check that they are sitting level. The tile surfaces themselves are often slightly undulating, so you may have to make judgments by eye when carrying out this process.

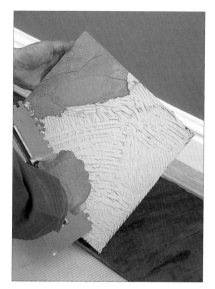

4 Because of slight variations in tile thickness, from time to time it may be necessary to either reduce or increase the amount of adhesive underneath a tile in order to make it the same level as the surrounding floor. Remove such tiles before the adhesive dries and adjust the levels accordingly.

5 Once all full tiles have been laid and are dry, you can deal with cuts around the edges of the room. Measure and mark each tile to fit, as shown in step 5 on p.203. While wearing goggles, use a tile-cutting saw to cut tiles to size. These saws may be obtained from hire centres and are usually required for slate tiles.

6 Grout the floor in the normal way, using grout recommended for slate. Make sure that the grout is firmly pressed into every joint. Wipe away excess grout with a damp sponge before using a grout shaper or wooden dowl to give the joints a neat finish.

7 Once the grout has dried, another coat of proprietary floor sealer can be applied in order to finish the floor. Once dry, the slate surface is ready for everyday use. A coat of sealer from time to time will keep a slate tile floor in good condition.

## HELPFUL HINTS

There can be considerable variations in colour between slate tiles, which can be attractive. However, when buying your tiles, it is important to make sure that they are all from the same batch. Even within the same batch of tiles, the colour may vary from one box to another, so it can be well worth mixing the tiles from different boxes before you start to tile. In this way, any small differences in colour will be diluted across the entire floor surface, reducing the risk of clear divisions, or lines, between tiles of one specific colour and those of a slightly different shade.

# LAYING A LAMINATE WOODSTRIP FLOOR

**YOU WILL NEED**
...............................................
Tape measure
Wood wedges
Hammer
Wood block
Sponge
Panel saw
Jemmy (designed for floors)
Pencil
Nail punch

**MATERIALS**
...............................................
Sheet underlay
Laminate woodstrip flooring
Wood glue
Moulding
Nails

*Woodstrip flooring has a wonderful polished appearance and comes in a variety of widths and designs.*

Laminate woodstrip flooring has become an increasingly popular option for home improvement. It complements modern or traditional homes and is an easy floor to lay, although there can be subtle variations in laying technique, depending on the type of floor you have purchased, and so it is important follow the manufacturer's instructions closely. Most of these floors are "floating" – there are no physical fixings between the laminate floor and the subfloor below. In this way, the floor can expand and contract slightly to deal with changes in atmospheric conditions without the boards buckling.

Woodstrip floors can be laid on most subfloors. If laying the floor on concrete, the screed must be completely dry – it can take several months before a new screed is dry enough for this type of flooring. Floorboards, plywood, chipboard or hardboard should be fixed securely. In the example below, the floor has been fitted with the original skirting board in place. Another option is to remove the skirting board before laying the flooring, then replace it afterwards, eliminating the need for a moulding (see step 7).

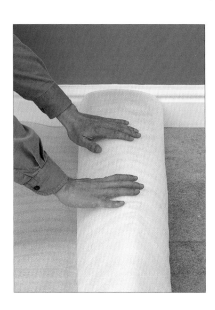

**1** Most laminate floors must be laid on sheet underlay, which is sandwiched between the boards and the subfloor. This sheet is simply rolled out and butt-joined across the floor surface. Generally, it does not require sticking down with any adhesive or tape.

**2** Beginning along one edge of the room, position a length of woodstrip flooring close to the skirting board. Use wedges, supplied with the flooring, to maintain a consistent gap between the boards and skirting board. This gap lets the floor expand with atmospheric changes without buckling the boards.

**3** These floors interlock with a tongue-and-groove mechanism. Use wood glue along the top of the tongue of the board, taking care not to allow the glue to get on to the surface of the board.

**4** Position the next length of floor and use a hammer and block to force the groove of the board onto the tongue of the previous one. Never use the hammer directly on a board because it will damage the tongue. Join subsequent boards in a staggered position as shown.

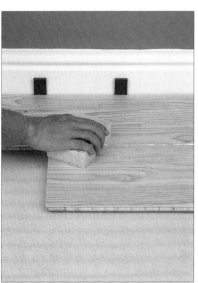

**5** Inevitably, some wood glue will be squeezed out of the join between the boards. Wipe this away immediately with a damp sponge; once it dries it will be difficult to remove from the floor surface.

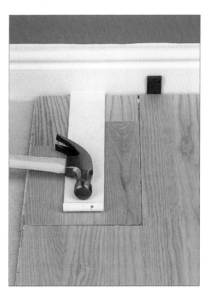

**6** When you reach the ends of subsequent rows of boards, it is necessary to cut them down to size before they can be positioned. In order to join the tongue-and-groove ends of the board, use a specially designed jemmy to knock the ends of the boards in to position.

**7** Once the floor is laid, remove the wedges from around the edges of the room and cover the resulting gap with lengths of moulding. Join this to the skirting board, rather than the floor surface, nailing it in position. Punch in the nail heads as required before filling, sanding and painting or varnishing.

## HELPFUL HINTS

Laminate woodstrip floors have several advantages over the similar effect produced by stripped floorboards, not least in their soundproofing possibilities. While you may not think of a wooden floor as ideal for soundproofing, the advantage with a woodstrip floor is that, because it is floating, you can place it on acoustic underlay to reduce sound penetration to floors below. It would be far more laborious to achieve the same effect with normal floorboards, as they would have to be taken up to lay soundproofing in the floor space below.

# PAINTING A FLOOR

## YOU WILL NEED

Hammer
Nail punch
Bolster chisel
Floor sander
Cloth or sponge
Paintbrush
Small artist's paintbrush
Caulking joints
Cartridge gun

## MATERIALS

Primer
Proprietary floor paint (two colours) or emulsion paint (two colours) and floor-grade varnish
Caulking joints
Decorator's caulk

*Adding a decorative border to a painted floor is a simple way of enhancing its effect and creating a very individual finish.*

You can give a room an attractive new look at a relatively low cost by simply painting the floor. Although concrete and chipboard floors can be painted, the best effects are usually achieved with plain floorboards. The floorboards must be clear of any other finishes such as stain or wax. If necessary, you can use a hired floor sander to remove any such layers (see pp.210–211).

You can use proprietary floor paints on floorboards, but ordinary emulsion paint is effective, as long as you apply a floor-grade varnish to protect it. The example here shows how you can use more than one colour to paint a pattern on the floorboards.

**1** Make sure that any protruding nail heads are knocked into the floorboard surface, using a hammer and nail punch. Secure any loose boards as required.

**2** Increase the board effect by simulating extra joins along the longer board length. Use a hammer and bolster chisel to cut an indentation across the widths of these boards at random intervals – these fake joins will be further enhanced when paint is applied.

**3** Give the floor a final sand to remove any rough areas before painting. This is especially important if the floor has not been sanded with a floor sander. A hand-held electrical sander is ideal for this, but be sure to keep it in line with the grain of the wood. Wipe away the dust with a damp cloth after you have finished sanding.

**4** Seal the entire floor surface with a good-quality primer, to provide a sound base for further paint application. Work the primer well into the wood surface and make sure that it has completely dried before you add the next coats.

**5** Using your first colour, paint alternate boards, taking care to be precise with the board joints and the fake joins that you made with the bolster chisel. Use a large brush and, if necessary, a small artist's paintbrush for any detailed work.

**6** Add the second colour to the rest of the boards, paying close attention to joints between the boards. Because of the primer coat, one coat of each colour may be enough, depending on how opaque you want the finish to be. If you are using emulsion paint, after it dries, brush on three coats of a floor-grade varnish.

## CAULKING JOINTS

In the example above, the joints between boards are left relatively open, but you can create a completely sealed surface by applying some decorator's caulk along the floorboard joints. Smooth it with a sponge or a damp cloth before it dries.

## CHILD'S ROOM

A painted floor is ideal for a child's bedroom, where you can produce a finish that is hard-wearing and not easily damaged (see p.93). You can have fun creating different patterns and designs to appeal to children. Maintenance is a matter of new paint from time to time; this offers the option of changing designs at a relatively low cost as the child grows.

# FINISHING WOOD FLOORING

## YOU WILL NEED

Hammer
Nail punch
Dust mask
Goggles
Ear protectors
Floor sander (hired)
Edging sander (hired)
Corner sander (hired)
Broom
Cloths
White spirit
Paintbrush

## MATERIALS

Nails
Wax or stain and varnish

*Stripped and stained floorboards produce a very natural look that blends in well with furnishings made of a similar material.*

The alternative finish to painting floorboards is to revive their natural look by sanding, then staining, and varnishing or waxing them. You will almost certainly need to use a floor sander. One can be hired on a daily rate, and it is normally possible to hire an edging sander and a corner sander in the same package.

Floor sanding is a messy task, and it is advisable to mask around doors to prevent dust travelling throughout the house. Open windows in the room where you are working and wear a dust mask, goggles and ear protectors. Sanders generally all work on similar principles – check the manufacturer's guidelines before you start.

**1** Before beginning to sand, make sure that all the floorboards are secured, and that there are no nails protruding from the floor surface, using a hammer and nail punch to sink them (see step 1 on p.208). Add extra nails as required, but take care not to damage pipes or cables below floorboard level.

**2** Use the sander, first across the floor at a 45-degree angle to the direction of the boards, and then at the opposite 45-degree angle. Finish by sanding along the floorboards with the grain; reduce the coarseness of the abrasive paper that you are using as you progress.

3 The large floor sander cannot to reach right up to the edges of the floor surface, so it is necessary to finish around the perimeter of the room with a specially designed edging sander. Hold on tightly to the hand grips as it can be difficult to control.

4 Just as the large floor sander cannot reach the edges of the floor, the edging sander is unable to get right into the corners. For this, use a corner sander which has a specially designed head to allow access into the apex of the corner.

5 Once sanding is complete, it is necessary to remove all the dust from the floor surface. The worst can be removed by simply sweeping up with a broom, then use a cloth dampened with some white spirit to pick up the rest of the dust and residue. You may need to do this several times.

6 If you are waxing the floor, the wax can now be applied. If you are staining the floor, as shown here, take care to stain the boards individually. Maintain a wet edge at all times, and only allow the brush to flow in the direction of the wood grain.

7 Once the stain has dried, the floor can then be varnished to give it a tough protective coating. Water-based varnishes are particularly effective and their quick drying times mean that more than one coat can be applied in a day.

## STAIN COLOURS

Most floorboards are made from softwoods, which are pale in colour. However, you can use coloured stains to make them darker and give the illusion that the floorboards are made from hardwood. This gives more flexibility when deciding on colour schemes for the room, increasing options for blending floor colour and room decoration (see p.29).

# SOFT FURNISHINGS DIRECTORY

## USING SEWING MATERIALS

**SEE PAGES** 214–215

A guide to the tools for soft furnishing projects, including multi-purpose tools and those specific for particular jobs.

## MEASURING FOR CURTAINS

**SKILL LEVEL** Low
**TIME FRAME** about 30 minutes
**SPECIAL TOOLS** None
**SEE PAGES** 216–217

Measuring up for curtains is essential to ensure you have enough material for the job.

## MAKING UNLINED CURTAINS

**SKILL LEVEL** Low to medium
**TIME FRAME** ½ day
**SPECIAL TOOLS** None
**SEE PAGES** 218–219

Lightweight, unlined curtains are relatively quick and easy to make and are ideal as long as a complete light blackout is not an essential requirement.

## MAKING A LOOSE CURTAIN LINING

**SKILL LEVEL** Medium
**TIME FRAME** ½ to 1 day
**SPECIAL TOOLS** None
**SEE PAGES** 220–221

A loose curtain lining makes it possible to wash the lining and curtain separately. Linings can also be transferred, so that if new unlined curtains are purchased, the lining from the old ones may be re-used.

## MAKING LINED CURTAINS

**SKILL LEVEL** Medium
**TIME FRAME** ½ to 1 day
**SPECIAL TOOLS** None
**SEE PAGES** 222–223

When a curtain fabric is not machine washable, there is little advantage in making a loose lining. Attached curtain linings will make curtains hang better; they are made using similar techniques to those used for loose linings.

## MAKING A FRENCH-PLEAT HEADING

**SKILL LEVEL** Medium
**TIME FRAME** ½ day
**SPECIAL TOOLS** None
**SEE PAGE** 224

Most curtain headings are finished with pencil pleats. Use a French-pleat heading if you wish to create a more ornate finish.

## MAKING TIE-BACKS

**SKILL LEVEL** Low to medium
**TIME FRAME** ½ day
**SPECIAL TOOLS** None
**SEE PAGE** 225

Tie-backs make an attractive decorative accessory for curtains, drawing them away from window recesses.

## HANGING CURTAINS

**SKILL LEVEL** Low to medium
**TIME FRAME** 2 hours
**SPECIAL TOOLS** None
**SEE PAGES** 226–227

Curtains are generally hung on curtain tracks or poles. Both mechanisms require some careful measuring when planning their positioning.

## MAKING A ROLLER BLIND

**SKILL LEVEL** Low to medium
**TIME FRAME** ½ day
**SPECIAL TOOLS** None
**SEE PAGES** 228–229

Blinds are an easy option that may be positioned next to a window or outside a recess.

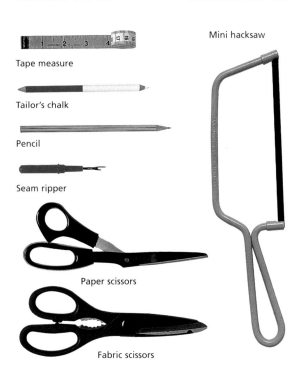

Tape measure

Tailor's chalk

Pencil

Seam ripper

Paper scissors

Fabric scissors

Mini hacksaw

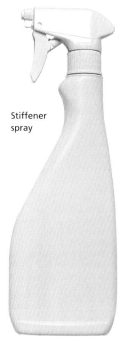

Stiffener spray

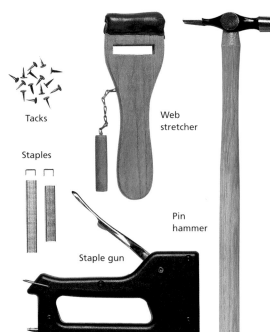

Tacks

Staples

Web stretcher

Pin hammer

Staple gun

## MAKING A ROMAN BLIND

**SKILL LEVEL** Medium
**TIME FRAME** ½ day
**SPECIAL TOOLS** None
**SEE PAGES** 230–231

Roman blinds are a more complicated variation on simple blinds. They have wooden dowels sewn into the blind fabric to create a drawing mechanism, with pleats of fabric on show when the blind is raised.

## MAKING A SQUARE CUSHION

**SKILL LEVEL** Low to medium
**TIME FRAME** 2 hours
**SPECIAL TOOLS** None
**SEE PAGES** 232–233

Cushions are one of the most common soft furnishing accessories, perfect for adding a splash of colour in a room. A simple square cushion with a zip fastening is an inexpensive, effective design, and it takes only a few hours, at the most, to make.

## MAKING A BACK-OPENING CUSHION

**SKILL LEVEL** Low to medium
**TIME FRAME** 2 hours
**SPECIAL TOOLS** None
**SEE PAGE** 234

An easy and alternative way of making a cushion cover, without the need for a zip, is to have a back-opening cushion. The fastening mechanism can be hook-and-loop tape, hooks and eyes, ties or buttons, or an overlap vent can be used.

## MAKING DECORATIVE PIPING

**SKILL LEVEL** Low to medium
**TIME FRAME** 2 hours
**SPECIAL TOOLS** None
**SEE PAGE** 235

Cushions may be given further decorative appeal by attaching piping around the edges. It is relatively simple to make your own piping, and it can be attached to new cushion covers or added to old ones as part of a revamp.

## MAKING A FITTED CUSHION

**SKILL LEVEL** Medium
**TIME FRAME** 2 hours
**SPECIAL TOOLS** Curved needle, thimble
**SEE PAGES** 236–237

Invariably, the fitted cushion in a comfortable chair needs replacing or recovering before any other part of the chair. Making a new cushion is straightforward, as long as you measure and make a pattern for a new cushion before you start.

## COVERING A DROP-IN SEAT

**SKILL LEVEL** Low to medium
**TIME FRAME** 2 hours
**SPECIAL TOOLS** Pin hammer, block of wood (or web stretcher, if you have one), staple gun
**SEE PAGES** 238–239

Whether you are replacing the worn covering on a drop-in seat or just changing the style to coordinate with a new decor, this is an excellent way of smartening up this type of dining chair and giving it a whole new lease of life.

## COVERING AN UPRIGHT CHAIR

**SKILL LEVEL** Medium to high
**TIME FRAME** ½ day
**SPECIAL TOOLS** None
**SEE PAGES** 240–241

Making a simple loose cover for an upright chair is a quick and easy way of changing its appearance, to create a piece of furniture that fits in with your colour scheme. It is also easy to remove and wash.

## MAKING A LOOSE SOFA COVER

**SKILL LEVEL** High
**TIME FRAME** 1 to 2 days
**SPECIAL TOOLS** None
**SEE PAGES** 242–245

A loose cover is a great way of giving a completely new look to an old sofa, as well as providing a cover that is easy to clean.

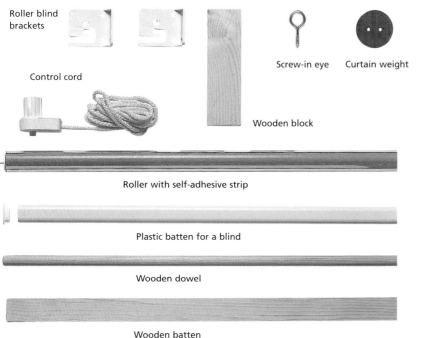

Roller blind brackets

Control cord

Roller with self-adhesive strip

Plastic batten for a blind

Wooden dowel

Wooden batten

Wooden block

Screw-in eye

Curtain weight

Pins and pin cushion

Needles

Curved needles

Needle threader

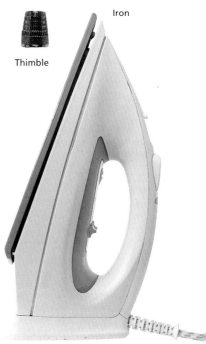

Thimble

Iron

# USING SEWING MATERIALS

As with all home improvement projects, it is important to have some understanding of the way in which soft furnishing tools and materials are used to achieve the desired result. Illustrated on these pages are the main features on a sewing machine and a selection of important materials required for the soft furnishing projects in this book, with a brief explanation of their use.

## SEWING MACHINE

A sewing machine will be the most expensive piece of equipment that you'll need to invest in, so it is important to take plenty of time when making your choice to ensure that you understand the machine's various features and the way it works. Although, in principle, sewing machines are the same, there are subtle differences between models, relating to how different stitches are selected and even simple tasks such as how to thread the needle. It is important to read the instruction manual supplied with the machine; if you are buying one second hand, you should make sure that the manual is included. The most important features to look for on any sewing machine are the functions for straight stitch, reverse stitch and zig-zag stitch. It is also necessary to have a normal presser foot, a zig-zag foot, a zip foot and some spare bobbins. The illustration below shows the main features on a typical sewing machine.

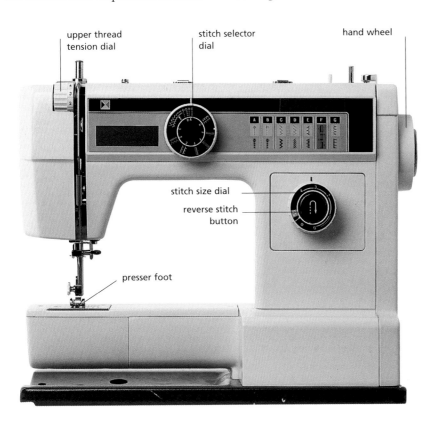

upper thread tension dial

stitch selector dial

hand wheel

stitch size dial

reverse stitch button

presser foot

## CURTAINS AND BLINDS

Very little special equipment is required for making curtains and blinds. You will need a tape measure, scissors, needles, pins and tailor's chalk, plus such items as curtain heading tape, hooks, hook-and-loop tape, buckram and thread.

### ◄ PIN HOOKS

These are inserted into the top of the fabric through the fabric, buckram and heading tape so that they are not seen from the front of the curtain. They are then hung on the rings or gliders of the pole or track in order to hang the curtain.

### ◄ PLASTIC CURTAIN HOOKS

These are used on heading tapes with pockets (pencil pleat). They are a cheap and lightweight alternative to metal hooks.

### ◄ ZINC CURTAIN HOOKS

Metal curtain hooks are stronger than plastic ones and are used on heading tapes with pockets. Where curtains are prone to jumping out of gliders, you can slightly squeeze the hooks with a pair of pliers to hold them in place more effectively.

### ◄ BRASS CURTAIN RINGS

These are sewn on to tie-backs so that they can be hooked in place on a hook on the wall.

### ◄ AUSTRIAN RINGS

These small plastic rings are used on blinds for threading cord through. They act as a guide for the cord when the blinds are pulled up. The rings are best sewn on by hand.

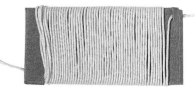

### ▲ BLIND CORD

Different weights and thicknesses are available according to the size of blind. A cord tidy can be used to hold cords neatly if they are not being wound around a cleat on the wall.

3 For sewing hems, use a standard presser foot with a needle that is heavy enough for the fabric; a standard 16 needle is ideal for most types. Choose a medium-length straight stitch and sew along the full length of both side hems.

4 On the wrong side of the fabric, mark 2.5 cm (1 in ) down from the top of the fabric, using tailor's chalk. Fold the top down to the mark and pin. Place the top of the heading tape 5 mm (¼ in) down from the folded edge and pin. Sew along both edges of the tape, tucking in the corner of the fabric to make a mitred corner.

5 Lay the curtain right side up. Measure from the top and mark the overall curtain drop with a pin. Mark the folds for the hem. The second fold should be about 9 cm (3½ in) from the overall drop mark and there should be about 5 cm (2 in) left for the first fold of the hem.

6 Weights are used on bottom hems or joining seams to make the curtains hang properly. Sew the weights into the bottom hem, just below the pin line for the first fold of the hem. The stitching will be hidden when the curtains are viewed from the front. The curtains are now ready to be hemmed at the bottom.

7 Turn up the hem following the marking pins (see step 5). Secure the two sides first so that the hems line up and line up the center seams of any joined widths of fabric. Hold the side hems and pull to create a little tension, which will make the remainder of the hem easier to fold and pin.

8 If your sewing machine has a backstitch feature, use this to sew the hems on patterned fabrics, or sew them by hand. On plain fabrics, a neater finish can be achieved by hand sewing. Slipstitch (see p.216) along the side of the hem, then along the sides of the top of the curtain to finish.

# MAKING A LOOSE CURTAIN LINING

**YOU WILL NEED**

Tape measure
Fabric scissors
Iron
Pins
Tailor's chalk
Sewing machine

**MATERIALS**

Curtain lining fabric
Thread
Loose-lining heading tape
Hooks

**SEE ALSO**

Using sewing materials
pp.214–215
Measuring for curtains
pp.216–217

Lining curtains increases the overall life of the fabric. Even if the curtains are not in direct sunlight, over time the light will make them fade and will cause general deterioration of the fabric. Generally, lining your curtains will improve the way they hang. In addition, it provides an extra layer of fabric at the window, which, in turn, improves insulation.

Detachable loose linings are simple to make and fit. They are attached to the back of the curtain with hooks, so it is easy to remove them. They are also transferable – if you change the colour scheme of the room and want new curtain fabric, you can simply use the old lining on the new curtains.

Some lining fabrics have a "black out" property, which makes them useful for rooms where the early morning sunlight streams in. They are most often used in children's bedrooms where the sunlight is causing sleep problems. To calculate the amount of lining fabric needed, see pp.216–217.

*A detachable loose lining will ensure that the curtains hang well – it also means they can be washed or replaced very easily.*

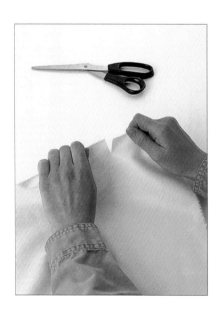

**1** Cut the lining, allowing for the hems, so that the finished size of the lining will be slightly smaller than the size of the ungathered curtain. Cotton linings can be ripped along the weave: cut into it at right angles to the selvedge, firmly grip each side of the cut, and rip directly along the weave. Press the edge flat after ripping.

**2** Turn and pin the side hem (see step 2, p.218). Because there is no pattern to follow on the lining, measure and mark with tailor's chalk or pins before pinning in place to ensure a straight hem. Sew along the hem, using a standard presser foot on the sewing machine and a straight stitch.

**3** Slip the heading tape over the raw top edge of the lining fabric so the raw edge is against the inside of the heading tape's fold. Pin. Fold the ends of the tape under before sewing. Sew across the cords at the tape ends where the two curtains will meet when they are hanging.

**4** Measure the hook-to-hem length of the curtain to which the lining is to be fitted. The lining needs to be 2.5 cm (1 in) shorter, so that it does not hang below the curtain. Allow a 5 cm (2 in) hem with a 4.5 cm (1¾ in) fold inside the hem.

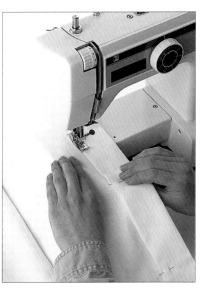

**5** The bottom hem can be machine stitched as it will not show when hung behind the curtain. Sew up the side of the hem, along the top, and down at the opposite end, using a medium-length straight stitch. Do a few stitches in reverse at the start and finish off the sewing line.

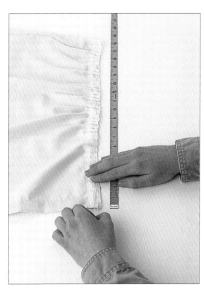

**6** Iron the lining. Pull the cords in the loose lining heading tape at the end that was not sewn across in step 3. Make the lining width 5 cm (2 in) less than the curtain width, so that the lining will sit behind the curtain without being seen. Tie a knot in the lining cords to secure them.

**7** The lining uses the same hooks as the curtains. Put each hook through the hole in the lining tape, then into the curtain tape. Once all the hooks are in place, the curtain and lining can be hung together on the same gliders or curtain rings.

## PRACTICAL LININGS

Loose-lined curtains are practical in kitchens, where the curtains usually need more frequent washing than in other parts of the house. The curtains and the linings can be washed separately with no worry about any difference in fabric shrinkage. In this traditional country kitchen (see p.10), floor-length lined curtains provide effective heat insulation.

# MAKING LINED CURTAINS

*Lining reduces the amount of light coming into a room, which can be useful in a bedroom that gets the early morning sunlight. Curtains will tend to hang better if the linings are attached.*

If your curtain fabric is not machine-washable, there is little advantage in having a loose lining. In these cases, it is as easy to attach the lining to the curtains when making them. The lining and the curtain fabric are simply stitched together at the side seams. The lining is cut narrower than the curtain fabric, so that the side seams are hidden at the back of the finished curtain. Both curtain fabric and lining are sewn to the heading tape at the same time. Double hems should then be pinned and stitched on both the curtain fabric and the lining fabric. Calculate the amount of fabric required following the instructions on pp.216–217.

1 Cut the lining fabric 10 cm (4 in) narrower and 2.5 cm (1 in) shorter than the curtain fabric. With right sides together, pin the lining to the curtain along one side 1.25 cm (½ in) in from the edge, ensuring the top corners meet squarely. Sew the side seam from the top, stopping 30 cm (12 in) from the bottom to allow for hemming.

2 Repeat for the opposite side of the curtain, then iron the side seams and turn right side out. Holding the top of the curtain, fold the side seams where the lining and curtain fabric are sewn. Holding the side seams together, fold the curtain in half so that the top corners of the side seams face each other and meet.

**3** The curtain fabric and lining will have a fold at the centre of the curtain where the lining fold is about 5 cm (2 in) shorter than the curtain fold. Mark both the curtain fold and the lining fold at the top of the curtain with tailor's chalk.

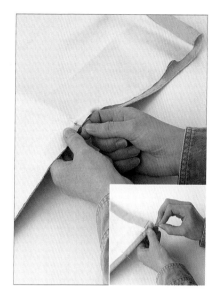

**4** Open out the curtain and pin the two marks together (this is the centre of the curtain). Measure and mark 2.5 cm (1 in) down from the top on the lining. Turn down the fabric and lining to the marks and pin, keeping the centre marks in line. Fold in 1.25 cm (½ in) fabric on the diagonal at the two top corners.

**5** Sew on the heading tape (see step 4, p.219). Mark the overall length and the hem length on the right side of the fabric (see step 5, p.219) and sew in the weights (see step 6, p.219). Turn in the bottom hem edges to make a mitred corner. The top corner of the hem should meet the seam.

**6** Measure the length of the lining, and mark it at the bottom so that it will be 2.5 cm (1 in) shorter than the curtain. Mark 5 cm (2 in) for the first fold of the hem and 6 cm (2½ in) for the second fold (see step 2, p.218). Sew the lining's hem as shown in step 5 on p.221.

**7** Slip stitch the corners of the curtain where they are pinned and sew up the hem as shown in step 8 on p.219. Where the corners of curtain and lining meet, pin them squarely in place, and slip stitch down the seam and continue about 2.5 cm (1 in) around the corner at the bottom to secure them.

**8** Make a note of half the curtain rail length. Pull the heading tape cords from the open end, pulling the pleats as tight as they will go (to make straighter pleats). Measure the cord and knot it at the half-rail length point. Let out the gathers so that they are even all along the curtain to the knot. The curtains are ready for hanging.

# MAKING A FRENCH-PLEAT HEADING

**YOU WILL NEED**

Measuring tape
Fabric scissors
Tailor's chalk and pins
Iron

**MATERIALS**

Fabric
Buckram
Thread

**SEE ALSO**

Using sewing materials
pp.214–215

There are various types of headings that can be used on curtains. While pencil-pleat heading is one of the easiest to use, French pleats create more of an impact, especially on plain fabrics. You can buy French-pleat (also known as triple-pleat) heading tape. However, the advantage of making your own is that you can make neater pleats. Instead of using heading tape, a strip of buckram – 10 cm (4 in) width is ideal – is attached to the fabric and then the pleats are made from the buckram and the fabric. When calculating the amount of curtain fabric, allow a minimum of double fullness (see pp.216–217), as each pleat uses 12.5 cm (5 in) of fabric. The gap between each pleat should be about 12.5 cm (5 in). Each curtain should finish with a pleat on the outside edge and have a gap with no pleats on the inside edge to allow the curtains to close properly.

**1** Make the curtains up to the point when heading tape needs to be attached (see steps 1 to 3, pp.218–219). Do not turn down the top. Line up the top edge of the curtain on the wrong side with the edge of the buckram. Using a zig-zag stitch, sew along the very top to join the buckram and the fabric.

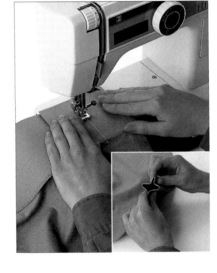

**2** Fold buckram and fabric over; pin in place. Sew a straight stitch, just above the zig-zag line. On the front of the curtain, mark with tailor's chalk, at right angles to the top, the lines where the pleats will be sewn (see Helpful hints). Pin and sew along the lines. Fold in to make each pleat (see inset).

**3** Fold each pleat in place down the depth of the buckram. To secure the pleats, sew across the bottom of each one just below the buckram, taking care as the needle will be going through six layers of fabric (or 12 if curtain is lined), or hand-sew the pleats in place. Use pin hooks at the back of the pleats to hang the curtains.

## HELPFUL HINTS

To mark pleats, start from the outside edge of the curtain and mark the first line 12.5 cm (5 in) in. Leave a gap and mark the next pleat. The gaps between the pleats must be even across the width, so they should be adjusted accordingly. Continue marking the lines along the length of the curtain. Pin the lines of each pleat so that they match on the back and front, keeping the fabric square at the top. The gap at the meeting edges of the curtains needs to be half the size of the others, so that the pleats are evenly spaced when the curtains are drawn.

# MAKING TIE-BACKS

**YOU WILL NEED**

Tailor's chalk
Fabric scissors
Pins
Sewing machine
Iron
Needles

**MATERIALS**

10-cm- (4-in-) wide buckram
Fabric
Thread
Brass rings

Tie-backs provide a simple, neat finish to curtains. As well as being decorative, they are a good way of holding the curtains away from the window to allow in the light. Measure around the curtain where you want to position the tie-back. Cut the buckram to this length, then cut one long edge into a curve. Use this as a template.

*Tie-backs can be made from the curtain fabric or from a plain fabric that complements both the curtains and the room's colour scheme.*

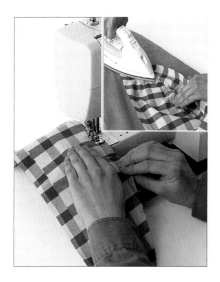

**1** Using the buckram template, mark and cut out two fabric pieces, adding a seam allowance of 1.25 cm (½ in) for the bottom and the sides and 4 cm (1½ in) for the top. Pin and sew the curved edges right sides together, starting and finishing 1 cm (⅜ in) from the end. Press the seam.

**2** Insert the buckram so that all the seam allowance is at the back of the buckram. Fold the top of the front piece of fabric over the top of the buckram and tuck in the excess fabric to give a neat edge. Pin in place. Tuck the sides in, making sure that all the fabric goes in behind the buckram. Pin in place.

**3** Using slip stitch (see Helpful hints, p.216), finish the tie-back by hand, making sure that the needle does not go through the buckram.

**4** Hand-stitch one ring on to each end of the tie-back, using doubled thread. You can then hang the rings on a hook positioned on the wall at the chosen level for the tie-back.

# HANGING CURTAINS

**YOU WILL NEED**

Pencil
Tape measure
Spirit level
Cordless power drill plus
drill bits
Screwdriver

**MATERIALS**

Curtain pole kit or track kit

Curtains are generally hung on either poles or tracks. Although these perform a similar function, there is a slight variation in how the two systems are fitted. Curtain poles come in many different forms and are made from all types of materials, such as iron or various types of wood. In most cases, the poles are held in place on the wall by specially designed brackets. For most windows, two brackets are enough, but for large windows or when the curtains are heavy, three or more brackets may be required.

Tracks are generally made from plastic and are more lightweight to handle. They use a number of small brackets to hold them in place on the wall, and they differ from poles in that the curtain can be drawn right the way along a track without interruption. (With poles, the brackets interrupt the curtain flow, so they must be placed in the right position to enable the curtains to be drawn unhindered.)

The initial part of the fitting procedure is similar for both curtain poles and tracks – a level guideline must be made on the wall surface to ensure the correct height for either the track or pole. After this step, the fitting procedure varies slightly for each mechanism. Pole brackets are fitted further away from the recess, but still on the pencil guideline. This is to ensure that curtains will be able to be pulled back away from the window recess when in an open position.

In most cases, the screw mechanisms for fixing, shown here, are all that is required to secure the tracks or poles in position. However, if the curtains are very heavy or the wall is not particularly stable, you may need to strengthen the fixing points. This can be done quite easily by injecting some resin into the holes drilled for the brackets, inserting the fixings and allowing the resin to dry before fixing either the tracks or poles.

## DRAWING GUIDELINES

**1** When positioning a curtain rail outside a recess, a suitable height above the top edge of the recess is generally about 5 to 7.5 cm (2 to 3 in). Use a tape measure to mark off this measurement directly above one corner of the recess.

**2** Use a spirit level aligned with this mark to draw a pencil guideline all the way along the top of the recess. Allow the pencil guideline to extend beyond the recess sides, as the curtain rail track or pole will always be longer than the width of the recess (see pp.216–217).

## FITTING A TRACK

**1** For a track, measure the required distance past the end of the recess at both ends, and mark off at equal distances along the pencil line to give positions for brackets. These distances will vary according to the length of the line, but brackets should be positioned about every 25 cm (10 in).

**2** At each point, drill a hole and fit the bracket. Screw it securely in place, ensuring that it is the correct way up. The screws and plugs required for fixing are normally supplied with the track.

**3** The track itself is simply clipped on to the front of the brackets. It may be necessary to tighten the adjustable screws on the brackets once the track is in place. End stops can then be positioned at each end of the track, so that once the curtains are hung they cannot slip off either end.

## FITTING A POLE

**1** Pole brackets are fitted further away from the recess but still on the pencil guideline (see step 1, left). First screw a metal-threaded plate on to the wall, then screw the base of the bracket on to the thread of the metal plate until the back face of the bracket is flush against the wall surface.

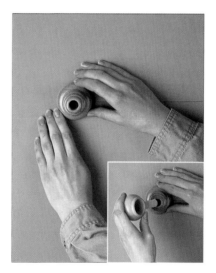

**2** Make sure the bracket is secure on the plate, but do not overtighten it. Slip the second part of the bracket into the first piece to act as a loop through which the pole is threaded. Once this loop is in position, secure it by inserting a grub screw through the top of the first part of the bracket into the loop neck.

**3** Once the other bracket has been fitted in place, thread the pole through the loops. Position the curtain rings so that one is on the outer side of each bracket. This will hold the end of each curtain in place when they are drawn. Position a finial on each end of the pole for decoration and to stop the end of the curtain falling off.

# MAKING A ROLLER BLIND

**YOU WILL NEED**

Tape measure
Mini hacksaw
Fabric scissors
Medium-grade abrasive paper
Sewing machine
Adhesive putty (such as Blu Tack)

**MATERIALS**

Roller blind kit
Fabric
Fabric stiffener spray
Thread

*A roller blind can be fitted inside a recess close to the window, as shown here, or outside the recess, so that it covers both the window and the recess.*

A roller blind is the simplest type of blind. They can be bought ready-made or made to measure, but you can make your own, using a kit. To calculate the amount of fabric required, measure the recess width and drop (see pp.216–217) and add 10 per cent for shrinkage, which may occur when spraying with fabric stiffener, plus an extra 30 cm (12 in) to the length for fitting the blind around the roller and batten.

**1** Fit the blind brackets following the manufacturer's instructions. It is not likely that the roller in a blind kit will exactly fit your window, so measure the width between the brackets and cut the roller of the blind to fit, using a mini hacksaw.

**2** Cut the fabric for the blind to a workable size (allow the 10 per cent for shrinkage and the extra 30 cm/12 in for the length). In a well-ventilated place, spray the fabric with the stiffener, following the manufacturer's instructions. Leave the fabric to dry.

3 When the fabric is dry and stiffened, measure the exact size required and mark with tailor's chalk, making sure that the marks are square. Cut the blind to size, taking care not to fold or bend it – although stiffened, the fabric will not be rigid. If you need to move the blind, roll it up.

4 Measure around the circumference of the batten. Use the measurement to pin a hem on the wrong side of the fabric to fit the batten. Before sewing the hem, insert the batten into the hem to check its fit and length. Mark where the batten needs cutting, if needed, then cut with the hacksaw. Sand off any rough edges.

5 Sew the hem using a straight stitch (with the batten removed). Use the same colour thread as the fabric because the stitching will show along the bottom at the front of the blind. Take care not to fold or bend the stiffened fabric while you are stitching the hem.

6 Peel the backing paper off the sticky strip on the roller. Making sure the fabric is square to the roller, attach the fabric to the sticky strip. Rub across the fabric to make sure it sticks. Roll the fabric onto the roller – hold the roller still with some adhesive putty, such as Blu Tack, while you are doing this.

7 Insert the batten into the bottom hem and attach the end bungs. Hang the blind on its brackets. Once it is in place, gently raise and lower the blind a few times to check that it is running square.

## ROLLER BLIND KITS

● Some roller blind kits are supplied with a wooden roller rather than the metal one shown. If using a wooden roller, the fabric can still be attached with a self-adhesive strip, but fixing it with a few staples, using a staple gun, makes it more secure.

● When making blinds, always use metal or wooden rollers rather than cardboard ones, which are also available. Cardboard rollers are not as strong and they tend to sag after a time, especially if the blind is hanging in a kitchen or bathroom, where there is a lot of condensation, which can make the cardboard damp.

# MAKING A ROMAN BLIND

## YOU WILL NEED

Tape measure
Tailor's chalk
Pins
Sewing machine
Needle
Saw
Abrasive paper

## MATERIALS

Fabric
Thread
Hook-and-loop tape (a piece the width of the blind)
Wooden dowels
Wooden batten
Austrian rings
Blind cord
Screw-in eyes

A Roman blind is a sophisticated version of a roller blind. It lies flat against the window but has deep, horizontal pleats when the blind is raised. It is attached to a batten secured above the window. A hanging system of cords threaded through rings on the back of the blind creates the pleats, which are formed by wooden dowels sewn into tubes on the back of the blind. The size of the pleats varies according to the number of dowels used – the more dowels, the smaller the pleats.

A Roman blind uses more fabric than a roller blind, as the tubes for the dowels and the side hems have to be sewn in. Calculate the fabric required by measuring the total area to be covered and adding a hem allowance at top, bottom and sides, plus an allowance for tubes, multiplied by the number required. If you need to, join fabric widths by using a zig-zag stitch along each edge, then joining with a straight stitch; press the seams open.

*A Roman blind can add a simple elegance in any room, complementing the walls, furnishings or floorcoverings.*

**1** Measure and mark the side hems. Pin and sew (see steps 2 and 3, pp.218–219). Turn down the top as for heading tape on curtains (see step 4, p.219). Sew the loop side of the hook-and-loop tape on to the back of the blind at the top where you have pinned, sewing all edges of the tape.

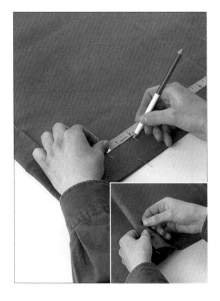

**2** Measure and mark with a pin where you want each dowel. Measure the circumference of a dowel to calculate the tube's size. For each tube, mark half the dowel's circumference plus a little extra on each side of each pin. Pinch together the marked lines and pin them, with the tubes on the wrong side of the fabric.

**3** Sew along the pinned lines, using a straight stitch, to form the tubes for the dowels. On the wrong side of the blind, sew a hem at the bottom that is wide enough for the wooden batten to be inserted.

**4** Hand-sew rings on to each of the tubes at equal distances from each edge. Wider blinds may need extra rows of rings in the middle. If uncertain about the number required, add an extra row of rings and extra cord. If the dowels show any sign of bowing after fitting, extra rings and cords can be added at that point.

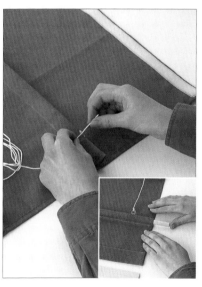

**5** Thread the cord through each line of rings, securing it with a knot on the bottom ring. Allow enough cord to go across to the side where the controls will be operated. Cut the dowels and the batten for the hem to the required length – just shorter than the finished width of the blind. Sand any rough ends and insert them.

**6** Screw the eyes into the bottom of the batten fixed over the window, placing them the same distance in from the edge as the rings on the blind. Stick the hook side of the self-adhesive hook-and-loop tape on to the batten; peel off the backing as you go. If the blind is heavy, staple the hook-and-loop tape for security.

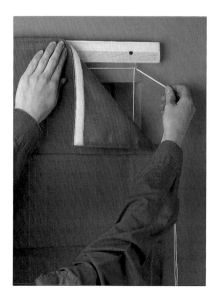

**7** Stick the hook-and-loop tape at the top of the blind on to the tape on the batten above the window. Thread the cords of the blind through the eyes under the batten. Thread the cord across the top to the side of the blind where the control cord will be operated. Wind the cords around a cleat on the wall to secure.

## DECORATIVE TOUCH

A Roman blind allows lots of light to flood through the bedroom window of a converted school (see p.15) during the day, then it makes an attractive focal point at night when the blind is lowered. Before fitting a Roman blind, make sure that the window is large enough to take the bulk of fabric created by the pleats when the blind is pulled up in the daytime.

# MAKING A SQUARE CUSHION

**YOU WILL NEED**

Tape measure
Tailor's chalk
Fabric scissors
Pins

**MATERIALS**

Fabric
Zip fastener (the width of
the cushion size)
Sewing machine
Thread
Cushion pad or other filling

*Cushions made from fabrics with unusual, interesting textures, in bold colours and designs, create a strong focal point in any room.*

Making your own cushions is a very simple way of adding a stylish – and colourful – finishing touch to a room. You can make them in an enormous variety of shapes and sizes – a simple square is one of the easiest – and they can be made from almost any fabric. If you want your cushion to be hard-wearing, choose your fabric accordingly. The cushion filling may be feathers, kapok (fibres from a type of tree), foam, synthetic fibres or polystyrene beads. Ready-made cushion pads come in many sizes and shapes, covered with fabric such as ticking or calico. For each cushion, you'll need two squares of fabric 3 cm (1¼ in) larger than the cushion size.

**1** Measure and mark on the fabric the squares for the back and the front of the cushion, adding (2 cm) (¾ in) to the width for seams, and 3 cm (1¼ in) to the length for seams and the zip. (If making several cushions from patterned fabric, try to mark out panels so that the pattern matches on each one.) Cut out the two pieces.

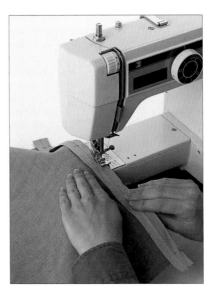

**2** Place one piece of fabric right side up and pin the zip along one length with the teeth of the zip fastener facing the fabric. Using a zig-zag stitch, sew the zip and fabric together. This prevents threads fraying and stops loose threads getting caught in the zip once the cushion is in use.

**3** Turn the fabric over and, along the zip length, mark a line 3 mm (⅛ in) deeper than the depth of the zip. Fold the zip back to this mark and pin in place. This forms a fold of fabric that hides the zip when the cushion is finished. Check that the fold of fabric is pinned flat against the zip on the right side before sewing.

**4** Using a zip foot, sew a line beside the teeth of the zip. Repeat steps 2 and 3, sewing the zip to the other piece of fabric on the other side of the zip. For zips with an attached slide, stop with the needle down through both fabric and zip. Lift the machine foot, move the slide past the needle, lower the foot, and continue.

**5** If using a zip off a roll, add the slide before pinning the edges of the fabric together at the seams, making sure that the top corners are square and that the folds of fabric that cover the zip are in place right up to the zip's teeth.

**6** Sew the seams together, using a straight stitch and a standard foot. Once the seams are sewn, sew around the seam edges, using a zig-zag stitch, to prevent fraying (changing the foot on your sewing machine, if necessary).

**7** Turn the fabric right side out. Insert a cushion pad and close the zip. If the cover fabric is not washable, you may wish to spray it with a fabric protector, which will help to keep it clean.

## STRONG INFLUENCE

Cushions can have a big impact on the decorative scheme. A single, well-chosen cushion made from a textured fabric can add considerable warmth to a cool, minimalist interior. Alternatively, cushions can soften the angular lines of a piece of furniture. These eye-catching ikat cushions bring a touch of ethnic style to a small modern living room (see p.29).

# MAKING A BACK-OPENING CUSHION

## YOU WILL NEED

Fabric scissors
Tailor's chalk
Tape measure
Pins
Sewing machine

## MATERIALS

Fabric
Hook-and-loop tape (the width of the pillow)
Thread

Cushion-cover openings do not necessarily have to be along one of the cover edges. A simple hook-and-loop tape fastening can be positioned across the middle of the back of the cushion. This is a particularly good type of fastening if your sewing machine does not have a zip foot. If you want to make a cushion with a centre-back opening, you need slightly more fabric than for a side opening because the back of the cushion is made out of two pieces of fabric, rather than the one piece shown in the square cushion on pp.232–233.

## ALTERNATIVE FASTENINGS

● If you prefer to use an alternative fastning to hook-and-loop tape, consider using hooks and eyes, pop fasteners (these can be bought individually or on a tape), ribbons, or buttons and button holes.

● An overlap vent may be used where no fastenings are required. To make this, allow at least an extra 2.5 cm (1 in) on the length of each of the back panels when cutting out. Tack the overlap in place before sewing up the side seams. When this is done, cut the tack stitches so that the cushion can be turned right side out.

**1** Measure and mark on the fabric the size of the front of the cushion, plus a seam allowance of 1 cm (⅜ in) on each edge. Measure and mark two back panels the same width as the front one, but half the length plus twice the width of the tape and 2 cm (¾ in) for the overlap and the hem.

**2** On each back panel, on the fastening edge, mark the hem allowance on the wrong side of the fabric. Pin the hems and sew in place, using a straight stitch. Place the two panels side by side with these hems overlapping and check that their total length is the same as that of the front panel.

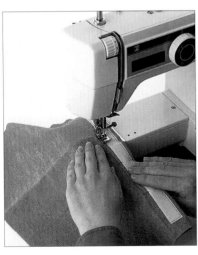

**3** Cut the hook-and-loop tape slightly shorter than the width of the cushion. On one back panel, sew the hook-and-look tape along the hem of the wrong side. On the second panel, sew the other side of the hook-and-loop tape along the hem on the right side of the fabric.

**4** Fasten the hook-and-loop tape. With right sides together, pin the front and back cushion pieces together, then sew them using a straight stitch. Sew with a zig-zag stitch around the edges to prevent fraying. Open the hook-and-loop fastening and turn the cover right side out.

# MAKING DECORATIVE PIPING

**YOU WILL NEED**

Iron
Tailor's chalk
Tape measure
Fabric scissors
Pins
Sewing machine

**MATERIALS**

Fabric
Thread
Piping cord (choose the width that suits the size of cushion you are making)

A piped edging highlights the shape of a cushion, giving it an elegant finish. When piping needs to bend around corners, it should be made from fabric cut on the bias. To mark bias strips, measure from the corner the same distance up the fabric as across, then draw a diagonal line to join the two points. This is the bias line. Using tailor's chalk, mark strips of identical width (enough to cover the piping cord plus a seam allowance) parallel to the bias line.

*Piping can be made from the same fabric as the cushion or from a contrasting colour.*

**1** Cut out the strips. To join strips, pin two together, right sides facing and matching the seam lines, so they form a V-shape. Sew together. Continue sewing strips together until the fabric strip is long enough to fit all the way around the cushion, with an allowance for joining.

**2** Fold the bias strip around the piping cord so the two edges meet. Sew alongside the cord to secure it in place using a zip foot or piping foot (either will work).

**3** To sew the piping on to the cushion, attach it to one side first. Place the piping on the right side of the fabric so that the edges line up and sew along the line that was made in step 2. Start at the back of the cushion so the join where the two ends meet will be hidden from view.

**4** At the corners, snip the seam allowance. To join the piping, trim the cord, then cut and fold under excess fabric; sew across. Place the second piece of fabric with the first piece, right sides together. Sew the same line, finishing as in steps 6 and 7 on p.233.

# MAKING A FITTED CUSHION

### YOU WILL NEED

Brown paper
Pencil
Paper scissors
Fabric scissors
Tape measure
Tailor's chalk
Pins
Sewing machine
Curved needle
Thimble

### MATERIALS

Foam (to a depth of your choice)
Wadding
Fabric
Thread

*A fitted cushion with a foam filling can transform a sagging old chair into a firm new one.*

A deep window sill can be made into a window seat by adding a fitted cushion, or a storage chest can be turned into an ottoman by making a fitted cushion for the top. However you use the cushion, the principles of measuring and making are the same. Make sure you choose a fabric that is strong enough to be stretched taut over a firm foam filling suitable for upholstery (the foam filling must comply with fire retardant regulations).

**1** Place a sheet of paper on the chair. With a pencil, mark the edges that the cushion will extend to. Where the paper will not lie flat around corners, cut into the paper from its edge. Cut out a template along the pencil line and use it to cut the foam and wadding. Alternatively, if the chair has a cushion, use it as the template.

**2** Make a second paper template by drawing around the first one and adding a seam allowance of 1 cm (⅜ in). Place this template on the fabric and draw around it with tailor's chalk. Repeat for a second panel. Mark the centres and corners of the template and fabric (see Helpful hints), then cut out the two panels.

**3** Measure the front, back and sides around the sewing line on the second template. Use these measurements to mark out the cushion's side panels on the fabric (see Helpful hints). The depth will depend on the foam used. Add seam allowances of 1 cm (⅜ in) around each side panel.

**4** With right sides together, pin the panels to make one continuous band. Sew the panels together, starting 1 cm (⅜ in) in from the edge each time (see Helpful hints). When the band has been sewn, fold the front panel in half, matching up the seams. Mark the centre fold with tailor's chalk. Repeat on the back panel.

**5** Pin the right side of the band to the right side of the top cushion panel, lining up the corners and centres and pinning to the corresponding marks. Pin in between as required. Sew a seam all round. Repeat on the bottom panel, but do not sew across the back panel. Sew the sewn seams with a zig-zag stitch (see Helpful hints).

**6** Turn the fabric right side out through the open seam. Cover the foam with the wadding and insert it into the cover, fitting it neatly into the corners. Pin the open seam together, maintaining the 1 cm (⅜ in) seam allowance. Follow the weave or any pattern where possible.

**7** Using a curved needle, slipstitch along the pinned seam (see Helpful hints, p.216). The curved needle will allow the stitch to be made into and out of the fabric in one move where there is no access to the back of the fabric. On heavier fabrics, you may need a thimble.

## HELPFUL HINTS

● Mark the centres and corners of the template and fabric, making sure that the centres line up with any pattern on the cushion fabric.

● If the fabric has a pattern, line the centre of the front side panel on the same pattern as the centre of the top cushion.

● When making the band for the side panels, start each join 1 cm (⅜ in) in from the edge. This makes it easier to sew on the top panel at the corners.

# COVERING A DROP-IN SEAT

## YOU WILL NEED

Pin hammer
Small block of wood
Fabric scissors
Tape measure
Tailor's chalk
Staple gun

## MATERIALS

Webbing, if necessary
Tacks
Firm chip-foam
Polyester wadding
Fabric
Platform cloth

*A new drop-in seat covering can transform an old dining chair, and it makes an excellent first project for practising your upholstery skills.*

Recovering a drop-in seat does not require a lot of fabric, so it is quite easy to change seat covers as part of general redecoration. You can even make a second frame to fit your chairs so that you can have drop-in seats to match the decor in both the kitchen or the dining room, if the chair is moved between rooms.

Calculate the amount of fabric required by measuring the width of the seat plus the drop on each side and 2.5 cm (1 in) on each side for turning in; repeat for the depth of the seat. The base of the seat is covered with platform cloth to give a neat finish that conceals the webbing and stuffing of the seat. Foam comes in different densities – choose a firm one for drop-in seats. When securing the webbing to the frame, it is a good idea to hammer three tacks in a row with a small gap between each one; then when the webbing is folded back to make a neat finish, hammer two more tacks into the gaps between the first ones.

**1** Drop-in seats will usually pop out easily (if not, give the seat a sharp tap on the base). Remove the fabric. If the webbing is worn out, remove everything from the seat frame – cover, stuffing and webbing. Work out how many lengths of webbing will be needed on the frame, allowing for a small space between each length.

**2** Mark on the frame the centre of each piece of webbing. Secure the end of the roll of webbing to the frame on one of the marks with tacks. At the opposite side of the frame, wrap the webbing around a block of wood to give some tension and secure this end. Cut the webbing, leaving excess to fold over.

3 Secure all the webbing lengths in one direction across the frame, then secure lengths the other way, weaving them in and out of the first lengths. Fold over the excess webbing at the ends of the lengths and secure each with two tacks, hammering them in between the three tacks under the fold. This gives a neat and secure finish.

4 Using the frame as a template, cut a piece of foam. Place the foam over the webbing. Cut a piece of wadding large enough to go over and down the sides of the piece of foam, but not covering the frame.

5 Cut the new covering fabric to fit over the foam, down the side of the foam and frame, and tuck 2.5 cm (1 in) under the frame at the front and back and widest point of the width. Draw a line 2.5 cm (1 in) in on the bottom back of the frame. Staple the fabric in place along the line, working from the centre out.

6 Pull the fabric at the centre front and staple it. Work out from the centre, maintaining the same tension from back to front while pulling slightly sideways, stapling each side of the centre in turn until 2.5 cm (1 in) from the corner. Secure the sides in the same way, keeping the weave or pattern straight from front to back.

7 At the corners, pull the fabric toward the centre and secure with a staple sideways to the corner. Fold and staple the excess fabric as flat as possible. The number of folds will vary according to the thickness of the fabric. Once the fabric is secure, cut any excess off at the corners without cutting too close to the staples.

8 Cut some black platform cloth the size of the frame. Fold in the edges and staple to the underside of the frame. The staples do not need to be as close together as on the top, as there is no tension on the platform cloth – its purpose is purely to provide a neat finish.

# COVERING AN UPRIGHT CHAIR

## YOU WILL NEED

Tape measure
Paper
Tailor's chalk
Fabric scissors
Pins
Sewing machine
Iron

## MATERIALS

Fabric
Thread

## SEE ALSO

Using sewing materials
pp.214–215

*You can transform a new or old desk or dining chair with a loose cover. Making this type of cover is straightforward – there are no arms or cushions to worry about. A loose cover is extremely practical as it can be easily slipped off for washing or cleaning.*

This loose cover is made from five panels – back and seat back, seat, skirt and two panels in the skirt. The back and seat back of the chair is one panel of fabric, folded over the top of the chair back. The amount of fabric required is calculated by measuring all the dimensions of the chair and drawing a cutting plan (see p.243). The fabric for the pleats at the front corners of the skirt must be included in the calculations (see step 1).

**1** Measure the height and width of the back and seat back; the depth and width of the seat; and the height and length of the skirt; include 32 cm (12 in) for each of the two pleats. Allow 1 cm (⅜ in) for all seam allowances. If the skirt cannot be cut from one width of the fabric, allow extra for joining the pieces. Cut out the panels.

**2** Place the panel for the back and seat back on the chair, wrong side out, and pin at the sides. Allow a seam allowance where the seat back will join the seat panel, and a hem allowance where the back panel touches the floor. Fold down each top corner (see inset) and mark a line across the top. This will give a boxed corner when sewn.

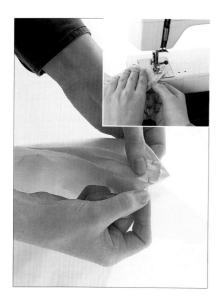

**3** Remove the back panel from the chair, sew the side seams that have been pinned, and press them open. Fold the top corner so that the centre of the fold and the side seam are in line. Pin in place along the sewing line, making sure that the seam is pinned open. Turn over and sew along the sewing line marked in step 2.

**4** Mark the centre of the fabric for the skirt. Measuring from the centre, mark where the corner will be. To make a corner pleat, measure and mark four equal distances of 4 cm (1½ in). Fold at each mark so that the two outside marks meet on the right side of the fabric. Pin the pleat. Repeat for the second front corner.

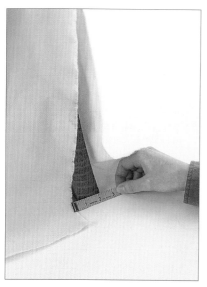

**5** Pin the skirt to the seat panel. Sew together, allowing for seams at the ends. Place the cover on the chair. Measure for a panel to be inserted each side where the skirt meets the back panel. If the chair legs are at an angle, these two panels will need to be wider at floor level. Cut out the panels, pin to the skirt, right sides together, and sew.

**6** Put the back and seat sections of the cover on to the chair, wrong side out, to make sure that they fit. Where the back and seat join, pin the two sections together. Remove them from the chair and sew them together.

**7** Put the cover right side out on the chair. Pin where the skirt meets the back. Pin at floor level where the hem needs to be turned up. Remove the cover from the chair, turn up, pin and sew the hems. Sew ties (see Helpful hints) down the side seams of the skirt and the back panel so they can be tied together.

## HELPFUL HINTS

● The ties for securing the loose cover can be cotton tapes, or you can make your own ties from the fabric that you are using to make the loose cover. To make the ties, sew little tubes of the cover fabric, with the fabric inside out, then turn them right side out, turn the ends under and sew them closed with slip stitch (see p.216).

● You can also use hooks and eyes or hook-and-loop tape to fasten the cover. If using hook-and-loop tape, you will need to allow slightly more fabric for the hems to give an overlap that will cover the tape.

# MAKING A LOOSE SOFA COVER

## YOU WILL NEED

Pencil
Graph paper
Tape measure
Fabric scissors
Pins
Tailor's chalk
Sewing machine
Hook-and-loop tape

## MATERIALS

Fabric
Thread

## SEE ALSO

Using sewing materials
pp.214–215

*A loose cover can give a whole new lease of life to a comfortable but well-worn sofa.*

To calculate the length of fabric required, you'll need to draw the dimensions of each fabric panel to scale on paper to make a cutting plan (see opposite). The fabric panels for the cover are fitted on the sofa and pinned with the wrong sides facing out before marking on the sewing lines. Use the seams on the existing sofa cover as a guide to where the sewing lines on the loose cover will need to be marked.

## MAKING A LOOSE COVER

1 Cut out all the pieces of fabric roughly. Make a mark on the wrong side of each piece if the weave is similar on front and back. Measure the width of the back of the sofa with a tape measure. Calculate the centre point and mark it with a pin at the top of the sofa.

2 Take the panel of fabric for the back of the sofa and measure and mark its centre point. Pin the centre of the fabric to the centre of the back of the sofa with the wrong side out. Pin the fabric in place on the back of the sofa.

*continued on page 244*

## MEASUREMENTS

Measuring up for a new cover must be done very accurately. Measure all the dimensions of your sofa as shown in the two illustrations below. These measurements form the dimensions of the fabric panels required to make the cover. Add seam allowances of 4 cm (1½ in) to each panel's measurements. The panels can be laid out on a cutting plan (see below). If the fabric has a large pattern, allow extra fabric for matching the design.

**1** Height of back panel

**2** Width of back panel

**3** Height of outside arm panel

**4** Width of outside arm panel

**5** Height of seat back to where it joins back panel, plus a tuck-in (at least the depth of cushion)

**6** Width of seat back to where it joins back panel

**7** Depth of seat and distance from floor, plus tuck-in

**8** Width of seat to where it joins outside arm panel

**9** Height and top of inside arm panel to where it joins outside arm panel

**10** Length, from back to front, of inside arm panel to where it joins outside arm panel

**11** Height of skirt

**12** Length of skirt

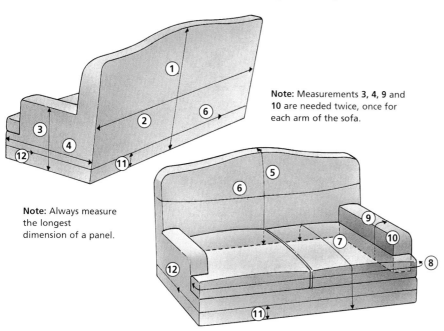

**Note:** Measurements **3**, **4**, **9** and **10** are needed twice, once for each arm of the sofa.

**Note:** Always measure the longest dimension of a panel.

## CUTTING PLAN

Before cutting the fabric, draw the dimensions of each fabric panel you have measured, including the seam allowances, to scale on graph paper to make a cutting plan. Where a panel is wider than the width of the fabric, you will need to add equal-size pieces either side of the panel or make the panel out of two pieces of fabric by joining them along the centre line of the sofa.

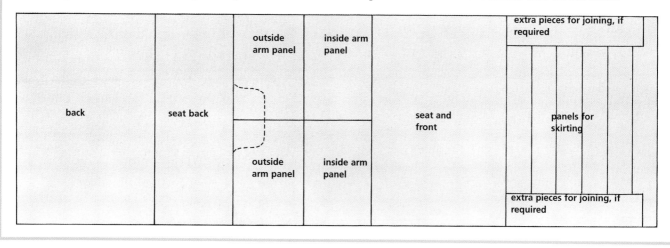

# MAKING A LOOSE SOFA COVER

**3** Remove the cushions. Mark the centre of the seat back panel and line it up with the centre of the back panel already pinned to the sofa. Pin the two panels together. Holding the excess fabric, mark the sewing line with tailor's chalk on the panels.

**4** At any points where the sofa is not square, there will be some excess fabric when the panels are pinned together. Cut away this excess fabric, leaving a seam allowance of at least 1 cm (⅜ in).

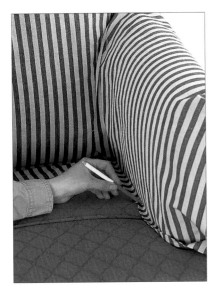

**5** Join the inside and outside arm panels in the same way as the back panels. Mark the sewing line on the seat back and inside arm panels where they meet the seat base. Pin and sew where the seat back and the inside arm panels meet.

**6** Replace the cushions and fit the seat panel, wrong side out, allowing for the tuck-in at the back and side of the cushions. Pin and sew the seat panel tucks to the seat back and inside arm where the sewing lines were marked.

**7** Sew the outside edges of the front of the seat panel to the side of the outside arm panel. Do this on each side of the sofa. Turn the cover right side out and fit it on the sofa, making sure that it is tucked in at the back and sides of the cushions so that it stays in place.

**8** Fold and pin the hems 1.25 cm (½ in) and 2.5 cm (1 in) on the back panel and outside arm panels so that they cannot be seen from the front of the sofa. The hems should be wide enough so that you can sew the hook-and-loop tape on to them.

**9** Pin the hook-and-loop tape in place on the right side of the hem on the outside arm panel, and on the inside of the hem on the back panel. Match up and fasten the two sides of hook-and-loop tape while it is pinned in place to ensure the best fit for the cover.

**10** Remove the cover and sew the hook-and-loop tape in place. Take care as the needle will now be sewing through the hook-and-loop tape and three layers of fabric.

**11** With the cover back on the sofa, check the position for the skirt to make sure that it will be in proportion to the overall size of the sofa. The skirt should have a seam allowance of 1 cm (⅜ in) at the top and a hem allowance at the bottom.

**12** Join enough skirt panels together to add up to three times the distance around the sofa plus end hems at each of the back openings. Pin pleats in place as shown, with each 2.5 cm (1 in) pleat using 7.5 cm (3 in) of fabric.

**13** On the right side of the cover, mark a line with tailor's chalk or pins 1 cm (⅜ in) down from where the skirt will join. Place the skirt right side down on the cover with the top of the skirt on the marked line (and the rest of the skirt above the line). Sew on the skirt, leaving a 1 cm (⅜ in) allowance.

**14** Turn the skirt back down the right way and press the bulky skirt seam. Turn up, pin and sew the hem on the skirt. When the cover is complete, turn it inside out. Using the sewing machine, zig-zag along all the seams to prevent them fraying and to give a neat finish.

# GLOSSARY

**A**

**ADOBE** Sun-dried, as opposed to kiln-baked, brick. Used for house-building in Mexico.

**ARCHITRAVE** The moulding that frames a door or window opening.

**B**

**BALUSTER** A post (one of a set) used to support a handrail along an open staircase.

**BALUSTRADE** The complete barrier installed along open staircases and landings. It consists of the balusters, newels and handrail.

**BATTEN** A thin strip of wood typically of 50 x 25 mm (2 x 1 in) softwood.

**BEAD OR BEADING** A type of moulding that has a half round or more intricate profile. It is often used for edging and as decoration.

**BROCADE** A heavy silk fabric with a raised pattern that is often highlighted with gold or silver thread.

**BUCKRAM** Thick, stiffened hessian material used for lining pelmets and tie backs.

**BUTT** To fit together two pieces of material side by side or edge to edge.

**C**

**CALICO** A white or unbleached strong cotton fabric.

**CHINTZ** A printed cotton fabric, usually glazed.

**CORNICE** A traditional, decorative moulding fixed at the junction between the walls and ceiling.

**COVING** A prefabricated concave moulding, often used as a cornice.

**CRAQUELURE** The fine network of cracks or crazing that can occur over time in the surface of paints or varnishes. It is an effect that can be recreated on modern items for a more aged look.

**CURTAIN DROP** The length of a curtain from the hanging system to the bottom edge.

**D**

**DADO RAIL** A traditional, decorative moulding, also called a chair rail, and usually made of wood, fixed to a wall at about waist height, originally to prevent furniture from marking the walls.

**DHURRIE** An Indian flat-weave rug, often with a geometric pattern.

**DISTEMPER** A primitive, opaque paint made from whiting or chalk dissolved in water and bound with animal glue.

**DOWEL** A round wooden peg, sometimes with grooves running the length of its surface. Used to plug holes or to form a joint by inserting it into holes in two pieces of wood.

**E**

**EGGSHELL PAINT** A paint that dries with a matt finish and is used for interiors.

**EMULSION PAINT** A water-based paint with a matt or sheen finish, used on interior walls and ceilings. It dries quickly and is easy to clean off paint and equipment.

**F**

**FANLIGHT** A window above a door, usually semi-circular and with glazing bars radiating out like a fan.

**FINIAL** A carved or moulded ornament on the ends of a curtain pole.

**FRETWORK** Pierced geometrical ornament of intersecting straight, repeated, vertical and horizontal lines.

**G**

**GLOSS PAINT** A solvent-based paint that dries with a hard, shiny finish. It is suitable for painting interior and exterior wood and metal. This type of paint needs a longer drying time than water-based paints and is harder to clean off paint equipment.

**GRAIN** The direction of the fibres in a piece of wood.

**GROUT** A water-resistant paste used for filling joints between tiles to seal the surface.

**H**

**HARDWOOD** Wood that comes from broad-leaved – usually deciduous – trees such as ash, beech or oak. This type of wood is typically hard; however, balsa is classified as a hardwood but is a soft, lightweight material.

**HEADING TAPE** A ready-made strip that is sewn to the top of a curtain and attached to the hanging system. It is used to gather the curtain.

**K**

**KEY** To roughen a surface, often by sanding, to provide a better grip for a material such as paint or adhesive.

**KILIM** A woven woollen rug with a geometric design from the Middle East or Central Asia.

**L**

**LIMEWASH** A traditional paint consisting of water, slaked lime and pigment used to paint plaster and stone walls.

**LINING PAPER** Plain paper used on walls under paint or wallpaper.

**LINTEL** A supporting beam across the top of an opening, such as a doorway, a window or a hearth.

**M**

**MASKING TAPE** An adhesive tape used for masking areas when painting.

**MASTIC** A non-setting compound that seals a

joint between two surfaces such as a tiled wall and a worktop, bath or shower tray.

**MATT FINISH** A non-reflective finish on a material such as paint or quarry tiles.

**MDF** Medium density fibreboard. A type of board made of compressed fine wood fibres.

**METAL LEAF** Very thin sheets of metal used for gilding woodwork and other surfaces.

**MITRE** A joint between two bevelled pieces that forms an angle, often a 45° angle.

**MOULDING** A narrow, usually decorative, strip of wood or other material. It is available shaped in different profiles. Skirting boards and dado and picture rails are types of moulding.

**N**

**NEWEL POST** Part of the balustrade, the wider post at both the top and bottom of a staircase for supporting the handrail.

**P**

**PATINA** A surface sheen resulting from years of handling, polish and dirt.

**PATTERN REPEAT** The distance between the centre of a mostif and the centre of the one directly below it.

**PELMET** A fabric-covered or decorative wood unit used to hide the top edge of

curtains or a structure such as the track of a sliding door.

**PILE** The fabric raised from a backing – often used to classify a carpet.

**PRIMER** A liquid substance used to seal a material, such as wood, metal, plasterboard and plaster, before applying an undercoat.

**PVA** A white, odourless glue that dries clear. It can be mixed with paint to seal the surface of objects.

**R**

**RAKU** Moulded Japanese earthenware, first produced in the fifteenth century.

**REBATE** A step-shaped recess in the edge of a workpiece, often as part of a joint.

**S**

**SHEEN FINISH** Also known as a silk finish, the amount of reflectiveness of a painted or other surface, midway between matt and gloss finishes.

**SIZE** A thin gelatinous solution used to seal a surface prior to hanging wallpaper.

**SKIRTING BOARD** A wood moulding used horizontally along the walls where they meet the floor.

**SOFTWOOD** Wood from coniferous trees, including cedar and pine.

**STAIN** A liquid that changes the colour of wood but

does not protect it. It comes in water-base, oil-base and solvent-base versions.

**STUCCO** A fine cement or plaster applied to walls and mouldings.

**SUGAR SOAP** A strong, alkaline-based liquid that is used for cleaning painted and other types of surfaces.

**T**

**TEMPLATE** Paper, card or metal or other sheet material formed in a specific shape or pattern to be used as a guide for transferring the shape to the workpiece.

**TERRACOTTA** A hard, unglazed earthenware that has been made from a brownish red clay of the same name. Terracotta can also refer to the colour typical of terracotta earthenware, which can vary from reddish brown to brownish orange.

**TERRAZZO** A polished finish for floors and walls consisting of marble or stone chips set in mortar.

**TIE BACK** A length of ribbon or cord or a metal bracket used to hold curtains clear of a window or bedhead.

**TOILE DE JOUY** A cotton fabric printed with figurative scenes in a single colour.

**TONGUE AND GROOVE** A joint between two pieces of material – such as floorboards or cladding –

in which one piece has a projecting edge that fits into a slot, or groove, on the edge of the other piece.

**TOP COAT** The last coat of a finish applied to a surface. There may be several coats underneath it.

**TROMPE L'OEIL** A style of painting or decoration where a picture is a convincing illusion of reality.

**U**

**UMBER** A natural earth pigment with a greenish-brown colour used in painting. Umber can be heated to form a dark-brown version, known as burnt umber.

**UNDERCOAT** One or more layers of a paint or varnish to cover a primer or hide another colour before applying a top coat.

**V**

**VALANCE** A short curtain used to hide a curtain pole or around a bed to conceal the base and the space below.

**VARNISH** A liquid applied to wood materials, it hardens to form a protective surface. It may be clear or coloured.

**VENEER** A thin decorative layer of wood applied to a less attractive base material.

**VERDIGRIS** A bluish green pigment obtained by scraping off the patina from copper that has been exposed to vinegar fumes.

# USEFUL ADDRESSES

**BRATS–MEDITERRANEAN PALETTE**
281 King's Road
London SW3 5EW
020 7351 7674
info@brats.co.uk
www.brats.co.uk
*waterbased, matt emulsion paints supplied in concentrated form in a range of vibrant colours.*

**DALER–ROWNEY LTD**
12 Percy Street
London W1A 2BP
020 7636 8241
www.daler-rowney.com
*A range of artists' materials, as well as decorators' paint brochures. Catalogue and mail order available.*

**DULUX**
Wexham Road
Slough, Berkshire SL2 5D2
01753 55055
www.dulux.com
www.dulux.co.uk
*Supplier of paints with advisory service.*

**FARROW & BALL**
Uddens Trading Estate
Wimborne, Dorset
BH21 7NL
01202 876 141
farrow-ball@farrow-ball.com
www.farrow-ball.com
*Modern and traditional paints and traditional wallpapers. Catalogue and mail order available.*

**FIRED EARTH PLC**
Twyford Mill
Oxford Road
Adderbury
Oxfordshire OX17 3HP
01295 812 088
enquiries@firedearth.com
www.firedearth.com
*Handmade floor and wall tiles, paints, fabrics, furniture. Catalogue and mail order available.*

**GREEN AND STONE**
259 Kings Road
London SW3 5EL
020 7352 0837
greenandstone@enterprise.net
*Artists' materials, including acrylic varnish, specialist brushes, casein paints, crackle varnish, gesso and gesso paints. Catalogue and mail order available.*

**PAINTABILITY**
Heneage Street
London E1 5LJ
020 7377 9262
*Stencils and paint effects sold only by mail order.*

**PAINT LIBRARY**
5 Elyston Street
London SW3 3NT
020 7823 7755
davidoliver@paintlibrary.co.uk
www.paintlibrary.co.uk
*96 paints designed for modern living. Includes metallic paint and perlescent glazes.*

**THE AMTICO COMPANY**
Head Office and Factory
Kingfield Road
Coventry CV6 5AA
024 7686 1400
www.amtico.com
*A range of vinyls replicating natural materials in traditional classical and comtemporary styles.*

**FORBO NAIRN**
PO Box 1, Kirkcaldy, Fife,
KY1 2SB Scotland
01592 643 111
www.forbo-nairn.co.uk
*Leading UK manufacturer of resilient flooring. Products include Marmoleum and Cushionflor©.*

**JUNCKERS LTD**
Wheaton Court
Commercial Centre
Wheaton Road, Witham
Essex CM8 3UJ

01376 517 512
www.junckers.com
*Solid and hardwood floors and worktops. Catalogue and mail order service available.*

**LASSCO**
**LONDON ARCHITECTURAL SALVAGE & SUPPLY CO LTD**
Saint Michael's Church
Mark Street
London EC2A 3PA
020 7739 0448
www.lassco.co.uk
*Bathroom and kitchen fittings and furniture, ceramics, doors, shutters, flooring, metalware, door furniture, panelling and carved woodwork, staircases and spindles, reclaimed flooring.*

**ORIGINAL SEAGRASS COMPANY**
Shrewsbury Road
Craven Arms
Shropshire SY7 9NW
01584 861 393
original.seagrass@virgin.net
www.original-seagrass.co.uk
*Supplies a range of 26 natural floorcoverings in seagrass, sisal, coir and wool.*

**PAUL FRICKER LTD**
Well Park, Willeys Avenue
Exeter, Devon EX2 8BE
01392 278 636
*Mosaic tiles and accessory materials. Catalogue and mail order available.*

**PARIS CERAMICS**
583 Kings Road
London SW6 2EH
020 7371 7778
www.parisceramics.com
*Handmade tiles, antique terracotta tiles, reclaimed floors and newly quarried limestone floors. Catalogue and mail order available; but visit a showroom if possible.*

**WINDSOR CARPETS LTD**
For nearest store ring:
0800 731 2889
www.windsorcarpets.com
*Carpet and flooring*

*specialists. Catalogue and mail order available.*

**ANNA FRENCH**
343 Kings Road,
London SW3 5ES
020 7351 1126
www.annafrench.co.uk
*Printed and woven fabric, wallpaper, borders and cut-outs in distinctive styles and handmade quality.*

**JOHN WILMAN LTD (COLOROLL)**
Riverside Mills
Crawford Street
Nelson
Lancashire BB9 7QT
01282 617 777
*Wall coverings, fabrics and bedding. Catalogue and mail order available.*

**BLIND FASHION**
Unit 8,
Treadway Technical Centre
Loudwater, High Wycombe
Buckinghamshire HP10 9RS
01628 529 676
www.bbsa-uk.com
*Made-to-measure blinds in a variety of styles, available in customers' own material.*

**CAREW JONES**
188 Walton Street
London SW3 2JL
020 7225 2411
www.carewjones.co.uk
*Suppliers of contemporary handmade furniture.*

**CHRISTOPHER WRAY LIGHTING**
591-593 Kings Road
London SW6 2YW
020 7751 8680
sales@christopher-wray.co
www.christopher-wray.com
*Offers a selection of over 6000 lights and lighting accessories in various styles.*

**THE CONRAN SHOP CONTRACTS**
22 Shad Thames
London SE1 2YU
020 7357 7703

www.giant.co.uk/conran.html
*Modern designer furniture
and accessories; offers
professional advice and
aftersales care.*

COUNTRY AND EASTERN
34–36 Bethel Street
Norwich NR2 1RN
01603 623 107
*A selection of old and new
Asian furniture, fabrics, rugs,
accessories and artefacts.*

HABITAT
For nearest store ring:
020 7255 2545
www.habitat.co.uk
*Contemporary furniture and
accessories.*

IKEA
For nearest store ring:
020 8208 5601
www.ikea.co.uk
*Modern Swedish furniture and
accessories.*

LOM BOK
4 Heathmans Road
London SW6 4TJ
020 7736 5171
*Supplier of Southeast Asian
furniture and accessories.*

MORGAN RIVER LTD
St Jude's Church
Dulwich Road
London SE24 0PB
020 7274 7607
*A wide range of attractive
office and contract furniture.*

RUGBY JOINERY
Watchouse Lane
Doncaster BN5 9LR
01302 394 000
www.rugby-joinery.co.uk
*Largest range of doors in
Great Britain. Catalogue and
mail order available.*

SPAZIO DOOR CO
Oaklands, Tenterden
Kent TN30 6NH
01580 763 593
*Folding doors, folding walls
and room dividers. Catalogue
and mail order available.*

CHALON UK LTD.
Hambridge Mill
Hambridge
Somerset TA10 0BP
01458 254 600
*Offers a wide selection of
kitchens. Also a showroom in
London.*

CRABTREE KITCHENS
The Sorting Office
17 Station Road
London N18 3DX
020 8803 3434
design@crabtreekitchens.co.uk
www.crabtreekitchens.co.uk
*Offers a wide selection of
bespoke traditional and
contemporary kitchens in
hardwoods and handpainted
finishes. Catalogue available.*

ISAAC LORD LTD
185 Desborough Road
High Wycombe
Buckinghamshire HP11 2QN
Cabinet fittings:
01494 462 121
Architectural ironmongery:
01494 459 191
www.isaaclord.s.com
*Cabinet and kitchen fittings,
door and window furniture
and fittings, locks and
latches, tools and decorating
products, paint mixing.
Catalogue and mail order
available.*

KEY INDUSTRIAL
35 Blackmoore Road
Ebblake Industrial Estate
Verwood
Dorset BH31 6AT
01202 825 311
www.keyind.co.uk
*Over 30,000 industrial and
domestic products. Ideal for
storage solutions. Catalogue
and mail order available.*

CRAFT SUPPLIES LTD
The Mill
Miller's Dale. Buxton
Derbyshire SK17 8SN
01298 871 636
*Wood, tools, accessories and
finishing supplies. Catalogue
and mail order available.*

WOODFIT LTD
Kem Mill
Whittle-le-Woods
Chorley
Lancashire PR6 7EA
01257 266 421
*Furniture fittings, doors and
storage solutions. Catalogue
and mail order available.*

THE COTSWOLD COMPANY
Admail 789, Riverside
Bourton-on-the-water
Gloucstershire GL54 2ZZ
0870 550 2233
www.thecotswoldco.co.uk.mg
*Stylish storage ideas for all
requirements available by
catalogue.*

THE DESIGNERS GUILD
267-271 Kings Road
London SW3 5EN
020 7243 7300
www.designersguild.com
*A wide selection of fabric and
wallpaper, classical and
contemporary upholstered
furniture, and accessories.
Orders delivered between one
and three days in Europe.*

HOUSE
PO Box 1748,
Salisbury SP5 5SP
01725 552 549
shop@housemailorder.co.uk
www.housemailorder.co.uk
*Mail order company offering
attractive, contemporary
home accessories.*

PEACOCK BLUE
PO Box 11254
London SW11 52N
020 7771-7400
*Mail order company
specializing in household linen.*

THE WHITE COMPANY
The Coda Centre
Unit 19C
London SW6 6AN
www.thewhiteco.com
*Mail order company
specializing in high-quality
white fabrics, household linen
and home goods.*

## FEDERATIONS AND ASSOCIATIONS

INTERIOR DECORATORS AND
DESIGNERS ASSOCIATION
LTD (IDDA)
1/4 Chelsea Harbour
Design Centre, Lots Road
London  SW10 0XE
0171 349 0800
www.idda.co.uk
*Professional advice on
working with designers and
designing your own home.*

INTERIOR DECORATORS
& BUILDING CENTRE
GROUP LTD
26 Store Street
London  WC1E 7BT
020 7692 6200
www.buildingcentre.co.uk
*Building information and
advice, and a comprehensive,
specialized bookshop.*

BRITISH BLIND &
SHUTTER ASSOCIATION
42 Heath Street
Tamworth
Staffordshire  B79 7JH
01827 52337
www.bbsa-uk.co
*Advice on all matters
concerning blinds and shutters.*

BRITISH CERAMIC
TILE COUNCIL,
BRITISH BATHROOM
COUNCIL
Federation House
Stoke-on-Trent ST4 2RT
01782 747 123
www.britishbathrooms.org.uk
*Information and advice on
all bathroom and tiling
matters; free fact sheets
available.*

THE LEAGUE OF
PROFESSIONAL
CRAFTSMEN LTD
10 Village Way
Rayners Lane
Pinner
Middlesex  HA5 5AF
020 8866 6116
*Information and advice on
professional craftsmen.*

# INDEX

Page numbers in *italics* refer to captions and boxes

# ACKNOWLEDGMENTS

**Photographic credits:**

The publisher would like to thank the following for their kind permission to reproduce their pictures in this book.
t=top, b=bottom, c=centre, l=left, r=right

Front Jacket: IPC Syndications; 2 Tim Street-Porter; 4-5 Peter Cook/ View; 6bl Ed Reeve/ Living etc/ IPC Syndication; 6br Chris Gascoigne/ View; 7bl Richard Glover; 7br Crowson Fabrics; 8–9 IPC Syndications: 10tr and bl Elizabeth Whiting & Associates; 11t Tim Beddow/ The Interior Archive; 11bl Elizabeth Whiting & Associates; 12t Henry Wilson/ The Interior Archive; 12b Elizabeth Whiting & Associates; 13t Camera Press; 13b Gary Hamish/ Arcaid; 14t Simon Upton/ The Interior Archive; 14b Elizabeth Whiting & Associates; 15t Camera Press; 15b Tim Beddow/ The Interior Archive; 16t Lucinda Symons/ Robert Harding Picture Library; 16b Edina van der Wyck/ The Interior Archive; 16-17 Colin Poole; 17t Henry Wilson/ The Interior Archive; 17b Camera Press; 18t Elizabeth Whiting & Associates; 18c IPC Syndications; 18b Andrew Wood/ The Interior Archive; 19t Colin Poole; 19b Chris Gascoigne / View; 20t Henry Wilson/ The Interior Archive; 20b Tim Beddow/ The Interior Archive; 21t Colin Poole; 21b Peter Cook/ View; 22l Tim Clinch; 22r John Miller/ Robert Harding Picture Library; 22–23 Paul Ryan/ International Interiors; 23t Axel Springer/ Camera Press; 23b John Miller/ Robert Harding Picture Library; 24l Camera Press; 24-25 Simon Upton/ The Interior Archive; 25r Nedra Westwater/ Robert Harding Picture Library; 25l Henry Wilson/ The Interior Archive; 26t Simon Upton/ The Interior Archive; 26b Clive Corless; 27t Colin Poole; 27b Tim Clinch; 28l Tim Beddow/ The Interior Archive; 28-29 Camera Press; 29tr Colin Poole; 29b Camera Press; 30t Wayne Vincent/ The Interior Archive; 30b Simon Upton/ The Interior Archive; 31t Denis Gilbert/ View; 31bl Tim Beddow/ The Interior Archive; 31cr Camera Press; 32-33 Chris Gascoigne/ View; 37br Paul 38c & bc IPC Syndications; 42bl Camera Press; 43bl Abode; 43br Abode; 44bl Camera Press; 45bl Camera Press; 45br Abode; 46bl Camera Press; 47bl Camera Press; 47br Tim Street-Porter/ Abode; 48bl Houses and Interiors; 49bl Abode; 49br Abode; 50tl Paul Ryan/ International Interiors; 50b Elizabeth Whiting & Associates; 51cl Camera Press; 51tr Robert Harding Picture Library; 51bc Amico Image Library; 51crb Fired Earth; 52r Camera Press; 52bl Robert Harris; 53tl Elizabeth Whiting & Associates; 53bl Paul Ryan/ International Interiors; 53cr & crb Anna French; 54cl Camera Press; 54tr Houses and Interiors; 54br Journal Fur Die Frau; 55cl Elizabeth Whiting & Associates; 55bl Elizabeth Whiting & Associates; 55cr Fired Earth; 55br Camera Press; 56cl Elizabeth Whiting & Associates; 56bc Andrew Wood/ The Interior Archive; 56–57 Camera Press; 57tc Elizabeth Whiting & Associates; 57tr Camera Press; 57bc Peter Cook/ View;58tr Houses and Interiors; 58–59 Circus Architects 1999; 59tr Camera Press; 59bc Camera Press; 60tl GE Magazines Ltd/ Robert Harding Syndication; 60–61b Camera Press; 60–61t Peter Cook/ View; 61b Chris Gascoigne/ View; 62t Simon Brown/ The Interior Archive; 62b Camera Press; 63t Elizabeth Whiting & Associates; 63b Peter Cook/ View; 64bl The Interior Archive; 64–65 The Interior Archive; 65tr Simon Upton/ The Interior Archive; 66tl Elizabeth Whiting & Associates; 66bl Elizabeth Whiting & Associates; 66–67 Camera Press; 67tr Henry Wilson/ The Interior Archive; 67br Elizabeth Whiting & Associates; 68cl IPC Syndications; 68c Robert Harding Picture Library; 68br Mosaic Workshop; 69tl Elizabeth Whiting & Associates; 69bc Elizabeth Whiting & Associates; 70tr Camera Press; 70bl Elizabeth Whiting & Associates; 71tr, bl, cr Paul Ryan/ International Interiors; 72-73 Richard Glover; 76 Paul Ryan/ International Interiors; 77tr Elizabeth Whiting & Associates; 77cr Elizabeth Whiting & Associates; 78c Tim Street-Porter; 78–79 Robert Harding Picture Library; 79tr Richard Glover; 79cr Paul Ryan/ International Interiors; 80l Camera Press; 80tr Camera Press; 81tr Camargue PLC; 81b Paul Ryan/ International Interiors; 82b Elizabeth Whiting & Associates; 82-83 IPC Syndications; 83c Camera Press; 83b Elizabeth Whiting & Associates; 84c Elizabeth Whiting & Associates; 84li, iii, iv, v Andrew Sydenham; 84lii Cucina Direct; 84lvi HOUSE; 84lvii, viii, ix, x Royal Doulton Plc; 85bl Colin Poole; 85tl Elizabeth Whiting & Associates; 85tr Elizabeth Whiting & Associates; 86 Tim Street-Porter; 87tr Elizabeth Whiting & Associates; 87cl Elizabeth Whiting & Associates; 87br Camera Press; 88c Tim Beddow/ The Interior Archive; 88b Camera Press; 88l Artisan Curtain Rails except (g) Clayton Munroe Ltd; 89tl Tim Street-Porter; 89br Peter Cook/ View; 90bl Camera Press; 90–91 Camera Press; 91bl Elizabeth Whiting & Associates; 91tr Simon Upton/ The Interior Archive; 92 Camera Press; 93tl Paul Ryan/ International Interiors; 93tr Paul Ryan/ International Interiors; 93cb Elizabeth Whiting & Associates; 93br Elizabeth Whiting & Associates; 94l a, c, f, g, Christopher Wray Lighting; b HOUSE; d,e, Andrew Sydenham; 94r Elizabeth Whiting & Associates; 95tl Elizabeth Whiting & Associates; 95tr IPC Syndications; 95b Camera Press; 96t IPC Syndications; 96bl Camera Press; 96br Elizabeth Whiting & Associates; 97t IPC Syndications; 97b IPC Syndications; 98bl Paul Ryan/ International Interiors; 98–99t Camera Press; 98-99b Elizabeth Whiting & Associates; 99tr Elizabeth Whiting & Associates; 99cr Henry Wilson/ The Interior Archive; 100 Camera Press; 101tl Paul Ryan/ International Interiors; 101tr IPC Syndications; 102l a, b Sottini; c-g West One Bathrooms; 102c Elizabeth Whiting & Associates; 102br Tim Street-Porter; 103tl Tim Street-Porter; 103bc Richard Glover; 103cr GE Magazines Ltd/ Robert Harding Syndication; 104tr Camera Press; 104b Camera Press; 105t Colin Poole; 105cr Camera Press; 106l a-d, f, h, k, l, n Tim Ridley; 106le, g, i, j, m Turnstyle Designs;106bc Elizabeth Whiting & Associates; 107tl Stephen Ward/ The Amtico Co. Ltd; 107bl Elizabeth Whiting & Associates; 107tr Simon Brown/ The Interior Archive; 108 Abode; 108tr Tom Leighton/ Living etc/ IPC Syndication; 109bc Morgan River; 110bc Colin Poole; 111tl Russell Sadur/ Robert Harding Picture Library; 111bc Russell Sadur/ Robert Harding Picture Library; 111tr Elizabeth Whiting & Associates; 112l all Cotswold Company; 112c Elizabeth Whiting & Associates; 112br Steel-Lok; 113t Elizabeth Whiting & Associates; 113br Elizabeth Whiting & Associates.

**All photographs in chapter 4** were taken by Tim Ridley, except 114–115 Crowson Fabrics; 130tc Lyn le Grice/ International Interiors;132tc The Stencil Store; 138tc 148tc Crowson Fabrics; 150tc Crowson Fabrics; 152tc Graham & Brown Wallpaper; 154tc Fired Earth; 155br Colin Poole;156tc Steve Sparrow/ Houses and Interiors; 158tc Arcaid; 160tc Mosaic Workshop; 162tc Mosaic Workshop; 166tc Nick Pope/ Rosalind Burdett; 168tc Elizabeth Whiting & Associates; 166–185 Tim Ridley; 170tc Steel-Lok; 172tc IPC Syndications; 176tc Key Communications; 183br Elizabeth Whiting & Associates; 192tc Amtico Image Library; 194tc International Stransky Thompson PR; 196tc Victoria Carpets Ltd; 198tc Victoria Carpets Ltd; 199br Elizabeth Whiting & Associates; 200tc Amorim UK Ltd; 202tc Fired Earth; 204tc Stonell Ltd; 206tc Kahrs Ash Stockholm; 208tc Paul Ryan/ International Interiors; 190-211 Tim Ridley;210tc Ducal of Somerset; 209br Paul Ryan/ International Interiors; 211br Colin Poole; 218t Next Plc; 220tr Fired Earth; 221br Elizabeth Whiting & Associates; 222t Harlequin Fabrics & Wallcoverings Ltd; 225tr Crowson Fabrics; 228t Eclectics; 230tr Eclectics; 231br Tim Beddow/ The Interior Archive; 232t Next Plc; 233br Camera Press; 235tr Andrew Martin/ Halpern Associates; 236t Kährs Birch, Glasgow; 240tc Paul Ryan/ International Interiors; 242tc Elizabeth Whiting & Associates

**Illustrations** on pages 34–35, 36–37, 41, 74–75, 77, 101 and 109 by Patrick Mulrey; 122–123, 147, 191, 217 and 243 by Chris Forsey; 40, 42–43, 44–45, 46–47 and 48–49 by Hytex. Mood board on page 39 designed by Nicholas Springman.

If the publishers have unwittingly infringed copyright in any illustration reproduced, they would pay an appropriate fee on being satisfied to the owner's title.

**Publisher's acknowledgments:**
We gratefully acknowledge the assistance of the following companies and individuals:

**Miles Hardware** 57 Glenthorne Ave, Yeovil, Somerset, BA21 4PN (01935 421281); **B.J. White** 4 Vale Road, Pen Mill Trading Estate, Yeovil, Somerset BA21 5HL (01935 382400); **Magnet Limited** Royd Ings Ave, Keighley, West Yorkshire BD21 4BY (0800 9171696); **Hewden Plant Hire** Station Road, Bruton, Somerset BA10 0EH (01749 812267); **Travis Perkins Trading Company Limited** Mill Street, Wincanton, Somerset BA9 9AP (01963 33881); **The Stencil Store** 20–21 Heronsgate Road, Chorleywood, Herts WD3 5BN (01923 285577/88); **The English Stamp Company** Worth Matravers; Dorset BH19 3JP (01929 439117); **Amorim Ltd** Amorim House, Star Road, Partridge Green, Horsham, West Sussex RH13 8RA (01403 710970); **Dovecote Gallery** 16 High Street, Bruton, Somerset BA10 0AA; **B J Haigh-Lumby** 1 High Street, Castle Cary, Somerset BA7 7AN (01963 351259); **Bruton Classic Furniture Co. Limited** Unit 1 Riverside, Station Road Industrial Estate, Bruton, Somerset BA10 0EH (01749 813266); **MGR Exports** Station Road, Bruton, Somerset BA10 0EH (01749 812460); **Polyvine Limited** Vine House, Rockhampton, Berkeley GL13 9DT (01454 261276); **The Fabric Barn** Clock House, Yeovil, Somerset BA22 7NB (01935 851025); **Aristocast Originals** 14A Ongreave House; Dore House, Industrial Estate, Sheffield, S13 9NP (0114 2690900); **Tile Wise Limited** 12–14 Enterprise Mews, Sea King Road, Lynx Trading Estate, Yeovil, Somerset BA20 2NZ (01935 412220); **The Amtico Company Limited** (0800 667766); **Dulux Decorator Centres** Altrincham, Cheshire, WA14 5PG (0161 9683000); **Kahrs (UK) Limited;** Unit 2 West, 68 Bognor Road, Chichester, West Sussex PO19 2NS (01243 778747); **Claire Minter-Kemp** Tom Dickins Fine Art, The Pump Room, Lower Mill Street, Ludlow, Shropshire (01584 879000); Mr S. Weatherhead, London House, 12 High Street, Wincanton, Somerset.

**Thanks also go to:**
Ann Argent, Tom and Hennie Buckley, Susan Clothier, Bill Dove, John Fives, Steve Green, George Hearn, David House, Richard Lane, June Parham, Michael and Sue Read, Ann Squires.

A special thank you to the following for all their help in putting the book together: Peter Adams, Antonia Cunningham, Susie Behar, Alison Bolus, Dorothy Frame, Thomas Keenes, Theresa Lane, Maggie McCormick, Katrina Moore, Tim Ridley.